Bilingualism: Basic Principles

Multilingual Matters

Please contact us for the latest information on all books in the series.
Derrick Sharp, General Editor, Multilingual Matters,
Bank House, 8a Hill Road, Clevedon, Avon BS21 7HH, England.

MULTILINGUAL MATTERS 1

Bilingualism: Basic Principles

(second edition)

Hugo Baetens Beardsmore
Vrije Universiteit Brussel

MULTILINGUAL
MATTERS LTD

British Library Cataloguing in Publication Data

Beardsmore, Hugo Baetens
   Bilingualism : basic principles. —— 2nd ed.
—— (Multilingual matters ; 1)
   1. Bilingualism
   I. Title   II. Series
   404'.2   P115

ISBN 0–905028–69–4
ISBN 0–905028–63–5 Pbk

Multilingual Matters Ltd.
Bank House, 8a Hill Road,
Clevedon, Avon BS21 7HH
England.

Typeset by Photo·Graphics, Honiton, Devon.
Printed and bound in Great Britain by
Colourways Press Ltd, Clevedon BS21 6RR.
Paperback bound by W.H. Ware & Sons,
Clevedon Avon.

Contents

Contents

Introduction

As with so many introductory works the present book grew out of a pressing need. Although there is a plethora of titles in the field of bilingualism, as the bibliography at the end of this book attests, there is no single introductory work to the study of bilingualism that is readily accessible or easily digestible. When I was faced with teaching a course on the subject it proved impossible to find a suitable introductory guide in English that would lead into the more refined theory and experimentation currently developing with ever increasing momentum. Indeed, there are relatively few general works on the topic at all. Perhaps the two most important books in this field are Weinreich's *Languages in Contact*, produced in 1953, and still a source of constant inspiration, and Haugen's *Bilingualism in the Americas: A Study and Research Guide*, published in 1956. Weinreich's book, although still readily available, is somewhat difficult for beginners and is also marked by the currents of thought prevalent in linguistic circles at the time of its conception. On the other hand, Haugen's book, although somewhat easier to approach, is no longer available for wide dissemination and also reflects the early stages of development in a field of study that is becoming increasingly popular.

Since these first major publications the number of papers and discussions of the subject have been spread in a disconcerting number of periodicals which often lead the beginner astray in that they assume familiarity with basic concepts and contentious points. There are, of course, collected editions of major developments in the field of bilingualism, such as those produced by Stanford University Press for papers by Lambert, Gumperz, and Haugen respectively, Fishman's work on sociological aspects of bilingualism. Hornby's combined overview of developments in the sociological, psychological and educational aspects. But all these pre-suppose a certain amount of familiarity with the field and cover such divergent aspects that the beginner is often left with a feeling of panic as he becomes aware of the need to fill in on basic concepts referred to in the often copious bibliographies.

It is to remedy this state of affairs that the present book has been designed with undergraduates especially in mind. It does assume some knowledge of the basic principles of linguistics since its primary concern is with the bilingual individual, though inevitably sociological considerations are touched upon, because the individual does not operate in a linguistic vacuum. On the other hand this book deals less in detail with societal bilingualism since my premiss is that sociological aspects of bilingualism should be approached only once an awareness of the individual linguistic phenomenon has been understood. As an introductory work it attempts to draw together much of the variegated information published in different sources since the early fifties and to direct the student, by means of the bibliography, to more detailed investigations considered of major significance.

The production of this work has been significantly helped by the impact draft versions have had on my students to whom I am indebted for their insightful reactions. Their response has enabled me to use the materials as a starting point for more detailed seminar work based on their original investigations, secure in the knowledge that they had grasped the complexity of bilingualism. I am also particularly indebted to Alan Thomas of the University College of North Wales, Bangor, for his critical reading of the manuscript and Professor Merrill Swain of the Ontario Institute for Studies in Education, Toronto, for her encouragement and counsel. Neither they, nor my students, are in any way responsible for the shortcomings that may still be found.

Hugo Baetens Beardsmore
Vrije Universiteit Brussel

Preface to the second edition

In revising and expanding the first edition of this volume I have been indebted to the reviewers who pointed out potential improvements which would extend some of the basic notions originally dealt with. Their comments have served as an encouragement to add information, clarify certain ambiguities and broaden the discussion of contentious issues. Since the first volume appeared the momentum of research into bilingual questions has increased and where more recent publications have added what are felt to be fundamental contributions to basic principles they have been incorporated. However, little new material has been added if it has been considered as more peripheral to the intention of providing the beginner to the field of bilingualism with the necessary tools for pursuing more in-depth personal investigation. A particular debt of gratitude is owed to Professor John Schumann of UCLA, California, for his comments on the draft of this second edition. Any remaining inadequacies are entirely the author's responsibility.

1 Definitions and Typologies

It is no easy task to start any discussion on bilingualism by positing a generally accepted definition of the phenomenon that will not meet with some sort of criticism. Bilingualism as a concept has open-ended semantics. Definitions are numerous and are continually being proffered without any real sense of progress being felt as the list extends. If we turn to just a few definitions their inadequacies immediately become apparent.

> "In ... cases where ... perfect foreign-language learning is not accompanied by loss of the native language, it results in bilingualism, native-like control of two languages. After early childhood few people have enough muscular and nervous freedom or enough opportunity and leisure to reach perfection in a foreign language; yet bilingualism of this kind is commoner than one might suppose, both in cases like those of our immigrants and as a result of travel, foreign study, or similar association. Of course one cannot define a degree of perfection at which a good foreign speaker becomes a bilingual: the distinction is relative."
>
> (Bloomfield, 1935: 55–56)

In this quotation there is a clear contradiction between what is said in the first sentence with reference to native-like control of two languages and the final sentence which mentions relative degree of ability.

Two of the major specialists in this branch of linguistics have attempted definitions which are probably deliberately vague and which consequently raise as many questions as those they attempt to avoid. Mackey, for example, states;

> "It seems obvious that if we are to study the phenomenon of bilingualism we are forced to consider it as something entirely relative. We must moreover include the use not only of two languages, but of any number of languages. We shall therefore consider bilingualism as the alternate use of two or more languages by the same individual."
>
> (Mackey, 1957: 51)

1

This statement is very similar to that by Weinreich who says;

> "The practice of alternatively using two languages will be called
> here BILINGUALISM, and the persons involved BILING-
> UAL. Unless otherwise specified, all remarks about bilingual-
> ism apply as well to multilingualism, the practice of using
> alternately three or more languages."
>
> (Weinreich, 1953: 5)

The extreme caution which such generalizations as the above reveal give
little information on how well two or more languages need to be known or
whether there are any gradations in bilingual usage depending on things like
speaking, writing, reading or listening abilities.

The following totally different type of definition provides a startling
contrast with the above but is not unique;

> "Bilingualism is the condition in which two living languages exist
> side by side in a country, each spoken by one national group,
> representing a fairly large proportion of the people."
> (Aucamp, 1926, in Béziers & Van Overbeke, 1968: 113)

Here the definition could well be considered as referring to contiguous
unilingual communities and have very little to do with bilingual speakers.

The above illustrations (for a broad critical discussion see Béziers &
Van Overbeke, 1968) show the potential confusion that definitions can
provoke. Nevertheless, the notion of bilingualism is well-established in the
minds of both the specialist and the layman, is the origin of passion and
polemics, and the source of widespread comment and enquiry. To some
extent the notion of bilingualism finds itself in the same category as the
elusive yet so familiar concept of the word; everyone knows what a word is
yet no one can give a satisfactory definition. Many linguists have tried to do
away with attempts to work on the basis of the word, building up their
understanding and explanation of language on foundations more amenable
to definable analysis and in a way this is a situation similar to the problems of
handling bilingualism. Just as in our bones we know what a word is,
inadequately definable though it may be, so most of us have an opinion as to
what bilingualism is, even though individual interpretations may vary
considerably.

Much pragmatic investigation in the natural sciences is beset with
similar difficulties of precision in definition yet this has in no way prevented
man from building up theories, conducting research and discussing certain
as yet elusive phenomena; it is perfectly feasible to treat the notion of

bilingualism in a similar fashion, bearing in mind that the field of investigation is evident but not as precise as one might wish.

One explanation for the difficulties in circumscribing the field of bilingualism is the multidisciplinary nature of the aspects involved (Hornby, 1977: 8). The various disciplines involved in analysing the phenomenon, be they linguistics, psychology, sociology or pedagogy, approach it from their own particular vantage point, leading at times to an appearance of confusion, though in fact this is not necessarily the case. Nevertheless, the term bilingualism covers a diverse series of programmes (Saville-Troike, 1973: 93).

Perhaps the greatest area of difficulty lies within the field of linguistics, accountable for, perhaps, by the general state of flux in which linguistic theory finds itself. Most widely accepted linguistic theories to date are grappling with the problems of understanding the functioning of a single language in the mind of the speaker, taking structure as a primary end in itself, and minimizing the significance of language use (Hymes, 1972: 272), though there are, of course, theoreticians with wider ranging ambitions. Bilingualism, on the other hand, must be able to account for the presence of at least two languages within one and the same speaker, remembering that ability in these two languages may or may not be equal, and that the way the two or more languages are used plays a highly significant role. Consequently a theoretical approach to bilingualism must of necessity have a broader and more all-embracing vision of speech behaviour than one that concentrates specifically and solely on structure. Much of the very reputable work conducted by linguists into the purely structural aspects of bilingual speech has resulted in a greater awareness of the *phenomena* of bilingualism, or of specific features in a bilingual's performance, but this has not necessarily led to any clear awareness of the fundamental difference between bilingualism and unilingualism, if it exists. This question will be the major area of investigation in this book.

As we have already seen from the definitions provided earlier it should be made clear from the outset that the term bilingualism does not necessarily restrict itself to situations where only two languages are involved but is often used as a shorthand form to embrace cases of multi- or plurilingualism. There is no evidence to suggest that the fundamental principles affecting language usage are any different whether two, three or more languages are being used by one and the same speaker, and the major question is whether they differ significantly from cases where only one language is being used.

Rather than attempting to provide a definition of bilingualism, which, in the present state of our knowledge about language in general, is likely to be unsatisfactory, most specialists prefer to work within the framework of a typology of bilingualism which allows for a clear delimitation of the particular area of investigation within a larger field. Typologies, which are descriptive labels, have the advantage of allowing the student to work within a clear frame of reference which is adapted to the need in hand and avoids the dangers of over-generalization to cases that cannot be easily circumscribed.

One of the most important distinctions to be made as the basis of any discussion in this field is that between *societal* and *individual bilingualism*. Societal bilingualism, an area extensively studied by Fishman (see Bibliography) and his disciples, is strictly speaking more involved with the sociology of language than with sociolinguistics or pure linguistics as developed over the past two decades, but there are points of convergence which make the findings of the sociological investigation of societal bilingualism relevant to the more linguistic issues implied in socio- and theoretical linguistics. In societal bilingualism the investigator is placing the accent primarily on understanding what linguistic forces are present in a community, their inter-relationships, the degree of connection between political, economic, social, educative and cultural forces and language. The scope of such investigation can be very wide and can lead to implications for language policy makers and language planners, educational strategists, social engineers and media or communications specialists. Basic to the study of societal bilingualism is the assumption that in complex, stratified societies many social differences are language-linked and that,

> "...language plays an important role in the differential social distribution of positive and negative social values of both a material and symbolic nature." (Kjolseth, 1978: 801)

For the student of bilingualism the societal aspects often form the background canvas which determines the relevance of his enquiry by clarifying the historical and social processes which lead to the existence of bilingual individuals. Even the microlinguistic case study of one bilingual speaker must normally be prefaced by a contextualization of the elements which brought about the presence of two or more languages in one speaker, often in the form of a simple case history, but sometimes leading to a complex description of both the background and the ways the two languages form part of the person's everyday life. For as both Bentahila (1983: 20) and Sharp (1973: 11) have pointed out, no two instances of societal bilingualism are likely to be identical in all respects.

The point where societal or group bilingual studies diverge most from the investigation of individual bilingualism is in the cases where one is examining multilingual federations, nations or societies whose major component elements consist of unilingual individuals living in close proximity. Such multilingual states as Belgium and Switzerland are clear illustrations of societal bilingualism based on the principle of territorial unilingualism (Mackey, 1976: 83) where the majority of the inhabitants are monoglots, though less obvious examples are those situations where isolated pockets of individuals do not speak the language of the majority of the inhabitants in their environment, as is often the case with immigrants. Even in multilingual societies of this nature, however, there are usually large numbers of individual bilinguals who function as linguistic mediators between the different groups present. It is these mediators who represent the link between societal and individual bilingualism.

One of the more comprehensive typologies of bilingualism that covers both major distinctions is that produced by Pohl (1965), though some of the labels he uses have not gained the widespread recognition they deserve. Among the more interesting types he lists are the following.

Horizontal bilingualism occurs in situations where two distinct languages have an equivalent status in the official, cultural and family life of a group of speakers and is mostly found, according to Pohl, amongst upper-level speakers such as the educated Fleming in Brussels (using Dutch and French), the Catalans (using Catalan and Spanish), and certain Québécquois (using French and English). Although such speakers might functionally differentiate their language usage there could also be considerable overlapping where either language might be used in very similar circumstances. For Pohl *vertical bilingualism* obtains when a standard language, together with a distinct but related dialect, coexists within the same speaker, though the more generally accepted term for this situation is *diglossia* which will be discussed in greater detail later (see p. 38). This pattern can be found in many parts of the world, including Walloon Belgium (Walloon and French), Germanic Switzerland (Schwyzertütsch and German) and Bali (Balinese and Indonesian). *Diagonal bilingualism* occurs with speakers who use a dialect or non-standard language together with a genetically unrelated standard language, as can be found in Louisiana in the United States (Louisiana French and English), German Belgium (Low German and French) and amongst Maori communities in New Zealand (Maori and English).

The link between societal bilingualism on the one hand and individual bilingualism on the other can be sought in the question discussed by Fishman (1965b): who speaks what language to whom and when? In cases where more than one language is being used by one and the same speaker we must find out what circumstances make him change over from the one to the other. The individual momentary choices must then be related to the larger stable patterns of choice that exist in the bi- or multilingual setting as a whole. This is done by examining the domain of language behaviour (e.g. the school, the family, the press, the administration), the topic of conversation within this domain, the role relationships between the interlocutors (e.g. superior to inferior, equal to equal, buyer to seller), the locale or setting of the interaction, and perhaps other factors (Fishman, 1972). If we now add to the multiple question of Fishman's put earlier that of how the bilingual operates in reality we move more clearly into the field of sociolinguistics as developed by people like Labov (1972), where grammatical structure is examined as forming a totality of sociologically and psychologically determined interaction variables. The social psychological dimension of the whole question has been principally worked upon by social psychologists like Lambert (1972a) so that by putting these different approaches together we can begin to get a composite picture of bilingualism as viewed from various disciplines.

One of the most difficult problems the student of bilingualism encounters is that of pinpointing just how bilingual a speaker must be in order to be considered a bilingual. Haugen (1953: 7) has suggested that;

> "bilingualism is understood... to begin at the point where the speaker of one language can produce complete meaningful utterances in the other language."

Although this statement may be intellectually adequate it does not seem to stand up to the test of common-sense reality. It is evident that many people can make a "complete meaningful utterance" or two in a foreign language without in any way being able to function, be it ever so minimally, other than in their primary language. Although I cannot ask the time or count up to ten in Spanish I can say "Buenas noches", "hasta la vista" and "mañana", which are complete meaningful utterances. Many a European teenager can reel off the words of a popular song in a foreign language yet could hardly hold an elementary conversation in the same foreign language. Theoretically, of course, it is true that the bilingual process has begun with these manifestations of other-language usage, though it is unlikely that native-speakers of that other language would consider this as sufficient proof of the beginning of bilingualism.

The above arguments should indicate that one of the most important factors to be borne in mind in discussing bilingualism of any type is that a notion of relativism must be introduced whereby the *degree of bilingualism* under analysis can be ascertained (Arsenian, 1937: 19). Now degree of bilingualism is not an easy thing to measure, though of course all language proficiency tests do this to some extent. However, such tests are usually geared to monoglot norms of a target language and often measure no more than discrete points of linguistic competence without really revealing to what extent the individual's functioning is adequate as a bilingual. The nature of the difficulties involved in this task can be gauged from the voluminous report by Kelly (1969) devoted to the description and measurement of bilingualism, from which no clear-cut definitive guidelines can be traced, though it is full of many useful insights.

Haugen's statement might be considered as providing a minimalist definition of bilingualism at the opposite pole to the maximalist viewpoint as put forward by Halliday, McKintosh & Strevens (1970). These authors talk of *ambilingualism* to describe the person who is capable of functioning equally well in either of his languages in all domains of activity and without any traces of the one language in his use of the other. For some people this type of person is the only "true" bilingual (Thiery, 1976) but in that case there may be very few "true" bilinguals around. As the discussion about ambilingualism is careful to point out, the complete ambilingual is a rare if not non-existent species, since the implication is that the speaker in question has lived a double life in which all of his activities in one language have been or could be reduplicated in the other. Since language functioning, be it only on the lexical level, is closely tied to the activities and experiences one goes through in life it is highly unlikely that a person who has concentrated his time on a particular set of activities in one language has had equal opportunity to do the same in another. Thus a highly competent speaker of two languages, such as a professional interpreter, may well be able to pass as a native-speaker in two languages with no traces of interference in either, but lexical availability is likely to be greater in one of the two in specific semantic areas. For even someone like this may find that when he is talking about a subject in a different language from that normally used to discuss it he may hesitate, perhaps only for a fraction of a second, before finding the precise term needed to develop the subject in the less-used language. Although such a speaker may well have two sets of lexical items available in his memory store, functional specialization of language usage will make those tied to one particular language more readily available than those from the other. Professional interpreters are trained to overcome this kind of difficulty but even these people are often found to work more easily from one of their languages into another according to the domain of activity, even if outside specific domains they are capable of functioning equally well in both directions.

The extent to which functional specialization is connected to linguistic conditioning can be illustrated by looking at the example of the so-called *natural bilingual* who has not undergone any specific training and who is often not in a position to translate or interpret with facility between his two languages. By natural bilingual, also known as *primary bilingual* (Houston, 1972) we understand someone who has picked up two languages by force of circumstances, either in the home as a child or by moving to a community where the speaker is obliged to work with more than one language, but where no systematic instruction in two languages has been provided. The latter case is sometimes known as *secondary bilingualism*, i.e. where a second language has been added to a first language via instruction. The author Julien Green is a case in point. Although he comes very near to being an ambilingual in that he can read, write, understand and speak equally well in French and English, his attempts to translate one of his own books led to failure. Thus although Julien Green represents a case of fluent and highly competent bilingualism this does not necesarily imply equal ease at handling all activities in all domains with the same facility. Functional specialization of language usage can even lead to momentary mental blockages where this is least expected, as when the perfectly competent bilingual who normally conducts a particular activity in one language is suddenly obliged to do so in another and cannot find the appropriate terms. The equation between a particular language and a specific activity may bring about a conditioning which impedes the ready availability of a term which in other circumstances may be on hand without hesitation. The sudden loss of ability to find a perfectly current term can even lead to situations where it is not only unavailable at the requisite moment in the "other" language but that its equivalent in the "primary" language (for that activity) also suddenly becomes inaccessible. The speaker may then be left with a precise image which he cannot render in either language except by some circumlocution. And yet to all intents and purposes this same speaker might well be a highly competent bilingual. What happens more frequently in such circumstances is that the expedient of borrowing from the language in which the activity dominates is resorted to, though this normally happens only if the interlocutor can interpret the borrowing. To illustrate this point is the example of a group of English- dominant bilinguals who worked in a French educational environment and referred to "ponderating" (Fr. *pondérer*) examination results in discussions in English, rather than using the term "weighting" with reference to marks. In theory this group of speakers' dominance configuration should have made the English term more readily available, though in practice it was the contextual environment which made the French term intrude. This process will be discussed further in our examination of interference and code-switching but is used here to show up some of the difficulties connected with so called ambilingualism.

Ambilingualism should not be confused with *equilingualism*, though there may be points of similarity. Equilingualism, alternatively called *balanced bilingualism*, occurs when a speaker's mastery of two languages is roughly equivalent and where this ability may match that of monoglot speakers of the respective languages if looked at in broad terms of reference. However, even in these cases the notion of balanced bilingualism should be treated with circumspection for, as has been pointed out by Fishman *et al.* (1971)

> "Bilinguals who are equally fluent in both languages (as measured by their facility and correctness overall) are rarely equally fluent in both languages about *all possible topics*; this phenomenon is invariably a reflection of the fact that the societal allocation of functions is normally imbalanced and in complementary distribution rather than redundant."

Moreover, Dornic (1978, 1979) has shown how untypical the balanced bilingual is once one looks beyond surface, impressionistic evaluations of ability in two languages, and that stress, fatigue, emotional upsets, etc., will bring out a hidden imbalance which might well be masked by good pronunciation and apparent accuracy under normal circumstances.

On the other hand, an equilingual may have a fairly balanced knowledge of two languages but is clearly discernible from two monoglot speakers, respectively, through possible traces of interference in both. In this case knowledge of the two languages is roughly equal but by monoglot norms of reference both may show signs of deviation. It might be, however, that monoglot terms of reference are irrelevant in the examination of the bilingual ability of an individual who functions equally well in two languages in a given society.

Although we have queried whether monoglot norms of reference are relevant in decisions on whether a speaker is bilingual or not, since they may well represent an exceptional, if not unattainable, goal for the vast majority of users of two languages, yet they still tend to represent the beginning and end point of all discussions on the question for many people. If they represent an idealized and often exceptional measure of ability, as is the case with the ambilingual, we might wonder how significant such types of bilingual proficiency are for investigation purposes. From the purely linguistic standpoint the ambilingual (if he exists, which I doubt) is not a particularly interesting case since there is nothing in the speech of such a person worth commenting on. In the hypothetical case of the ambilingual with a "perfect" mastery of two languages in all fields of activity with no traces of interference there will be no phonological, morphological or syntactic features peculiar to either language that will be distinguishable from the speech produced by separate monoglots. From the psychological or sociological point of view such cases would be interesting, of course, since we would want to know how such a speaker achieves this feat and how this successful functioning in two languages affects his life, but from a purely linguistic standpoint there is little worthy of comment. The second point that makes the study of the flawless bilingual less relevant is that he is not representative of a very large class of bilingual speakers; the vast majority of people who by force of circumstances or by choice manipulate more than one language do reveal significant differences in the quality of speech produced, sometimes in both the languages involved but more often manifesting greater ease and ability in one than the other. In fact, it has been stated that the vast majority of cases are those of the *non-fluent bilingual* (Segalowitz & Gatbonton, 1977) where clear divergences from monoglot speech are detectable in at least one of the languages used. Thus the non-fluent bilingual represents a more useful case for investigation in both sociological and linguistic terms.

The obsession with monoglot norms of reference has led to the notion of *semilingualism,* an extreme variant of *double semilingualism* (Haugen, 1977), which, although conceptualized by earlier workers in the field, has been considerably propagated by Skutnabb-Kangas & Toukomaa (1976). Now the notion of semilingualism has led to considerable controversy and should be treated with great caution by anyone approaching bilingual studies; moreover, it should not be confused with what Hockett (1958) labels as *semibilingualism* and which he understands as *receptive bilingualism* (see p. 16) accompanying productive monolingualism.

The idea of semilingualism as widely propagated has been based on comparisons of performance of Finnish immigrant children living in Sweden in their Finnish and Swedish with monoglot children living respectively in Finland and Sweden and noting that their ability in both languages shows signs of considerable retardation. The work referred to above goes further to indicate that the retardation on the part of the bilingual immigrant children, when compared with their monoglot peers, may become a permanent feature among the immigrants, leading to social stigmatization representing a life-long handicap to the psychological, social and moral development of the bilingual.

The case of semilingualism is a problematic one on several counts, and is being ever more contested as the term filters through to the lay public and gets bandied about in an irresponsible fashion. It may well be that inadequate development of either of a bilingual's languages may be attributable to the peculiar social circumstances of certain immigrant populations where ghetto-like conditions isolate the speaker from the rich linguistic environment of the host community, driving him back into the more restricted world of the home-group. This home group, cut off as it is from the varied range of linguistic input that would have been available in the country of origin, could well be the origin of certain atrophied language development. T'Sou (1981b) is one of the few researchers to get the controversial debate into proper perspective (although many others are involved in refuting or defending the notion of semilingualism) by discussing the case of what he calls SWONALS or speakers without a native language. Such people are culturally displaced individuals who are isolated adults in a foreign environment, and indeed T'Sou rejects the idea of the occurrence of this phenomenon in pre-pubescent children. Adult SWONALS are people who suffer language loss in L1 without compensatory gain in L2, whereas much of the more notorious work on so-called semilinguals is based on inadequate comparisons of children with monoglot peer groups as a reference norm which fail to pay attention to the fact that with children bilingual competence is still in the stage of development and that divergences between monoglots and bilinguals are to be expected, if only in the disparity in input of linguistic models. Baetens Beardsmore (1983a) has shown how evidence purporting to reveal semilingualism in bilingual children is often inadequate, as have many other scholars (see below). On the other hand, T'Sou looks for internal grammatical evidence to prove the type of semilingualism he refers to, rather than insisting on comparative criteria of the type used by the protagonists of the concept, which may only give part of the picture. In so doing he takes into account the possibility of the bilingual norms of the type referred to by Oksaar (1983) which may be different from those prevalent in monoglot communities.

The debate about semilingualism has long been developed around the type of bilingual education to be provided for Finnish immigrants in Sweden, yet studies of bilingual education in other parts of the world, although not specifically dealing with immigrants, contradict the evidence put forward to support the notion, notably the case of immersion programmes in Canada (Swain & Barik, 1978; Swain, 1980; Swain & Lapkin, 1982). In immersion programmes, of whatever type they may be, English-speaking children from middle-class backgrounds receive all their instruction, or part of it, in French in the first few years of schooling, yet do not become semilingual; although their knowledge of French is not comparable to that of their monoglot French-speaking peers, they show no retardation in their development of English once the time factor is taken into consideration. When the level of competence in English is correlated with age and amount of input received it is found that any initial retardation is made up over a period of time. Children in immersion programmes end by having an equivalent mastery of English to that of their peers and a better mastery of French than children who had gone through a standard French-as-a-foreign-language programme, so that instead of being semilingual they achieve a certain degree of French-English bilingualism at no cost to their first or dominant language. Similar levels of success have been documented for other bilingual education programmes in European Schools (the network of establishments set up for the children of European civil servants and using up to seven teaching languages with every child compulsorily receiving instruction in at least two—Baetens Beardsmore, 1979a, 1980a; Baetens Beardsmore & Swain, 1985). On the other hand, as Genesee (1984) has pointed out, the successful bilingual education projects referred to above do not completely contradict the unsuccessful cases highlighted by Skutnabb-Kangas and others.

Swedish reports on semilingualism have caused a considerable amount of polemic amongst those involved in bilingual education (cf. Brent-Palmer, 1979, and the reply by Skutnabb-Kangas & Toukomaa, 1979, or Edelsky *et al.*, 1983 and the reply by Cummins & Swain, 1983). It would seem that the notion of semilingualism has been influenced by the deficit hypothesis put forward by Bernstein (1971) in which the social-class-determined notions of restricted and elaborated code account for different linguistic behaviour. However, the criticism of Bernstein's hypothesis (Labov, 1970; Ammon & Simon, 1975: 96–120; Dittmar, 1976: 29–101) and the sociolinguist's appraisal of the integrated nature of bilingual behaviour make it difficult to accept the notion of semilingualism in its crudest form without certain restrictions. For, although many bilinguals' performance in two languages may well differ distinctively from that of two separate monoglots, in terms of the total range of abilities the bilinguals may well achieve a similar, if different repertoire. This aspect will be dealt with in more detail in subsequent chapters. Although it may well be that the bilingual does not possess a complete repertoire of each separate language he uses, owing perhaps to functional specialization determined by the circumstances of his life experience, his total range across both languages is likely to be similar to that of a monoglot. As long as the tools with which one measures bilingualism are those used for measuring the one speaker/one language behaviour patterns, one is bound to come across some difference, lag, deviation or whatever, in at least one of the languages involved. Ever more scholars are pointing out the nebulous nature of the idea of semilingualism, including Paulston,

> "Semilingualism does not exist, or put in a way which is non-refutable, has never been empirically demonstrated." (Paulston, 1982: 54),

Oksaar (1983), who dismisses the concept as a mere catchword which is of no use for unbiased research, and Ekstrand (1979, 1983) who has discussed the lack of empirical support and theoretical foundations for the notion. Perhaps the final word on this term should come from one of its major protagonists, Skutnabb-Kangas, who states,

> "In the scientific debate the word has outlived its usefulness and should go",

and further

> "I do not consider semilingualism to be a linguistic or scientific concept at all. In my view it is a political concept." (Skutnabb-Kangas, 1984: 248–49)

The concept may perhaps have some restricted usefulness for dealing with those cases where, through social deprivation, a speaker is unable to acquire sufficient mastery of a second language in order to function adequately in that language and at the same time fails to develop, or loses control of, his first language through isolation or insufficient linguistic stimulus. Such is the case of the Chinese SWONAL described by T'Sou (1981b), an adult immigrant to the United States with few contacts with either Chinese or English speakers and whose linguistic development was one of accelerated creolization. Certain people in Wales have been described as having "two second languages" instead of one first and one second but here, too, one must not forget the possibility of bilingual norms arising in a mixed language community as found in certain Welsh counties. What is unfortunate about the catchphrase appeal of a term like semilingualism is that by focussing attention solely on linguistic norms it masks socio-psychological phenomena which are probably far more significant in accounting for particular differences in a bilingual's two languages. For it is at times almost impossible to maintain full native-like ability in L1 when living abroad, both because of the different sociocultural environment in which the language has to be used and because of the mere presence of another language which will impede the usage of L1.

The idea of semilingualism lies perhaps at the opposite pole from that of ambilingualism and should no more represent a yardstick for average bilingual ability than the irrelevant perfectly balanced case. If only one of the speaker's two languages is inadequate by monoglot norms there is no case for semilingualism. If both languages are marked as different from monoglot norms there is still no case for semilingualism, since such norms might be irrelevant in a society where everyone shares the bilingually-marked speech patterns. Nor is there a case for semilingualism if one notices bilingually-marked speech patterns in the speaker's two languages but fails to account for this in terms of socio-economic status, age, opportunity for use of language, interaction patterns, time devoted to language learning and the nature of the environment.

Two very useful and highly refined definitions of more marginal types of bilingualism have been developed by Dorian (1982); the first, *low-proficiency semi-speakers*, is introduced here to dispel any possible confusion with what has preceded, and to be distinguished from the second category of *near-passive bilinguals*. Dorian investigated inhabitants of a small speech island in East Sutherland made up of fisherfolk descendants bilingual in English and Scottish Gaelic who are surrounded by English monolinguals. All the fisherfolk descendants are bilingual, some of their fellow-villagers are English monoglots, while a certain number of the inhabitants do not fall into either clear-cut category. The latter are succinctly described as follows:

> "Semi-speakers are individuals who have failed to develop full fluency and normal adult proficiency in East Sutherland Gaelic, as measured by their deviations from the fluent-speaker norms within the community. At the lower end of the proficiency scale they are distinguishable from near-passive bilinguals by their ability to manipulate words in sentences: reminded of a forgotten Gaelic noun or verb, for example, they can nearly always build it into an intelligible Gaelic sentence, whereas near-passive bilinguals can rarely do so (although near-passive bilinguals know a good many lexical items and short phrases). At the upper end of the proficiency scale, semi-speakers are distinguishable from even the youngest fully fluent speakers of East Sutherland Gaelic by the presence in their speech of deviations from the local grammatical norms (recognized as 'mistakes' by fluent speakers), and by the frequency of such deviations, as well as by the presence of a marked degree of analogical levelling and a tendency to eliminate syntactic redundancies." (Dorian, 1982: 26)

These two categories of individual are not considered as monoglots because of their outstanding receptive control of East Sutherland Gaelic and their knowledge of the sociolinguistic norms which operate within the Gaelic-speaking community. This could be observed from their ability to understand everything, appreciate jokes, grasp significant titbits of gossip, etc., even though they themselves said very little. Such speakers' active usage of Gaelic tended to be restricted to formulaic utterances which were always appropriately placed in conversations, or else they would produce semantically integrated but grammatically deviant sentences which they might not be able to finish but which were often rounded off by a fluent Gaelic speaker. Whatever the degree of proficiency of semi-speakers and near-passive bilinguals they were definitely members of a bilingual speech community and therefore fell outside the classification of monoglots.

The emphasis that has been placed upon what the speaker does with his languages in the society in which he lives leads to the idea of *functional bilingualism*. This term can be interpreted in two ways, a minimalist and a maximalist interpretation. Under the minimalist interpretation a person can be called functionally bilingual if he is able to accomplish a restricted set of activities in a second language with perhaps only a small variety of grammatical rules at his disposal and a limited lexis appropriate to the task in hand. The marginal types referred to earlier are extreme examples of functional bilingualism as seen from the minimalist end of the scale. More generally, though, one could say that a minimalist version of functional bilingualism is close to that of languages for special purposes, as, for example, when certain jobs require a minimal working knowledge of another language, e.g. airline pilot English as used at international control towers, the French of *haute cuisine* for people in the catering industry. This type of linguistic knowledge is fairly easy to acquire, does not involve the intensive investment in time and tuition that a more pronounced and wide-ranging set of abilities involves and can be taught in specially designed courses that concentrate solely on the limited objectives of producing a speaker who can function primarily in his first language and over a restricted range in his second. The cost-effectiveness of achieving these limited goals has led to an increasing interest in the promotion of languages for special purposes and the creation of specialized working groups and journals to investigate this particular field (Gorosch, 1978). Many people would not accept this minimalist interpretation, however, as representing a form of bilingualism.

The maximalist interpretation of functional bilingualism comes much nearer to widely held views on what is involved in being bilingual, since it covers a wide range of activities and capacities in two languages. In this case the speaker is able to conduct all of his activities in a given dual linguistic environment satisfactorily. Note that there is no reference to norms in this explanation, since such a speaker may well use patterns that are completely alien to the monoglot reference group and show heavy signs of interference in phonology, morphology, lexis and syntax. However, to the extent that these do not impede communication between speaker and listener they do not get in the way of functional bilingualism. It may well be true that the majority of adult bilinguals who have learned their second language late in life fall into this category. Although they may not possess sufficient command of nuanced expression in the second language to operate in the same way that a monoglot would, they nevertheless succeed in understanding almost everything they read and hear, and speak and write sufficiently coherently for their interlocutors to appreciate their message.

The narrowing down of the range of ability implied in the preceding paragraphs leads to the notion of *receptive bilingualism*, which in itself could be considered as one form of functional bilingualism. This particular description fits the person who understands a second language, in either its spoken or written form, or both, but does not necessarily speak or write it. An alternative term for this case is *passive bilingualism,* though this is not favoured by specialists involved in language learning because it is felt that any language decoding activity implies active neurological processes where the mind is filtering and organizing the stimuli it receives into meaningful patterns. Receptive bilingualism is relatively easy to acquire, particularly for the older learner, and is a less time-consuming learning task in that it does not involve the laborious acquisition of language patterns that must be at ready command for fruitful conversation or written communication with a speaker of another language. Moreover, its long-term effects tend to be greater in that the ability to understand a foreign language can linger on far longer than the ability to speak or write one. Indeed, there are many cases of schoolday learners or university graduates in a foreign language who have lost the ability to communicate their ideas in the learnt second language but who have little difficulty in reading or understanding it.

Even native speakers of a language who emigrate to a foreign country and have little opportunity to keep their first language actively in use may, after a considerable period of absence from their home country, find that they are no longer readily able to communicate with ease in their first language. They often have less difficulty in reading newspapers and letters from their home country or in understanding their original compatriots. This situation can arise even when the emigrant learns the second language after adulthood, though it is rare for adult emigrants in this situation to have completely lost the faculty to produce utterances in their first language. People like this have been called *dormant bilinguals* by Grosjean (1982: 239). What is often the case is that after a period of acclimatization in the community of origin the language that has lain dormant for a considerable period of time is re-activated. It is a moot point whether one should, for example, consider the Estonian immigrant to the United States, who may not have used his first language for thirty years or more in a productive fashion, as a receptive bilingual in Estonian and a productive bilingual in English. Under the correct environmental stimulus such as a holiday in the country of origin, such speakers usually become productive again in their first language.

The case of the young child who is transferred to another linguistic environment at a very early age, say five years, is not quite the same. It is well known that young children removed to a community where there is no further stimulus in the first language can completely and rapidly lose the ability to manipulate that language or even understand it. It is not clear whether re-activation of the first language is easier in such cases than if the child had never had any knowledge of it, though some slight information on this question is reported by Tits (1948).

The promotion of receptive bilingualism in teaching programmes is slowly gaining ground because of its manifest advantages in time investment. In many universities across the world courses in reading ability in foreign languages form an essential component of many studies. In certain circumstances receptive abilities in reading and comprehension are even used to foster cross-lingual communication among people who speak and write only in their first language. For this policy to be a viable proposition in cross-cultural communication it implies that two linguistic communities liable to have frequent contacts advocate the same policy of mutual receptive bilingualism, and indeed this situation can be found in Belgium and Canada. In these countries public oratory is often conducted by members of parliament in their respective first languages but the services of the interpreter are often dispensed with for listening purposes. In this way two speakers may conduct a dialogue in two different languages yet both understand each other perfectly adequately. The advantages of this type of situation are that they allow each speaker to express his ideas with the precision of his native language ability and to conduct business efficiently.

A receptive ability, particularly of the auditory comprehension type, however, often accompanies a more limited productive ability and in circumstances where language loyalty is not involved or where great precision is less important there often arises a tendency on the part of one of the interlocutors conducting a dialogue involving speaking in a different language from the partner to switch to the partner's language. This can be explained by the fact that for most people cross-language communication based on receptive bilingualism is an unrealistic situation in which it feels abnormal to conduct a dialogue in a different language from that used by the partner. The move towards the speech patterns of one's interlocutor in a converging direction is known as *linguistic accommodation*, discussed with specific reference to bilingual contexts by Hamers & Blanc (1983: 183–207). The factors that determine the move away from communication based on a receptive pattern towards the use of one language for both speakers are multiple and include the degree of intimacy in the interaction (the more intimate the setting or relationship the greater the tendency to use the same language); the relative productive knowledge of each speaker involved (the one with the better command tending to switch more readily); the prestige of each language (the more prestigious tending to take over); attitudinal patterns towards each language (one community often expecting the other to be more or less bilingual than itself); the size of the group interacting (where the majority of speakers of one language might influence the minority present from the other language to switch to coalesced unilingual usage, though this is not always the case); and individual personality traits. A concrete illustration can be taken from the situation which might arise in Dutch-French interaction in bilingual Brussels. In the informal setting of, say, a cocktail party, speakers from the different language groups might well start off by using their own individual languages in communicating with each other. Very quickly this pattern may be broken, with the likelihood that the Dutch speaker will change over to French since it is tacitly assumed by both groups that the Dutch speaker is likely to know French better than his counterpart knows Dutch, and because French may for a variety of subtle reasons be considered as prestige-laden. These factors may well combine to over-ride the numerical strength of representatives of each language group present so that the presence of perhaps only one French speaker in the group could lead the Dutch speakers to switch. The above example should not be over-generalized but serves to illustrate the inter-relationship between societal and individual bilingualism in determining particular bilingual communication patterns.

The counterpart to receptive bilingualism is the situation where speakers not only understand but also speak and possibly write in two or more languages, i.e. *productive bilingualism*. Most foreign language teaching programmes are designed potentially to lead to productive bilingualism, though whether they do so or not depends to a large extent on the point at which one considers a person can handle the second language with enough facility to be classified as a bilingual. What is apparent from observation is that the development of receptive bilingualism outpaces that of productive bilingualism in the same way that its long-term effects seem to be greater. Productive bilingualism does not necessarily imply that the individual is capable of both writing and speaking two languages to the same level of proficiency. Such equivalent ability is largely determined by the learning circumstances. Some people are able to speak and understand two languages with almost equal facility without necesarily being able to write either of them adequately, while others can write only one with any degree of accuracy though they may speak two. Certain productive bilinguals may be able to write relatively easily in two languages but not speak with equal fluency in two, though often the ability to use the written form productively implies relative ease in oral abilities. However, one need only think of scholars of classical languages to realize that it is perfectly possible to write in a language one does not speak. On the other hand, in the same way that receptive bilingualism may be restricted to oral/aural skills, productive bilingualism need not imply *biliteracy* and indeed in many parts of the world where bilingualism is prevalent the speakers may not be able to read or write in either language. The classification of an individual as a productive bilingual makes no statement about his degree of competence in two languages since this is not a qualitative term. The user might speak and write his two languages in a manner that clearly reveals that he is not a monoglot user of either of them, or else he might speak and write only one of the two with traces of measurable distinctiveness. Since many biliterate bilinguals who regularly use their two languages do so in clearly differentiated circumstances, it is perfectly feasible to envisage the productive bilingual who speaks language A better than he writes it and writes language B better than he speaks it. By "better" here we mean, of course, with greater ease or with less disparity from the monoglot norms of reference. Situations like this are prevalent in countries where formal education is conducted in a language different from that of everyday life, particularly if the home language has no written form.

The typologies discussed up to this point lead to possible combinatory patterns for bilingual ability across the four language skills (see Table 1).

Thus a type 1 productive bilingual could manipulate the four basic language skills in two languages while a type 4 productive bilingual would be illiterate but could understand and speak two languages, while a type 5 productive bilingual might be the sort of person who speaks and understands a tribal language that has no written form but reads and writes a language acquired via book learning but which he has never had the occasion to hear or use (possibly a rare case). On the other hand, a type 3 receptive bilingual would be the classical scholar who only has the occasion to read and write a dead language.

TABLE 1 *Patterns of Individual Bilingualism*

Language Skills	Productive Bilingualism								
	Type 1		Type 2		Type 3		Type 4		Type 5
Listening comprehension	L1	L2	L1	L2	L1	L2	L1	L2	L1
Reading comprehension	L1	L2	L1	L2	L1	L2			L2
Oral production	L1	L2	L1	L2	L1	L2	L1	L2	L1
Written production	L1	L2	L1						L2

Language skills	Receptive bilingualism								
	Type 1		Type 2		Type 3		Type 4		Type 5
Listening comprehension	L1	L2	L1	L2	L1		L1	L2	L1
Reading comprehension	L1	L2	L1		L1	L2			L2
Oral production	L1		L1		L1		L1		L1
Written production	L1		L1		L1	L2			

Mackey (1976: 418–27) provides a far more detailed method for describing an individual's bilingualism which takes into account both the changing nature of patterns of language usage across time and the nature of interaction as determined by setting, domain, style, degree of intimacy, etc. In this method the amount of time spent using the two languages can be estimated, not only along the scale of the four language skills, but also with reference to siblings, ancestors and descendants, in-group acquaintances and out-group contacts, as well as in terms of the nature of the activity, e.g. recreation, instruction, prayer, daydreaming.

Pohl's (1965: 347) list of bilingual types includes *symmetrical bilingualism*, which coincides with the notion of productive bilingualism discussed earlier with the difference that it implies equal competence in both languages (i.e. balanced). His description of *asymmetrical bilingualism* coincides with the different types of receptive bilingualism we have presented. It might be useful, however, to retain this label to describe the situation which at first sight may seem exceptional but in fact is not so rare. This is the case of the student of a foreign language who has probably learnt via a standardized model and can make himself understood (in spite of a trace of accent and certain structural or lexical inadequacies) but who has difficulty in understanding what is said to him by native speakers. The French student of English, for example, who arrives in the north of England for the first time may have immense difficulties in understanding the inhabitants of, say, Newcastle, whereas the latter will have little difficulty in understanding their visitor. Although we are dealing with a form of productive ability on the part of our French student it differs from the standard situation where productive ability subsumes receptive ability; here there is obviously a receptive ability as far as standard English is concerned but this is not adequate for the Newcastle situation so that the idea of asymmetrical bilingualism neatly defines the circumstances. (Alternatively this could be described as one particular instance of bilingualism without diglossia, see p. 39. Usually this situation is only a temporary one to which rapid adjustment can be made. It might also be useful to consider as a form of asymmetrical bilingualism the situation in which one of the languages involved is no longer spoken, as with ancient Egyptian, so that it is impossible to go beyond the receptive reading and the productive writing skills.

The different types of bilingualism examined so far show the relative nature of the concept quite clearly but say nothing about how well a person needs to master one of the four skills in order to be considered as bilingual. We have also seen that the minimalist definition of the onset of bilingualism is of little practical help in solving this question (see p. 6). A useful way of describing the pre-bilingual state is to talk of *incipient bilingualism* (Diebold, 1961), which we would like to use as follows. Since it is generally accepted that receptive bilingualism precedes productive ability in the basic language skills there is some stage in the acquisition of a second language when the person is beginning to unravel the patterns of that language either at the decoding or the encoding level. This early or pre-bilingual stage can potentially lead to successful receptive or productive skills, the extent to which it does so depending on learning opportunity, amount of exposure to the second language and motivation to progress in its acquisition. It is possible that the majority of school learners of foreign languages can be considered as incipient bilinguals in that they are potential users of a second language but may never be in a position to want to use it or feel confident enough to do so in a real-life situation. Although still a somewhat imprecise notion it can be a useful way of describing people who have some knowledge of a second language which is not considered adequate for them to be ranged under the category of either receptive or productive bilinguals.

As one progresses through the different types and levels of ability, from the incipient, through the receptive to the symmetrical or asymmetrical productive stages, one can see a pattern of increasing complexity of skills developing. The speaker whose ability to function in a second language increases with its use is in a position of *ascendant bilingualism*, while if he no longer uses one of his two languages for a period of time and begins to feel some difficulty in either understanding or expressing himself with ease is in a position of *recessive bilingualism*. Dormant bilinguals referred to earlier (see p. 16) are one example of recessive bilingualism, though the most typical example of the latter case is the school learner of a foreign language who may have attained considerable skill but who in later life no longer has any contact with that language and gradually loses whatever ability might have been acquired. Such situations can even arise with people who have specialized in foreign languages, such as university graduates, or who have lived in a foreign country for a period of their lives but who later lose all contact with and use of a particular language. The older generation of Indonesians who under colonial rule had a regular use for Dutch but who since independence have had less and less need for the language illustrate this situation particularly well. Similar to recessive bilingualism is what Sawyer (1978) has called *covert bilingualism* but which refers more to a socially imposed attitudinal disposition to conceal one's knowledge of a given language rather than the loss of a language due to lack of practice, though the concealment may end in language loss. Covert bilingualism tends to occur in situations where a minority group, under the pressure of social stigma, undergoes a process of assimilation to the majority group's language and in the quest for upward social mobility will conceal the cultural attributes as well as the language of origin. Increasing signs of ethnic vitality amongst minority groups in all parts of the world are tending to minimize the occurrence of covert bilingualism on a societal level, though it may still arise on the individual level (see p. 88). Alternatively, community-based linguistic antagonisms may lead some to deny knowledge of a given language as illustrated by Hamers & Blanc (1983: 191), who describe how Flemings in Belgium may refuse to give tourist information in French to someone perceived as a Belgian, but comply if the enquirer is identified as a foreign French-speaker.

It is useful to distinguish the categories described above from similar designations which do not quite cover the same circumstances. The first is that of *additive bilingualism* as defined by Lambert (1974) in which the second language brings to the speaker a set of cognitive and social abilities which do not negatively affect those that have been acquired in the first language but where the two linguistic and cultural entities involved in being bilingual combine in a complementary and enriching fashion. Such a situation is brought about when the society in which the individual evolves attributes positive values to both languages and considers the acquisition of a second language as an extra tool for thought and communication. This form of enrichment language learning has been typical of the educated élite right down the ages (Lewis, 1976) from the time when the ancient Romans considered knowledge of Greek and Latin as an essential feature of the civilized citizen, through the Franco-Russian bilingualism described by Tolstoy under the Tsars to contemporary Singapore where Mandarin and English are given complementary positive status. Whatever the reality of the teaching situation may be, it is also the principle of additive bilingualism which serves as the intellectual justification for much of the mass foreign language instruction conducted in the majority of monoglot schools today.

The opposite situation arises with *subtractive bilingualism,* where the second language is acquired at the expense of the aptitudes already acquired in the first language and where, instead of producing complementarity between two linguistic and cultural systems, there is competition. This situation is prevalent in societies where the sociocultural attributes of one of the languages are denigrated at the expense of those of the other, which has a more prestigious socio-economically determined status. This situation is often found where ethnolinguistic minorities are present and is most easily brought about when schooling is conducted in a language different from that spoken in the home environment. Subtractive bilingualism can also be the origin of sociopolitical tensions in communities where linguistic identification and language loyalty play a significant role, and it accounts for the present dwindling in numbers of Welsh speakers in the United Kingdom, the decline of Irish in Eire and even the domination of world languages like English and French in former colonial territories.

At this stage it should be pointed out that bilingualism need not necessarily be coupled with *biculturalism,* though most successful bilingual educative programmes strive to make the two coincide. It is perfectly feasible to learn a foreign language without acquiring any of the cultural attributes implicit in that language, though the learner's resultant behaviour may appear somewhat strange to a native speaker of that language. Much of the friction across different linguistic communities can arise out of situations where speakers of two languages have acquired two sets of linguistic patterns but then proceed to use the second set with the cultural values of the first. At the least this can give rise to bewilderment on the part of the interlocutor, who is likely to interpret linguistic cues as coinciding with the cultural implications which are familiar to him; at the worst it can lead to interpretations of ignorance, rudeness or arrogance. Moreover, the further one progresses in bilingual ability the more important the bicultural element becomes, since higher proficiency increases the expectancy rate of sensitivity towards the cultural implications of language use.

Fitouri (1983: 214–15), in his attempts to distinguish between purely linguistic and purely cultural attributes prevalent amongst a population of

Ara'ic-French bilingual schoolchildren in Tunisia, distinguishes between four types of individuals:
1. bicultural bilinguals
2. monocultural monolinguals
3. monocultural bilinguals
4. bicultural monolinguals.

To illustrate the fourth category he gives the example of the children of immigrants whose parents have given up the use of their original language but who have maintained their customs, beliefs and value systems which they continue to transmit within the home through the medium of the language of the outside wider community.

One frequent example of lack of concordance between bilingual ability and cultural awareness is the misuse of taboo terms in the second language because their equivalents in the first language may be fairly anodyne in connotation or because the speaker is not sensitive to the implications of the taboo terms in the second language. A more subtle illustration of the intertwining of language and culture is to be found in the difficulties encountered by speakers of German or Dutch with the correct use of "Please" and "Thank you" in English, to which they often attribute the functions of the German "Bitte", "Danke schön", or the Dutch "Alstu-blieft", "Dank U". In German and Dutch the equivalent of "Please" is often used when handing something over and speakers of these languages often feel at a loss in English if this pattern cannot be carried over in the same type of situation. When they do so by using "Please", however, the speaker's reaction is likely to be one of interpreting the linguistic cue as an initiation to a request or to a requirement of further information, leading the listener to query this Germanic cultural feature by "Please what?". The uses to which "Thank you" are put also differ widely between English and other languages; for example, in turning down an offer in French "Merci" is sufficient to indicate that something is not required and can be interpreted as "Non, merci", whereas in English its equivalent "Thank you" is more likely to be interpreted as "Yes, thank you", implying acceptance. Thus it can be seen that without bicultural awareness the speaker can quite unwittingly achieve the opposite of the desired goal and may not communicate effectively in two languages. Van Overbeke (1976: 115) calls this phe-nomenon "interference which affects sociolinguistic behaviour". Awareness of the cultural facet in language learning has led to the development of the theory of *communicative competence* (see pp. 44, 136) and most serious programmes of bilingual education contain this bicultural element. More-over, in many circumstances where mixed ethnic groups are in contact it is essential to actively foster biculturalism beyond that which might be inherent in the language component itself of a two-language curriculum in order to minimize the effects of subtractive bilingualism.

The illustration just given of the relationship between language and meaning leads to discussion of the preoccupation of psycholinguists with the semantics of bilingual speech and their account of some of the differences in usage between different types of bilingual speaker. Analysis of the relationship between signs and meaning was triggered off by Weinreich (1953, 9-11) who distinguished between three types of bilingualism. In type A the signs of each language separately combine one unit of expression with one unit of content, e.g.

In type B the signs combine one single unit of content with two units of expression, one for each language, e.g.

In type C the meaning unit is that of the first language with its corresponding unit of expression and is the same for the equivalent unit of expression in the second language, e.g.

Type C would be a manifestation of *subordinate bilingualism* and would describe the case of the bilingual who exhibits interference in his language usage by reducing the patterns of the second language to those of the first (Paradis, 1977b: 238). Later research on Weinreich's original analysis collapsed types B and C into one category with Ervin & Osgood (1954) formulating a hypothesis whereby the original type A situation was called *co-ordinate bilingualism* and the types B and C together were called *compound bilingualism*. The new dichotomy has gained some anchorage in discussions about bilingual functioning but has led to increasing controversy and confusion with the passage of time so that it requires some attention in the drawing up of our typologies. Ervin & Osgood's hypothesis was based on the environmental or acquisition context in which the languages had been learned. For a compound bilingual, where two sets of language signs were associated with the same set of representational mediation processes, this came about as a result of having learned a foreign language in the traditional school situation (and via the intermediary of the first language) or else through the individual's growing up in an environment where two languages were spoken more or less interchangeably by the same people in the same situations. For the co-ordinate bilingual, where the two languages corres- pond to two independent meaning systems, this came about by learning two languages in totally differentiated circumstances, e.g. one in the home and the other outside, or where the second language was learnt in a totally different cultural environment from the first.

It was the work of Lambert *et al*. (1958) and Jakobovits (1968) which extended the dimensionality of the distinction so as to embrace not only aspects of the semantic functioning of bilinguals but also the lexical, syntactic, phonological, cultural and attitudinal aspects. However, in a critical appraisal of experiments designed to test the hypothesis Macna- mara (1967a) found both contradictory results and an inadequate explanation for the way in which the compound bilingual managed to keep his two languages apart. Attempts to accommodate these findings were made by concluding that the compound-co-ordinate opposition was a relative one more readily reflecting a continuum in which the same individual possibly behaves in a co-ordinate fashion during some activities or at certain periods of his life and in a compound fashion at other times (Lambert, 1969b). Paradis (1977a) relativizes further between compound, co-ordinate and subordinate to explain different types of bilingual behaviour. For Jakobovits (1968: 31) the extreme example of a co-ordinate bilingual would represent linguistic schizophrenia where there is complete functional independence in all aspects of the speaker's two language systems, while with the pure compound the two language systems are so fused that

> "the second language represents a mere alternative channel for
> the overt manifestation of the same underlying system repre-
> sented by the 1st language" (Jakobovits, 1968: 31).

In other words, the extreme example of a compound bilingual would be a translation machine!

Earlier experimental evidence, alluded to by Macnamara, had already raised doubts as to the adequacy of the hypothesis in predicting the separated (i.e. interference-free) use of languages by either compounds or co-ordinates as well as the difficulty in classifying people in either category. According to Paradis (1977b: 244) compounding is mostly predominant in phonology in the speech of normal bilinguals, where the person uses one and the same phoneme in both languages as a blend of the actual phonemes of each separate language. An English-French bilingual, for instance, will produce an /i/ which is neither the English /I/ nor the French /i/ but a mixture of the two, and this in both languages. Consequently, to the extent that a subject possesses a compound system he does not speak either language quite like a native monoglot; this type of situation is encountered mainly amongst communities where two languages are in permanent contact and it might lead to a recognizable contact dialect of each language.

In spite of the attempt to clarify the distinction (e.g. by the re-introduction of the subordinate case by Paradis) it would seem that the hypothesis does not allow for the reconciliation of conflicting cases of bilingual development. Ervin & Osgood had indicated that the compound bilingual was one who had acquired the two languages in childhood in a context where both were used almost interchangeably by the same persons. Such cases do exist but fail to account for other speakers in the environment who might well use one language exclusively and who presumably also influence language development.

Awareness of the contradictory evidence surrounding the distinction led Lambert (1969b) to modify his original conception of compound-co-ordinate bilingualism so that

> "compound bilinguals were defined as those brought up in a thoroughly bilingual home environment from infancy on, while co-ordinates were those who had learned the second language at some time after infancy, usually after ten years of age, and usually in a setting other than the family." (Lambert, 1972a: 308)

Based on this assumption and on differences in ability noted between early as opposed to late bilinguals, Baetens Beardsmore (1974a) suggested that the compound language system represented that which reflects the *acquisition* of 2 × L1 during the vital formative years of the child's linguistic development. This falls in with the ideas on the language acquisition device, or LAD, as put forward by Chomsky (1965: 56 and 206) and Lenneberg (1967: 142–87) which indicate that there is a critical age of 11± years for the development of language in the monoglot. Language learning beyond this age appears to involve some different processes so that the co-ordinate language system would be that which reflects an *acquired* L1 during the formative years, to which has been added a *learned* L2 at some stage beyond the critical age of 11± years. The above differentiation between the two systems was at the time felt adequate to explain how in the co-ordinate case the two languages might correspond to two independent meaning (and other) systems. It was also thought to account for the interference-free behaviour of the compound bilingual who has not necessarily acquired only one set of representational mediation processes, but two, whose nature would still be different from the two sets (one acquired, one learned) of the co-ordinate.

Since the above publications doubts have been expressed on the relevance of Lenneberg's LAD hypothesis which led to the reformulation of the nature of compound and co-ordinate bilingualism; Krashen (1973; 1975) has criticized the critical age hypothesis, as have Ekstrand (1979) and Felix (1982) in their detailed analysis of early and late bilingualism in both natural and classroom environments, so that the theoretical foundations of the discussion are shaky.

The confusion around the whole issue of compound-coordinate-subordinate bilingualism has led some researchers to question the validity of the entire hypothesis. Diller (1970), in a review of the literature, has noted that at least three contradictory definitions have been used and that experimental evidence does not confirm any distinction. He concludes that the notion of compound and co-ordinate bilingualism is a conceptual artifact, while Shaffer (1976) further suggests that research into bilingualism should proceed without assuming that the distinction has been established. It would be wise to take these warnings into account, particularly since the careful investigation into bilingual neurological processes by Albert & Obler (1978), although not discarding the notions, does not convincingly establish their significance.

The preceding discussion on different types of mental processes which may affect bilingual output highlighted a significant difference between *early* and *late* bilingualism which has received considerable attention in the specialist literature (see Chapter 4). By early bilingualism is meant the acquisition of more than one language in the pre-adolescent phase of life, what Haugen (1956: 72) calls *infant bilingualism*, Swain (1972) describes as "bilingualism as a first language", and Adler (1977) terms *ascribed bilingualism*. Late bilingualism occurs when the first language is acquired before the age of more or less 11 and further languages are learned at some age beyond this period (what Adler, 1977, calls *achieved bilingualism*). One could further refine this age-determined distinction by referring to cases where two languages are present from the onset of speech as *consecutive*, or *early consecutive bilingualism*, and cases where the second language is added at some stage after the first has begun to develop as *early* or *late successive bilingualism*. McLaughlin (1984: 101) calls *simultaneous bilingualism* the case where a child is introduced to a second language before the age of 3 and successive bilingualism when it is added beyond this age, while admitting that this cut-off point is somewhat arbitrary.

A considerable amount of research has been conducted into the acquisition of more than one language by very young children, succinctly overviewed in McLaughlin (1978; 1984). The pioneer in this field was Ronjat (1913) who described the bilingual development of a child up to the age of 4 years and 10 months in a situation where a clear distinction was made between language and interlocutor on the principle of one person = one language. Ronjat's son, Louis, learnt German from his mother and French from his father and went through the following developmental stages. Initially Louis' pronunciation seemed to be based on a unified phonological system in that his pronunciation was the same in both languages. In both languages there was a parallel development in phonetics, morphology and syntax and the child soon became aware of his bilingualism and translated messages from one language into the other. At a later stage in his life the child's usage reflected functional specialization brought about in part by schooling, with Louis preferring French for technical expression and German for personal literary expression. His development was not accompanied by retardation in general linguistic progress and loans from one language into the other were isolated cases.

The most important analysis of early bilingualism is that conducted by Leopold (1939-49) in which the author's daughter, Hildegard, was systematically observed in the first two years of her life and less systematically up to the age of 15 years 7 months. Hildegard was brought up in the United States in English and German (her father's language) and became dominant in English because of the richer environmental stimulus provided in this language. Although she showed considerable signs of interference in both languages in different phases of her development from the age of 2 onwards, she too began quite early to use only one of her two languages according to the language of her interlocutor. Interference from English into German was particularly noticeable in the lexis and syntax but less evident in pronunciation, morphology and word formation. Again no negative effects were found in the general linguistic and mental development of the child which could be attributable to the simultaneous acquisition of two languages.

A third significant investigation of early bilingualism is that conducted by Rūķe-Draviņa (1967) into the development of her two children brought up in Latvian and Swedish. In this case the children were confronted with Swedish after their first language had been established in the home environment, but at a very young age, and Swedish represented the language of the outside world, friends, play groups, etc. As with the cases cited earlier these children began to distinguish between the two languages in their lives very early in life, towards the end of the third year. They kept both distinct in function, depending on their interlocutors. It appeared that the first language acquired, Latvian, maintained strong emotional ties, even when Swedish became more developed so as to dominate in lexical and structural complexity.

Two rather different studies of early bilingual development describe cases in which the second language gradually displaces the first (subtractive bilingualism), as frequently happens when young children are removed to a new linguistic environment and have decreasing contacts with their first language. Kenyeres & Kenyeres (1938) describe the case of their daughter, Eva, who spoke Hungarian (the family language) and a little German up to the age of 6 years and 10 months when she moved to Geneva and began school in French. After 10 months she spoke French as well as a native speaker except for a few deviant verb forms and French gradually began to take the place of Hungarian, continuing to develop in step with the child's intellectual progress. Interesting results from this study show how Eva manifested similarities with monoglot linguistic development, as well as significant differences. It was noted that there was no transitional step by step build up of language abilities in the second language as occurs when children learn one language only, that there was more reflection on language structure, and that the first language often served as a support in the learning of the second. Unlike late bilinguals, such as adult learners of a foreign language, there was less reliance on the articulatory habits of the first language in acquiring the pronunciation of the second.

The second case of early (successive) bilingualism is that described by Tits (1948) of a Spanish refugee girl who was taken in by a Belgian family and who spoke only Spanish on arrival but was sent to a French school at the age of 6 years and 4 months. She rapidly adapted to her new linguistic environment, showed no signs of retardation in intellectual development or in her articulation of French and after 93 days declared to her guardians that she had forgotten her Spanish. The latter tried to keep Spanish up in the home environment but with a relative lack of success.

The two examples just discussed reveal an interesting area of investigation for students in this field, namely that of language loss. It is known that this can occur swiftly and perhaps definitively with young children who sever all connections with their original language environment. What is not clear is whether relearning the original language at some later stage in life occurs with any greater ease than is the case with people learning a second language for the first time. A study of this type of situation has been conducted on a very young child (3-4 years) by Berman (1979) but more information is required on older people in similar circumstances. Nor is it clear how quickly the process of language loss occurs, what the critical age for avoidance of language loss may be or, in the case of adults who lose contact with their language of origin and become "rusty", how long it takes to re-activate the dormant abilities. Ancillary to all these questions is the study of language loss among late learners of a second language, i.e. the school learner of a foreign language.

Cohen (1975b) studied young children who were forgetting a second language after a limited period of non-exposure and produced tentative findings which suggested that the things learnt last were those first forgotten, while the rate of forgetting appeared to be faster than the rate of learning. The volume edited by Lambert & Freed (1982) addresses itself to both societal and individual aspects of language loss, trying to incorporate the meagre information to date into a wider frame of reference by linking up language attrition with language acquisition, language use and language maintenance. Both the summary chart of findings from research on language loss and the detailed bibliography provided in this collection of papers should represent a useful resource tool for those interested in delving deeper into this very necessary and relatively unchartered area of bilingual studies.

A more recent case study of bilingual development in children is Saunders' (1982) account of the acquisition of German and English by his two sons, Thomas and Frank, which, although avowedly anecdotal, is not merely impressionistic but based on a broad overview of the literature as well as on tests. It represents an unusual departure from the classical case studies mentioned earlier in that although the principle of one parent—one language was applied in providing the input, with the mother speaking English, the father, who represented almost the sole source for German in an almost exclusively monolingual environment in Tasmania, was not a native speaker of German but a professional linguist. The account reveals how in these somewhat unusual circumstances successful bilingual proficiency can be achieved, even though the lack of peer interaction made the children's output in German somewhat monostylistic, i.e. adult-like. As this book was designed mainly to dispel some of the worries that might arise among parents confronted with bilingualism for the first time it is particularly strong on answering practical questions about the effects of dual language acquisition on cognitive and emotional development, on its effects on family and community relationships for the child and on how to provide compensatory strategies for achieving near equilibrium in proficiency when the "other" language, in this case German, is not prevalent outside the home.

An important contribution to childhood bilingual development is the study carried out by Fantini (1985) who has documented the Spanish-English development of his son, Mario, over the first ten years of his life. This study is uniquely interesting on several counts, primarily in that it differs from the classical investigations by concentrating on the developmental *sociolinguistic* aspects of the learning process, without ignoring purely linguistic dimensions. Particularly important here is the account given of the ways in which the socialization process affects bilingual acquisition and the determination of the relevant social factors which triggered Mario's switching from one code to another. An incidental point of interest, though minor in the overall study, is the fact that Mario was sporadically exposed to a third language, Italian, and Fantini shows how the third language interacted with the other two to produce some interesting features of integration into the overall bilingual developmental process, thereby providing rare gems on trilingual acquisition. This study confirms some of the earlier findings (e.g. that Mario had achieved complete separation of languages by the age of two years and eight months, an early development of metalinguistic awareness and no negative associations connected with his bilingual status in predominantly monolingual out-of-home environments) but goes further in revealing the rapid development of code-switching which was done appropriately by the third year, the acquisition of age-appropriate styles which distinguished between peer usage and adult usage and important comments on speech variation even within limited bilingual ability. Fascinating information is also provided on the nature and frequency of interference which is linked to the developmental process, revealing how sparse this tended to be according to the different levels of linguistic analysis and how this changed in directionality, over time and according to contextual variables such as interlocutor, setting and topic. Fantini's sociolinguistic approach also examined Mario's proficiency in each language as compared with that of monolingual children to see whether his knowledge and use of Spanish and English differed from or resembled that of monolingual speakers. The results of several tests, combined with school reports and comments from various observers of the child showed that by age ten he had successfully developed dual language systems and was judged an acceptable and competent member of each of two cultures.

It is generally accepted that early bilingualism has many advantages over late bilingualism from the viewpoint of linguistic competence in the two languages, though documented examples of the negative consequences of such cases do exist (cf. for example, Lebrun & Hasquin, 1971; Skutnabb-Kangas & Toukomaa, 1976). However, it would seem that in most cases where the consequences are less positive they can usually be attributed to social and psychological factors coupled with educational strategies that have not sufficiently taken into account the many variables involved in achieving successful bilingualism. A critical appraisal of experiments, and their defects, which purport to reveal the negative aspects of bilingualism, particularly in education, can be found in Balkan (1970).

Many specialists have demonstrated the positive aspects of early bilingualism, both for the ease with which it can be achieved and the superior level of attainment when compared with late bilingualism, particularly with respect to the acquisition of a flawless, native-like accent and intonation patterns in more than one language. Although increasingly called into question, Lenneberg's (1967) analysis of the biological foundations of language, which was devoted to monoglot circumstances, provides many arguments applicable to the early acquisition of two or more languages and reveals the great plasticity of the nervous centres relevant to speech in the pre-adolescent child. It also attempts an explanation of the gradual loss of language learning ability with ageing, which perhaps accounts for the apparent greater difficulty noted with late bilinguals in achieving a competence in the second language which completely masks influences from the first. Other neurolinguists (Penfield & Roberts, 1959; Glees, 1961) have tended to confirm the relationship between the development of cerebral mechanisms and verbal behaviour which stress the fact that young children have a capacity for acquiring new linguistic mechanisms which older people do not have. According to Titone (1972), although two languages can be acquired from the very onset of language development, the optimum age for the introduction of early consecutive bilingualism would appear to be between four and five years, particularly when the parents themselves are not in a position to provide the necessary input. At this age the imitative capacities of the child are at their highest development and receptivity to socialization by means of verbal communication is at its greatest. Titone (1972: 93–138) summarizes the arguments in favour of early bilingualism as follows: motivation to communicate is very great with young children who also enjoy playing with language and are less inhibited than older learners in the manipulation of sounds, words, structures, etc.; young children have an extremely sensitive perception of highly nuanced differences in sounds, which, coupled with their imitative capacities, lead to the ready assimilation of distinctive differences between languages which might escape the attention of the older learner. There is little evidence based on reliable experimentation that early bilingualism in itself can have negative effects on the development of the personality, though many observers have erroneously attributed to bilingualism personality problems which have become apparent or been exacerbated by bilingualism but which in fact may be due to sociocultural factors. There is also little evidence to show that early bilingualism need have negative cultural effects on the child, provided that different cultures are not presented as conflicting but are allowed to integrate harmoniously. This may be difficult to achieve in certain social conditions but should not be automatically considered as a bilingual problem (see Chapter 5). On the linguistic side early bilingualism may in the initial stages lead to a lower level of vocabulary development per language than in monoglots. This is only revealed, however, if one looks at the two languages involved separately. When both languages are examined the total lexis representing the total conceptual vocabulary of the bilingual child may even be greater than that of the monolingual (Doyle *et al.*, 1977: 28).

Many of the advantages listed above are more difficult to realize with the late bilingual, but not necessarily absent. Awareness of the differences between the two categories of speaker should lead to a more careful appraisal of how one sets about describing, measuring and promoting the same or similar goals. Strong evidence as to the difference between early and late bilingualism has been given by Genesee *et al.* (1978), where in a small-scale but refined experiment the authors have shown how early bilinguals are less inclined to keep their two linguistic systems functionally distinct or segregated than is the case with late bilinguals. The experiment suggested that the phonetic, syntactic and semantic components of the adolescent bilingual's language processing may be more differentiated neurophysiologically than those of the infant and childhood bilingual; with early bilinguals meaning appeared to play a pre-eminent role in the interpretation of lexical stimuli, whereas late bilinguals appeared more able to circumvent semantic forms of processing. (For further discussion of these points, see Chapter 4.)

The debate on the overall desirability of introducing bilingualism early or late in the child's educative process (see Chapter 5) has been refined to some extent by experimental evidence which revealed that on certain linguistic and cognitive skills the older learner was at an advantage. Swain (1981b) analysed test results for anglophone children learning French and showed how in some aspects of learning a second language the older pupil who had begun schooling in the foreign language at ± age 13 compared favourably with the younger pupil who had begun at ± age 5. The older learner was found to be superior in reading comprehension tests while the younger pupil was better in listening comprehension tasks; measurements using cloze procedures for testing grammatical competence revealed the two types of pupil to be almost equal. Interpretations of these findings were that the older learner is more cognitively mature, more able to abstract, classify and generalize in formulating and applying L2 rules; the older learner has already acquired the skills of reading and writing and needs only to learn the different surface realizations of these skills in L2. The older learner also has a greater "world knowledge" which he can transfer to L2.

In further studies designed to try to explain this difference, Swain (1981b) and Cummins, (1979; 1980), distinguish between "basic inter-personal communicative skills" or BICS, and "cognitive and academic aspects of language proficiency" or CALP, which are significant for under-standing differentiated progress rates for early and late bilinguals. CALP refers to the demands inherent in the educational system, such as literacy skills, whereas BICS refers more to language use which reflects mani-festations such as oral fluency, accent and certain aspects of sociological competence. Swain and Cummins also argue that CALP is cross-lingual and that once its features have been learned they are applicable to any language context. In this way the older learner can more easily transfer the abilities required for handling decontextualized language as implicit in literacy activities, once they have been acquired in L1 (see Chapter 5 for the later developments of these hypotheses).

It should be noted that in the presentation of the different types of bilingualism so far great care has been taken to avoid mention of the "mother tongue". This has been deliberate, since in many cases it is irrelevant to talk of a mother tongue in the widely accepted layman's understanding of the idea. To many, mother tongue often means the language best known which is assumed to be that first learnt. If one looks at the early infant bilingual there may have been more than one language from the outset so that neither is best known, while in other cases the language first learnt may, through force of circumstances, not be the one best known in later life. For an illustration of the potential confusion around the concept and usage of the terms "mother tongue", see Skutnabb-Kangas, 1984: 12–57.

Dodson (1981) uses the concept *preferred language* as a substitute for the notions of dominant language, mother tongue or L1 since it brings out clearly the varying nature of bilingual proficiency. For Dodson the preferred language is determined by factors which change the significance of a given language across time, according to the subject's case history, and in line with subjective self-assessment of relative fluency. This is a subtle concept which should not be dismissed lightly since it takes into account questions of repertoire and domain; a bilingual might well have one preferred language for one set of activities, another for another, his preferred language for all activities may change with time, or else may partially change so that, for example, prayer and mental arithmetic might have the same preferred language throughout life whereas informal social interaction might change preferred languages according to individual circumstances. This viewpoint strongly underlines the view put by Mackey (1970a: 554) that

> "bilingualism is not a phenomenon of language; it is a character-istic of its use. It is not a feature of the code but of the message. It does not belong to the domain of *langue* but of *parole*."

Very little attention has been given to the other widely-used non-specialist ideas of "perfect bilingualism" since these tend to imply value judgements of linguistic ability which are often difficult to circumscribe. Pohl (1965: 347) claims that it is absurd to talk about a perfect bilingual just as it is to talk about a perfect unilingual. In circumstances where it is felt necessary to make a distinction between the language first spoken or that in which the speaker feels greater ability, it is wiser to indicate this in terms of dominance or preference, or if L1, L2, etc., are used, to show that the numbers refer to order of acquisition in consecutive bilingualism.

Now that a long list of different *types* of bilingualism have been discussed it would perhaps be useful to go back to our initial preoccupation with definitions and see whether some one formula can bring as many of them together as possible. Béziers & Van Overbeke (1968) gave a review of many of the inadequacies of previous attempts at definition and went on courageously to formulate a new one. The result is rather all-embracing, tending to cover the maximum number of cases discussed up to now with the advantages and defects implied in such an undertaking. For these authors

> "Le bilinguisme est un double moyen nécessaire ou facultatif de communication efficace entre deux ou plusieurs 'mondes' diffé-rents à l'aide de deux systèmes linguistiques."
> (*"Bilingualism is a double means of efficient communication, imposed or freely chosen, between two or several 'worlds', using two linguistic systems."*) (Béziers & Van Overbeke, 1968: 133)

This statement covers the complete range of possibilities from the minimal-ist starting point indicated by Haugen to the maximalist case put forward by Halliday, McKintosh & Strevens, as well as different levels of bilingual competence at any stage in between. It imposes no restrictions about the nature, purity or equivalence in linguistic knowledge in either language, except the indication that communication must be efficient. It does not even imply that one has to speak a second language, since the person who speaks one but understands two can possibly communicate efficiently by means of two linguistic systems — in this case there is at least one-way communication from the speaker of language A to the listener who speaks language B but also understands language A.

The usefulness of this definition is that it allows one to view bilingualism as a cline with no clear-cut limits other than those of the pure monoglot at one end and the perfect ambilingual at the other. Its weakness is that one still has to place the type of bilingualism under discussion once the definition has been given. In this way the student of the question has to fix his own limits along the cline and accommodate his explanations within the framework he has set himself. On the other hand the definition can be extended to allow for the interpretation of bilingualism along lines that fit in with the investigation of what are generally considered monoglot speech communities.

The homogeneity of the monoglot speech community is never as clear-cut as superficial observation might lead one to assume, as has been shown by Labov (1972) in his investigation of New York English. Not only are there frequently considerable dialect differences within one speech community, but within each dialect group there are also significant varieties in language form according to the functions to which the language is being put. These functional differences, sometimes called registers, are the varieties of a given dialect that are conventionally distinguished by the subject matter or use to which the language is being put. The register of the law, or of the church, significantly differs in English from that of a letter or an informal chat and the differences may be of substance as well as of form. High Church Anglicanism, for example, is characterized by differences in grammar, lexis and pronunciation from any other form of English use, as for example in pronoun forms (*Thee, Thou*), verb morphology (*The hour cometh and now is...*), lexis (*the handmaiden of the Lord, verily I say unto you*), as well as the particular intonation often associated with corporate prayer. It might be argued that these differences are not significant when compared with bilingual behaviour across two languages, since many educated speakers of English can call on any of these relatively infrequent elements at will so that they form part of their global mental grammar of English. That they do not do so unless called upon by profession or proclivity is merely a question of availability, not of substance. Nevertheless, a vast number of native speakers of English are conceivably never in a position to place any of these elements in their speech with any more ease than certain types of bilingual who are expected to switch to another language according to function.

When one moves to differences in dialects within one language, one is confronted with a similar situation of formal and functional separation. It is well known that linguistic borders are quite often arbitrary, as are the groupings of dialect families under one national language umbrella. The inhabitants of the Dutch-German border area are respectively classified as speakers of Dutch or of German depending on which side of the national frontier they may find themselves. Yet internal evidence from analysis of the dialects in question often reveals that they are more closely related to each other than to the respective national languages under which they are classified. In other words it may well be that the Dutch dialect speaker on the western side of the common frontier has more features in common with his German neighbour than he has with a Dutch inhabitant of Amsterdam. It may also imply that the Amsterdamer has just as much difficulty in communicating with his compatriot on the Dutch border as he has with the German national on the other side. This situation has consequences for the notion of language distance by which bilingualism is sometimes measured.

As one moves through different dialect varieties of a language one moves along a scale of differentiation which may lead to the point of mutually unintelligible dialects. Once mutual unintelligibility has been reached one is faced with the same conditions as pertain to bilingualism. In many nations a situation exists where speakers of a dialect which differs considerably from the national standard are obliged to learn this national standard for purposes of education and wider communication beyond the region. Such is the situation in German Switzerland where a regional form of German, Schwyzertütsch, is spoken but where standard German is used in print, the media and education. Such cases of *bi-dialectalism* tend to be a one-way process in that the speaker of a standard variety of a national language rarely feels the need to learn the non-standard variety whereas the opposite is more frequent. Bilingual societies are similar in that usually only one of the groups in contact feels the need to learn the language of the other. It is rare to have stable two-way bilingualism in equal proportions across two language groups (Mackey, 1976: 30). The bi-dialectal situation, more prevalent than is often imagined, has led to the notion of *diglossia* as put forward by Ferguson (1959: 336);

> "Diglossia is a relatively stable language situation in which in addition to the primary dialect of the language, which may include a standard or regional standard, there is a very divergent, highly codified, often grammatically more complex, super-posed variety, the vehicle of a large and respected body of literature, heir of an earlier period or another speech community, which is learned largely by formal education and is used for most written

and formal purposes, but is not used by any sector of the community for ordinary conversation."

Diglossic situations can be found all over the world, as in the Arabic-speaking countries where a *High* form of Arabic is used for education, religion and formal communication, and a *Low* form for informal contacts and local usage. This Low form differs from region to region and may vary so considerably from the High form as to be almost unintelligible to a speaker of a different Low form from another part of the Arab world. In Greece the *demotic* form of Greek is reserved for High situations and the *katharevusa* for Low situations, though the dichotomy is gradually being eroded. In Belgium it may be a Flemish or Walloon dialect that serves in Low situations with standard Dutch or French in High situations.

The relationship between diglossia and bilingualism becomes apparent when one thinks of the relationship between dialects of one language and bilingualism in terms of the cline described earlier. If two dialects of an umbrella language are mutually unintelligible and differ considerably from the standard, one is clearly in a state of diglossia and theoretically at least in a potential state of bilingualism. Fishman (1967: 34) has stated that

"Bilingualism is essentially a characteristic of individual linguistic behaviour whereas diglossia is a characterization of linguistic organization at the sociocultural level"

and has drawn up a theoretical framework for analysing situations where either or both may co-occur in a particular sociocultural context. Thus one can have situations of bilingualism with and without diglossia and diglossia with and without bilingualism as illustrated in Fishman's schematic representation:

TABLE 2

		Diglossia	
		+	−
Bilingualism	+	Both diglossia & bilingualism	Bilingualism without diglossia
	−	Diglossia without bilingualism	No diglossia No bilingualism

The diglossic component of this Table, implying a subdivision into High and Low forms, fits into the bilingual component depending on whether the High language is genetically related to the Low or not.

To illustrate the possibilities represented in Table 2 we can look at the case of a complex urban setting such as Brussels where two standard languages are present, French and Dutch, together with dialect variants of each, some indigenous to the city and some brought in by Walloon and Flemish immigrants (Baetens Beardsmore, 1979c). The linguistic forces present in the city can be broken down as in Table 3.

TABLE 3 *Linguistic Forces in Brussels*

Category of Speaker	Diglossia	Bilingualism
1. Indigenous upper-level French monoglot	–	–
2. Indigenous lower-level French monoglot	(+)	–
3. Indigenous bilingual	+	+
4. Indigenous Dutch monoglot	–	–
5. Flemish immigrant	+	(+)
6. Walloon immigrant	(+)	–

The indigenous monoglots, be they upper-level French-speakers (category 1) or Dutch speakers (category 4 — these belonging to lower-level social groups since the upper-level indigenous Dutch monoglot is a relatively rare occurrence in Brussels), share the features of no diglossia and no bilingualism. However, the French monoglots will mainly use a High, prestige form, while the Dutch monoglots, an ageing and diminishing sub-group, will probably use a Low, dialectal form of Dutch in most of their activities. Category 2, the indigenous lower-level French monoglot, may be diglossic (hence the brackets) if he uses a form of French marked by contact and interference features from Dutch in the more intimate aspects of his daily life, reserving the High form of French for official transactions; on the other hand, he may well only master the Low, regional form of French productively and only handle standard, High French receptively. His nearest counterpart is the Walloon immigrant to the city (Category 6) who may or may not be a Walloon dialect speaker in Low circumstances, using High French elsewhere. The indigenous bilingual (Category 3) generally speaks a Low form of a Dutch dialect in more intimate communication and some variety of French in High circumstances characterized by a certain degree of formality. Finally, the Flemish immigrant (Category 5) usually masters a dialect and a standard form of Dutch, making him diglossic in the Dutch component of his social behaviour, but he may also use French in High circumstances since this is the numerically dominant language in the city.

Although this overview is somewhat simplistic (see Baetens Beard-smore, 1983b) it illustrates the complex intertwining of diglossia, individual and societal bilingualism in a small geographic area. Within the field of bilingual studies there has been a certain amount of polemic concerning the definition and the applicability of diglossia to certain social contexts, especially where creoles and pidginized forms of languages are in contact with other speech patterns (see particularly French scholarly debates on this in the reviews *La Linguistique*, 1982, and *Langages*, 1981).

In a re-appraisal of the relationship between bilingualism and diglossia, Fishman (1980) added two further dimensions to the general debate. What intrigued him were the ethnocultural implications of the presence of two languages in diglossic functioning, bearing in mind that just as bilingualism is primarily concerned with individuals, so biculturalism is an individual asset or debit. Culture, for Fishman, refers to norms pertaining to all of human behaviour, belief and valuation. On the societal level of diglossic functioning, determined by institutional forces, there is a potentiality for *di-ethnia*, where ethnicity is to be understood as the more restricted set of behaviours, values and beliefs related to membership in a particular people. It would seem that di-ethnia is a rare phenomenon since it is difficult to reconcile ethnic values of say, black African society and white western society, though Fishman quotes the example of certain sectors of the Moslem world where traditional behaviour, dress, diet and values dominate most of life but where modern economic and technical roles require different dress, diet and languages. Biculturalism, on the other hand, may or may not accompany bilingualism, as we have seen earlier (see p. 23).

The complex picture that emerges from any discussion of bilingualism, where individual language use is closely inter-related with social forces, brings into focus the point made at the outset of this chapter that bilingualism is a relative concept with no clear cut-off points. If we accept that bilingualism is situated somewhere along a cline which ranges from non-diglossic monolingualism, through bi-dialectalism to the use of two distinct languages at varying levels of ability, then it is clear that some of the phenomena that have traditionally been considered as exclusive to bilingual behaviour may well manifest themselves amongst categories of speakers other than manipulators of two distinct languages.

Summary

In an attempt to circumscribe the field of investigation covered by bilingual studies a typological frame of reference has been presented which clarifies some of the ambiguities inherent in over-generalized definitions of bilingualism. Particular emphasis has been placed on the fundamental distinction between societal and individual bilingualism, with the accent on the latter, though without neglecting the interlocking nature of the sociological and linguistic aspects of using two or more languages. Starting from a minimalist standpoint which defines the onset of bilingualism, different degrees and types of bilingual ability have been reviewed until the maximalist position is reached whereby bilingualism is equated with equal native-like mastery of two or more languages. For the individual speaker, examples have been given ranging from the initial stages of incipient bilingualism, through such types as receptive and productive bilingualism, ascendant, to indicate a progressive development, recessive, to indicate diminishing ability, additive and subtractive bilingualism dependent on the effect on the primary language, as well as equilingualism and ambilingualism which indicate different types of advanced ability. The relativistic status of bilingual ability has been underlined, highlighting distinctions between early and late bilingualism, and varying types of language dominance in the manipulation of the four basic linguistic skills. Attention has been carefully drawn to several polemical questions in connection with definitions and typologies, particularly the arguments around semilingualism, compound and co-ordinate bilingualism. Within the larger framework of societal bilingualism, individual cases have been described in terms of symmetrical, asymmetrical, vertical and horizontal bilingualism, leading into the discussion of the relationship between bilingualism and diglossia. In this field the linguistic aspects of dual language usage cannot be dissociated from sociological questions, so that biculturalism and di-ethnia have also been taken into account as factors determining both degree of bilingualism and the nature of bilingual usage.

2 Interference and Code-switching

The preceding typology and analysis of factors intervening in the scientific discussion of bilingualism allow the student of the subject to decide what specific type of bilingual behaviour he intends to investigate and to narrow down the scope of enquiry to manageable proportions. In this chapter we shall pay attention to the purely linguistic elements relevant to such investigation. These must of necessity be those features which distinguish the speech of a bilingual from that of a monoglot. It could be argued that the speech of an ambilingual with perfect mastery of two languages which makes him indistinguishable from two separate monoglots is of no interest to the student of bilingualism, since he will manifest no linguistic characteristics that can be investigated. Although this achievement may be of interest to the psycholinguist, particularly in the quest for an understanding of how this feat is achieved, or to the sociolinguist for an understanding of how such ambilinguals operate their two codes successfully, there is no significant evidence of deviance from the monolingual norm in either language. Our field of investigation lies with the more prevalent type of bilingual, the one who betrays his binguality in either or both of his languages. Here a choice will have to be made based on criteria discussed in the previous chapter as to what type of non-fluent bilingual one is going to investigate at a particular stage of development in the range of bilingual competence. It is clear that an examination of the speech characteristics of the incipient bilingual will differ significantly from that of the balanced bilingual, though there may well be points of convergence. At this stage, however, our task is to concentrate on identifying the specificity of bilingual speech in order to intensify our awareness of what it is we are looking at. Much of what will be said in this chapter will be based on the pioneering work of Uriel Weinreich's *Languages in Contact* (1953) and Einar Haugen's *Bilingualism in the Americas* (1956), both of which represent milestones in the development of the linguistic study of bilingualism, to which we will add examples of more recent thinking.

Since our major concern here will be with the observable features of bilingual speech this has implications for the theoretical approach to the question. For if one examines the observable features, one is of course commenting on performance rather than on competence, to use the transformational-generative dichotomy. Such an approach might be called into question by the pure theoretician but it would seem that there is little choice open to the student of bilingualism since, as Chapter 1 has shown, it is difficult to define the ideal bilingual speaker-hearer and his competence. Moreover, there are communities in many parts of the world where it is impossible to talk about an ideal speaker-hearer either in one or two languages who functions in a homogeneous group in the way posited by theoreticians of monoglot behaviour. There are tribes in the north-east Amazon where the normal scope of linguistic competence covers a control of at least four languages, a similar situation pertaining in South-east Asia where the ideally fluent speaker is often multilingual, though with restricted specialization of function in each language. It is cases like these that have led many students of bilingualism to reject the straightforward notion of linguistic competence as the quest of their investigations in favour of that of communicative competence as developed by Hymes (1972). For the field we are looking at this notion is of particular significance since it covers not only the knowledge possessed by the user of the formal code of a particular language or languages but also the social implications of choice within and across the languages involved. Both elements are important in examining bilingual behaviour since they allow for the examination of *structure*, the primary goal of the pure theoretician, together with *use*, and more specifically the way one speaker may use more than one language.

In bilingual studies one is interested not only in grammaticality with respect to linguistic competence, but also in acceptability with respect to performance, which can be judged by providing answers to the following four basic questions:

    a) whether (and to what degree) something is formally *possible*;
    b) whether (and to what degree) something is *feasible* in virtue of the means of implementation available;
    c) whether (and to what degree) something is *appropriate* (adequate, happy, successful) in relation to a context in which it is used and evaluated;
    d) whether (and to what degree) something is in fact done, actually *performed*, and what its doing entails."

(Hymes, 1972: 281)

In examining a bilingual's use of English using the criteria outlined above one would first have to find out whether other speakers of English do the same or similar things with the language in the same or similar circumstances or not. If the bilingual is in a monoglot native-speaker English environment the answers to the four criteria test may well be different from those that would apply in an English-other-language bilingual community of the type found, say, in Singapore or Montreal. The theory of communicative competence takes into account the interaction of grammatical systems (what is formally possible), psycholinguistic systems (what is feasible in terms of human information processing), sociocultural systems (what is the social meaning or value of a given utterance), and probabilistic systems (what actually occurs). Canale & Swain (1980a: 20) illustrate these points by showing how a given utterance may be ungrammatical with respect to a particular grammar (e.g. *the was cheese green* with respect to standard English), unacceptable or awkward in terms of a particular perceptual strategy (e.g. *the cheese the rat the cat the dog saw chased ate was green* with reference to a perceptual constraint on processing multiple centre-embedded clauses), inappropriate in a particular social context (e.g. saying *good-bye* in greeting someone), or rare in a particular community or situation (e.g. saying *may God be with you* instead of *good-bye, bye-bye*, and so forth in ending a routine telephone conversation). Now it could well be that in a bilingual community where English is one of the components of the majority of speakers' linguistic profiles different criteria of possibility, feasibility, appropriateness and actual performance apply and these could be accounted for in the same way that the examples quoted can be analysed for the monoglot English-speaking community, thereby allowing for a more comprehensive approach to bilingual behaviour than one based purely on linguistic competence. In so doing one can more readily integrate the observable features of bilingual speech into a theoretical frame of reference than is the case which relies on intuitive assumptions about the idealized grammar of a difficult to define ideal bilingual.

The observable elements of marked bilingual speech have traditionally been classified as *interference* phenomena, an omnibus term that requires further clarification. Originally the concept of interference referred to the use of formal elements of one code within the context of another, i.e. any phonological, morphological, lexical or syntactic element in a given language that could be explained by the effect of contact with another language. However, the notion of communicative competence as outlined above has widened the scope of enquiry beyond the purely formal linguistic elements to include other features of linguistic behaviour which can possibly distinguish a bilingual from a monoglot. Thus it is doubtful whether every departure from the monoglot norm by the introduction of elements extraneous to a given language should be seen as interference. The social implications of language choice available to the bilingual may so operate that the same speaker will behave differently depending on the type of interlocutor involved and the make-up of the linguistic community. For instance, a bilingual in communication with another bilingual who shares the same linguistic background may feel free to use both of his language repertoires on the assumption that communication may well be enhanced by using elements from two languages—if so there is no question of impaired communication brought about by what has traditionally been considered as interference. On the other hand, the same bilingual speaker in conversation with a monoglot may not feel the same liberty and may well attempt to maximize alignment on monoglot norms by consciously reducing any formal "interference" features to a minimum. If so, his communicative competence may vary in function of the interlocutor, being perhaps more efficient with some partners than with others — "more efficient" by the monolingual norm — but not by the bilingual norm, for which comprehension is unimpaired in conversation with bilingual interlocutors. Indeed, with the bilingual partner so-called interference may be the norm, particularly for registering familiarity, solidarity, etc.

If we accept the notion of interference in the restricted sense as consisting of the observable features of one code used within the context of the other, we may still fail to observe pertinent elements of bilingual behaviour which distinguish it from that of monoglots. In an ideally organized investigation of bilingual speech those things that are done by monoglots but *not* done by bilinguals using the same languages should also be looked into, though this is a more subtle area of investigation. It has been noted that non-native speakers of a language may avoid using certain constructions for which they feel no need or perhaps which present them with a degree of problematic complexity which can be circumvented by the use of alternative and simpler constructions without in any way betraying their lack of ease in that language (Baetens Beardsmore, 1970). The avoidance of the *passé simple* in French or the so-called question tag in English might well escape the attention of the observer and in no way betray bilinguality or non-nativeness if alternative correct constructions are used in their stead, but may well represent a deviation from what a monoglot might do in the same circumstances. Rejection patterns such as these might be called *negative interference,* and are probably only detectable via lengthy investigation based on comparative frequency counts. What the competent bilingual has done in circumstances like these is that he has brought his *strategic competence* (see p. 131) into play, i.e. has made use of the resources available to achieve his goals.

The widening of the notion of interference alluded to above can be further extended to cover other areas of bilingual behaviour which are not so clearly marked by formal features. In the field of semantics it has been shown by Lambert & Moore (1966) that the associations attached to terms used by bilinguals do not necessarily coincide with those of monoglot speakers in that part of the associations of the cognate word in each language are present in some bilinguals' minds. Differences like these are not readily observable in the flow of bilingual speech and are not formal features in the sense alluded to earlier, but are nevertheless significant. Their presence in the bilingual can only be explained in terms of contact between two semantic systems and they represent another type of interference to be discussed later.

At this point it is useful to consider how increasing observation of characteristic bilingual behaviour and the resulting awareness of the regular, frequent and even normal occurrence of features from language A in speech primarily conducted in language B has led certain scholars to reject the term interference as misleading. This is because interference has negative connotations implying deviations from monoglot norms, yet in many bilingual communities reflections of one language in speech in the other are perfectly acceptable and have no such connotations. Moreover, studies of bilingual acquisition in both children and adults have shown how what has traditionally been called interference is a normal developmental process which may disappear with time or remain a permanent feature of bilingual output. Clyne (1967) has produced some of the clearest arguments for discarding the term "interference", particularly with reference to the lexis, preferring the more neutral terms of "transference" and "transfers" to refer to elements of language A present in extracts of discourse primarily conducted in language B.

Although many scholars agree that "transfer" is a more positive way of indicating such features, the majority of authors still use the term interference, as we will in our further discussion, if only to clearly distinguish from another, similar phenomenon discussed below which would be masked by the sole usage of the more neutral notion of transfer. We hope this will not confuse readers.

A further problem connected with the delimitation of the concept of interference, even at the formal level, is that of deciding when the use of elements of one language within the context of another ceases to be interference but represents a switch in language, or *code-switching*. Haugen (1956: 40) rejects the switching from one language to another for stretches of discourse in the middle of a conversation as no longer representing interference, but this raises the question of how large a chunk of language must be before falling into the category of code-switching. The following example of a conversation between two people who share the same pair of languages, English and Spanish, would be classified as code-switching but not as interference by Haugen's definition;

> "**Secretary:**   Do you have the enclosures for the letter, Mr Gonzalez?
> **Boss:**   Oh yes, here they are.
> **Secretary:**   Okay.
> **Boss:**   Ah, this man William Bolger got his organisa-tion to contribute a lot of money to the Puerto Rican parade. He's very much for it. ¿Tu fuista a la parada?
> **Secretary:**   Si, yo fui...?" (Ure, 1974: 233)

To what extent is the insertion of a couple of utterances in Spanish in a dialogue primarily conducted in English different from the following example, where individual lexical items from French are inserted into a Dutch syntactic structure?

> "De pompier militaire van de staat... loop partout me ne vitesse zoo rapide as de chemin de fer." (*The state military fireman ... runs everywhere with the speed of a railway*)
> (Baetens Beardsmore, 1978a)

This illustration reveals an intermingling of two codes so great as to make it difficult to decide whether we are dealing with lexical interference, recurrent code-switching, symbiosis, a creole or something else. It could be argued that the last example is basically one of lexical interference since the basic structural pattern is a Dutch one with slight syntactic re-arrangement (*pompier militaire* instead of *militaire pompier*). One might also argue that the largest measurable unit of interference is precisely that found under the classification of code-switching as illustrated in the Spanish-English example earlier, where whole sequences of one language are inserted into the context of another. Western literature provides many examples of the latter, notably Tolstoy's *War and Peace*, where the conversation of the Russian aristocracy is heavily intermingled with stretches conducted partly in French and partly in Russian. Phenomena of this kind have been attested since the Middle Ages in literature produced in Germany, France, Britain, the Low Countries and elsewhere (Forster, 1970), reflecting sociolinguistic phe-nomena that can be attested outside the literary sphere in thriving bilingual communities all over the world. In Chapter 4 we will take a theoretical look at the distinction between code-switching and interference, but for the present purpose it is sufficient to note the similarity in external, measurable phenomena.

As McClure (1981) has pointed out, there is no consensus among researchers as to what constitutes a code switch. Some scholars have been concerned with the alternate choice of codes occasioned by shifts in factors, such as topic, setting and participants, known as "situational shifting", while others concentrate on the linguistic constraints which determine the nature of the change of code. Further confusion may arise when one reads the small number of articles that prefer the terms *code-mixing* to refer to occurrences of what others variously call borrowing, interference, transference or code-switching. For example, McLaughlin (1984: 96–97) distinguishes between code-mixing to refer to switches within sentences and code-switching to refer to changing language over phrases or sentences, while Hatch (1976: 202) maintains there is no sharp distinction between mixing and switching. On a purely practical basis, founded on the proportion of articles using the above terminology, and to avoid confusion in this book, code-mixing will not be further referred to, since it appears to be the least favoured designation and the most unclear for referring to any form of non-monoglot norm-based speech patterns.

Code-switching is not arbitrary but rule-governed (see pp. 75–81) and depends on factors such as topic, code being used, situation and participants. For such switches of stretches of utterances to take place, the minimal bilingual community must exist, by which is meant that at least two interlocutors must share the same pair of languages. Should only one of the speakers be bilingual it is more likely that a switch from one language to another would not occur since it would imply a breakdown in communication. Thus there might well be a difference between the Spanish-English example and the Dutch-French example in that in the latter case the speaker and listener might not have two languages at all at their disposal but only one consisting of mixed elements. The following two examples are taken from contexts in which the participants shared the two languages involved in the code-switch. The first begins in French and ends in Dutch and was noted in the Brussels bilingual setting:

> "On a beau au lavoir. Chic, / 't was tijd" (*It's fine at the laundry, nice/ it was high time*)". (Baetens Beardsmore, 1971c: 48)

The second example cropped up in a conversation between Dutch-English bilinguals in the middle of an otherwise all English set of exchanges:

> "The one / mee zijne lange neus" (*the one with his long nose*)".
> (Baetens Beardsmore, 1979c: 119)

Had the listeners in both cases been monoglots it is highly unlikely that the switch in language would have taken place. Under Haugen's restricted definition of interference it is not clear whether the last two examples should be considered as part of the field of study or not. Yet it is difficult to see any difference in kind between these two examples and the previous Spanish-English case where the change-over clearly occurs at the sentence boundary.

A further problem with the notion of interference is pinning down the stage when an element extraneous to a particular code by monoglot norms but consistently present in bilingual speech has stopped being a question of interference. The "pompier militaire" example given earlier comes from a unilingual environment in which French lexical elements are permanently present in the local Dutch dialect. To deal with cases like these one should rather talk of *integration*, , i.e. the *regular use* of material from one language in another in the form of an established loan, particularly when no alternative "non-foreign" element is known or used. The use of the French "blasé" in English or the English words "building, smoking" in French are similar examples (cf. Haugen, 1956: 55 for further examples). Diachronically, of course, such loans must be considered as interference since at some time in the development of the language (or dialect) they must have been imported from outside, though for the present-day state of the language this can no longer be considered to hold. It has been claimed, moreover, that the opposition between synchrony and diachrony is not relevant to bilingual studies (Mackey, 1976: 310–12) because by its very nature bilingualism is a relatively unstable phenomenon where the use of two languages is in rapid evolution within both the individual speaker and the community.

One claim is that the difference between integration and interference can be recognized by the phonological and morphological shape of the term under examination. If the term has been assimilated to the patterns of the host or recipient language it can be considered as integrated; for example, the original French word "liqueur" ['likœr] is often pronounced [lik'juə] in English. If on the other hand the term has not been completely integrated into the regular patterns of the host language it can be considered as an element of interference. But this yardstick is not completely satisfactory. In bilingual communities made up of a large number of speakers who share the same linguistic background, norms of pronunciation and word formation may not be the same as those of the respective monoglot standards since all speakers follow some bilingually determined patterns. Terms borrowed from one of the languages may in such circumstances follow standard monoglot norms, be re-aligned on patterns determined by the borrowing language or fall somewhere in between the two according to some community-based bilingual norm. The sociolinguist might argue that decisions on interference or integration depend on both the formal aspects and the frequency and nature of usage in a particular community. Take the case of certain borrowings in the French-Dutch contact situation of Brussels. Many highly educated, monoglot French speakers in Brussels use the Dutch term "sterfput" to indicate "a draining well, cesspool" instead of the standard French "puisard". Depending on their degree of sensitivity to pronunciation features they may render this as [ster'pyt] or ['sterfpyt], the first being more "French" in form than the second. Now by monoglot norms of reference "sterfput" can be considered only as an interference element replacing "puisard", yet the fact that "puisard" is either not known or not used in French in the Brussels context implies that "sterfput" must be considered as an example of integration, since the alternative form from standard French is absent in the community. Thus by sociolinguistic criteria the shape of the word does not influence its categorization as an integrated form since that form nearer to the original Dutch pronunciation, ['sterfpʌt], is also used by some.

From the above it can be seen that integration is a question of degree, the more a particular term of foreign origin is used in a bilingual's speech (and also in that of the monoglot, too) the more integrated it must be. Mackey (1976) suggests that the range of integration can be measured on a usage scale going from 0 to 100%, with the lower end of the scale tending to reflect interference and the upper end integration.

Our illustration of the distinction between integration and interference has been taken from the lexis but it is useful to enquire whether the same distinction does not hold good for other levels of linguistic analysis. The whole question will depend on the type of bilingualism under investigation and the methodology being applied. If one is studying the speech of an ascendant bilingual during some transitional phase there are likely to be phonological, morphological, syntactic and lexical features in the second language which clearly owe their existence to patterns in the first language. In terms of interference and integration the second language which is undergoing the borrowing is known as the *recipient language* while the first is known as the *source or donor language*. Thus a foreign accent in the second language may be considered as reflecting interference from the first or donor language if one is using monoglot norms of reference. The examination of speech of representatives of stable bilingual communities in which accent or any other feature is often marked as revealing bilingual characteristics may be a different case. Here the community norms prevalent in the bilingual society may be more significant than monolingual reference points, in which case the marked distinctive features possibly reflect integration rather than interference. If large masses of speakers in the bilingual community share the same distinctive speech characteristics they have probably been stabilized and integrated into regional speech patterns.

The interference/integration dichotomy becomes more important when one turns to what might be called *residual bilingual* communities, as in a society where large masses of speakers have shifted from using one language to the exclusive use of another via an intermediary bilingual phase. Mass language shift of this type can occur as swiftly as in three generations, with the first generation using language A exclusively, the second being bilingual in languages A and B, and the third being unilingual in language B (Van Loey, 1958). Immigrant communities often undergo this process, brought about by subtractive bilingualism operating in the middle generation, though it also accounts for the anglicization of large parts of Wales and the shift from Dutch to French predominance in Brussels. If one examines the type of French spoken today in Brussels it will be readily distinguishable from that used by a Frenchman, whether his Belgian counterpart is a bilingual or not. This distinctiveness noticeable even among the majority of monoglots in Brussels cannot directly be attributed to interference since they know little or no Dutch, though historically speaking what distinguishes Brussels French from that spoken in France is attributable to Dutch influence. Thus what was originally a question of interference must now be considered as one of integration.

To illustrate how integration reflects itself, together with code-switching phenomena, in *residual* bilingual communities one could look at two identifiable linguistic groups from Brussels (for further details, see Baetens Beardsmore, 1983b) who, although they know little or no Dutch, clearly manifest Dutch influences in their speech. The first group of speakers represents educated middle and upper middle class French monoglots, the second lower middle and lower class French monoglots, who are both readily distinguishable from their counterparts in France by their restricted use of code-switching and their more regular use of integrated residual bilingualism features.

Group 1

a) Upper-level French monoglots in Brussels may occasionally operate code-switching, usually in the form of loanwords (see p. 57) for affective reasons such as humour, irony, denigration, etc. Given that the terms in question are culture-tied they are to some extent integrated, though they have been classified under code-switching since the users are generally conscious of their "intrusive" nature in French. Examples are terms and expressions like *moedertaal* (referring to the Dutch language, literally "mother tongue"), *platteland* (the Flemish countryside, literally "flat country"), *zinneke* (mixed breed, literally "mongrel"), *vogelpik* (the game of darts), *Walen Buiten* (a slogan used by some Flemish nationalists, literally "Walloons get out").

b) There are few traces of residual bilingualism in the phonology of this group as a whole, pronunciation of French being of a regional type similar to other varieties found in metropolitan France, and what Warnant (1973) calls *français neutralisé*.

c) Lexical traces of residual bilingualism in the form of integrated items for which no standard French equivalent is either known, or used, often manifestations of loanblends or loan translations (see p. 57), are relatively restricted in number (see Table 4) (sources for all illustrations, Baetens Beardsmore, 1971c; 1983b).

d) Syntactic traces of residual bilingualism in the speech of this group tend to form part of the general environment of Belgian French as a whole and are relatively restricted in number. Individual upper-level French monoglots who are aware of the non-normative nature of certain of these turns of phrase might well avoid them, though the short list below is fairly representative;

—*goûter* used with an object complement to signify *avoir le gout de* in expressions like *ça goute l'orange* on the Dutch model of *smaken, het smaakt naar sinaasappel* (to taste of something);

—*goûter* used without a complement as an equivalent of *plaire* in expressions like *ça goute, ça te goute?* on the Dutch model of *smaakt het?* (Does it taste?);

—avoir + adjective (e.g. *avoir facile, avoir difficile*) where the adjective functions as an object complement or as an adverbial to replace the standard French *faire facilement, avoir des difficultes* based on the Dutch equivalent *het makkelijk, moeilijk hebben* (to find things easy, difficult);

—a tendency to use adverbials in initial position without emphatic stress, based on Dutch word order rules, e.g. *malheureusement ils ne l'ont pas trouvé = jammer/spijtig hebben zij het niet gevonden*; in standard French the preferred construction would be *ils ne l'ont malheureusement pas trouvé* (unfortunately they didn't find it).

Group 2

This category of lower-level French-speaking monoglots is more readily identifiable in Brussels and probably represents the dominant linguistic category in the city, though there are no statistics available to support this estimation. All the features listed for group 1 are present in this sub-category's speech, to which should be added the following representative elements.

a) Code-switching in the form of loanwords and loan expressions may be more prevalent in that many speakers in this category feel freer to add

TABLE 4

Brussels French	Standard French	Dutch Origin	Translation
bac	récipient en forme de cuve ou boîte	bak	receptacle
bloquer	réviser	blokken	to revise
buser	(faire) échouer aux examens	buizen	to fail exams
couque	gâteau, brioche	koek	cake
drache	averse	dretsen	shower
drève	allée plantée d'arbres	dreef	tree-lined avenue
doufe	lourd (temps)	dof	muggy weather
ket	'titi' bruxellois	ket	local boy
kot	chambre d'étudiant, débarras	kot	student room
pape	bouillie, boue, colle	pap	pudding, glue
rim-ram	remue-ménage	rim-ram	fuss and bother
sterfput	puisard	sterfput	drain
zwanze	blague, farce	zwans	practical joke
ce n'est pas du spek pour ton bec	ce n'est pas tøn affaire	't is geen spek voor uwen bek	it's none of your business
avoir un oeuf à peler avec quelqu'un	avoir un compte à regler avec quelqu'un	een eitje met iemand te pellen hebben	to have a bone to pick with someone
avoir des jambes en flanelles	se sentir faible	flanellen benen hebben	to feel weak at the knees
avoir une boentje pour quelqu'un	avoir un faible pour quelqu'un	een boentje hebben	to be keen on someone
frotter la manche à quelqu'un	flatter	iemand de mouw vegen	to get round someone

local colour to their informal speech by using Dutch origin items. As with the first group the insertion of Dutch elements is often done for affective reasons and varies from speaker to speaker; mild expletives may be used, e.g. *niks mendale* ("nothing doing"), *godferdom* (a swearword), as well as consciously selected humorous or denigrating terms like *pei* ("old bloke"), *trut* (a simple-minded, backward female), *klette* (idiot).

b) The phonology of group 2 is more strikingly marked by residual bilingualism, particularly in the prosodic features. Tonic stress tends to be more strongly differentiated from weak stress than is the case in standard French, thereby affecting the melodic curve of the phrase. Often the prosodic features of this group's speech coincide with the melodic curve of local Dutch, even though the speakers in question know little or no Dutch.

Vowel quality also shows traces of residual bilingualism, particularly in the back rounded half-closed /o/ and half-open /ɔ/, which both tend to be slightly centralized, slightly lowered and nearer to their Dutch equivalents. Similarly front open /a/ and back open /ɑ/ tend to collapse into a unique intermediary open vowel similar to the Dutch a-sound, resulting in little distinction between the vowel quality of *manne* and *âme*, even though there is a length distinction.

c) It is particularly in non-formal speech usage that group 2 tends to reveal greater receptivity towards non-standard French lexical items. To the list already given for the first category of speakers (see Table 4) should be added the following elements as illustrations.

TABLE 5

Brussels French	Standard French	Dutch Origin	Translation
clache	chauve	kletskop	bald head
clouche	motte	kluts	dollop
dik	gros	dik	fat
fla	faible, mou	flauw	feeble
un scheer	une 'touche'	scheer	a "pick-up"
stuk	morceau	stuk	piece
blouche	bosse	bluts	dent
encore toujours	toujours	nog altijd	still
à tantôt	à tout a l'heure	tot straks	see you later
crolle	boucle	krul	curl

d) Syntactic features which should be added to those listed for the first group of speakers in Brussels include the following;

— the use of the periphrastic future with *aller* as an auxiliary verb in *ça va aller?* (standard French *ça ira?*) under the influence of Dutch future constructions, e.g. *zal't gaan?* (Will that be o.k?);

— the use of prepositions adverbially on the basis of Dutch (or Flemish dialect) so-called pronominal adverbs, e.g. *quand vous avez fini avec = waneer je daarmee gedaan hebt* (when you've finished with it);

— the use of prepositions adverbially where the construction coincides with a Dutch verb form which includes an adverbial element, e.g. *prendre avec = meenemen, donner avec = meegeven, mettre dessus = opzetten* (take with, give with, put on);

— the use of prepositions which coincide with Dutch syntax (or Flemish) dialect, as is the case with all our examples) and which are more concrete than the particles and prepositions used in standard French, e.g. *on est occupé avec vous?* (standard French *on s'occupe de vous?*) = *is iemand met U bezig?* (Is someone looking after you?), *j'étais sur le tram* (standard French *dans le tram*) = *op de tram* (on the tram), *la fenêtre donne sur la rue* (standard French *dans la rue*) = *het venster geeft uit op de straat* (the window gives out onto the street), *il s'amuse avec ses jouets* (standard French *s'occuper de, s'amuser de*) = *hij houdt zich met zijn speelgoed bezig* (he's busy with his toys);

— the frequent use of what are known as *chevilles* in French, or lubricators functioning like question tags in English, which coincide with the functions of their translated equivalents in Dutch and which are almost totally absent from standard French, e.g. *tout de même, quand-même, seulement, une fois, comme ça*, as in *tu ne vas tout de même pas me dire que. . .* = *je gaat me toch niet zeggen dat. . .* (but you're not going to tell me that. . .), *vas seulement voir = ga maar kijken* (just go and look), *il m'a dit une fois, comme ça, que. . .* = *hij heeft me zo eens gezegd dat. . .* (he just told me that. . .).

From what we have been developing so far it should have become apparent that any discussion of interference/transfer and code-switching requires both a linguistic and a sociological or extra-linguistic approach, as has been pointed out by Weinreich (1953: 3) and many others (cf. Rickford, 1986) and indeed there are many who claim that the nature of the social contact is more important than the nature of the linguistic systems in determining both the direction and the extent of interference. This point should be consistently borne in mind on reading what follows, since although the emphasis in this chapter is placed on identifying linguistic phenomena these should always be appraised against the backdrop of social constraints.

Lexical Transfer

For certain purposes of investigation it is useful, however, to examine data initially on the assumption that specific features noticeable in bilingual speech represent interference, even if at some later stage the investigator might wish to reconsider his data as representing integration. This is particularly true if the aim is to highlight the specificity of bilingual speech as opposed to that produced by monoglots. In the lexical field it appears that interference can take on different forms and will affect different lexical categories in varying ways. Most studies of lexical interference have revealed that nouns are most easily transferred from one language to another while structure or function words are less easily transferred (Haugen, 1956: 59). Between languages that have similar syntagmatic patterns it appears that after nouns it is verbs, adjectives, adverbs, prepositions and interjections which are transferred in decreasing scale in the order listed, with pronouns and articles showing the greatest resistance to transfer (Haugen, 1972a: 177). When transfer does occur it may take different forms. Nouns may retain their source language shape, be partially assimilated to the recipient language or be complete *loan translations*, whereas verbs, adjectives and adverbs are less likely to keep their original form in the process of transfer.

A fairly well established classification of the different types of transfer has been provided by Haugen (1956: 59–60). This classification is based on the degree or manner of integration of a particular element. On the phonemic level there is a division into *unassimilated loans* (where there is no adaptation to the phonology of the recipient language), *partially assimilated* and *wholly assimilated loans*. Coupled with this phonemic division is a morphemic distinction between loans that show no morphemic substitution, those that show partial substitution and those with total substitution. An item that shows no morphemic substitution is known as a *loanword*. An illustration of this is the name given to the game of darts in Brussels French as a replacement for the standard French "fléchettes". Many Brussels bilinguals use the Dutch-origin word "vogelpik" in their local variety of French. Whether the term is phonologically assimilated to French, giving the pronunciation [vogel'pik], or pronounced on the local Dutch dialect pattern ['vouɣalpik], will depend on the individual speaker's social origins, linguistic background and general sensitivity to French phonological patterns. In cases where only part of the phonemic shape of the transfer is imported these are known as *hybrid loanwords* or alternatively, *loanblends*, illustrated by the English "plum pie" adopted in Pennsylvania German as [blaumǝpai], where the English morpheme [pai] has been imported but the local German [blaumə] has been substituted for "plum" (Haugen, 1972: 165).

The third classification for a transferred lexical item is that of *loanshift* in which morphemic substitution occurs without any importation from the donor language. Loanshifts are alternatively known as *loan translations* or *calques*. The English "skyscraper" has been imported into Dutch as "wolkenkrabber", into German as "Wolkenkratzer", into French as "gratte-ciel", into Spanish as "rascacielos", all of which are illustrations of loanshifts. The term loanshift has also been used to describe the semantic displacement that occurs when a native term is applied to a novel cultural phenomenon that has been imported and is referred to by an existing term in the recipient language that acquires new semantic features. Thus American Portuguese uses "pêso", originally meaning "weight" in Portuguese, with the significance of "dollar". It is perhaps wise to distinguish between a loanshift of this kind and the case where semantic confusion arises between words of similar form in both source and recipient languages, so as to be near homonyms, but with clearly distinct semantics. Many French speakers of English, even with an advanced knowledge of the language, frequently use the English "library" with the meaning of the French "librairie" = "bookshop", leading to semantic ambiguity. Many similar examples among second language learners could be found, and although such cases are evidence of loanshifts it would perhaps be clearer to refer to them as loan translations which reveal influences of what Van Overbeke (1976: 120) calls both *inter- and intralinguistic interference;* by interlinguistic interference is meant the obvious connection between French and English in the above example, while by intralinguistic is meant the analogical semantic process that is in operation within one of the languages involved, in this case English, and where the semantics of library is re-aligned under the influence of the relationship to books. Interference of this subtle type increases in proportion to the degree of similarity of features between the two languages. In other words, the greater the difference between the two languages the easier it is to keep lexical items apart and interference-free.

Continuing on the assumption that lexical transfer, whatever form it may take, is to be measured in terms of the donor and recipient languages seen as idealized norms, we may note with interest what areas of human activity lend themselves most readily to transfer. The traditional classification of lexical items into semantic fields will reveal the permeability of a recipient language to lexical transfer and there are certain indications that specific conditions lend themselves to the transfer of words in conditions of language contact.

The relative prestige of the two languages involved will determine their permeability to transfers and also the nature of transfer. It is generally felt that the more prestigious language transfers more readily to the less prestigious in terms of quantity, though other elements discussed later may affect this general principle. Factors determining the relative prestige of two languages are sociological in nature and often shared by the whole community. It is the relative high prestige held by English in Uganda which accounts for the Luganda borrowing from English of "doctor" in the form "ddokita", even though the indigenous term "omusawo" could cover the same semantic functions adequately (Mosha, 1971: 293). Relative prestige does not necessarily imply a one-way transfer pattern from the high-rated to the low-rated language since investigations in many parts of the world have shown how transfer can occur from a deprecated into a more prestigious language in connection with items that have negative connotations. The relative low prestige of the donor language adds expressivity to the pejorative associations implied in the use of the transfer. French speakers in Belgium often attach negative associations to Dutch based on a complex of socio-economic and historically determined factors; consequently, many insults, nicknames, swearwords, etc., borrowed from Dutch dialects can be found in the regional French of both monoglot and bilingual Belgians (Baetens Beardsmore, 1971c: 355–56). Herbillon (1951: 16–26) noted that almost a third of the terms transferred from Dutch into Walloon French in Belgium had deprecatory overtones, while Lanly (1962: 95) observed that in contact situations obscenities and vulgar expressions easily lend themselves to transfer. This might also be explained by a residual feeling of sensitivity to vulgarity which is masked by borrowing an offensive term from another language. However, it is also true that many speakers who borrow obscenities from another language are not aware of the strong associations connected with the term in the donor language or else attribute the milder overtones held by the equivalent term in their own language to the translated element in the other language. French speakers of German often use "Scheisse" on the mistaken assumption that it has the relatively anodyne connotations of "merde", its denotative equivalent, when in fact the German term is far stronger. This example of *semantic interference* operative in the less well-known language is another illustration of inadequate communicative competence as reflected in a lack of awareness of the cultural implications of semantic values.

A further illustration of the transfer of elements from a less prestigious to a more prestigious language (in the eyes of the speakers of the latter, of course) can be seen from the fact that the French used in Switzerland readily borrows terms of German origin to disparagingly designate women, thereby increasing the pejorative association connected with the use of the transfer. Cases of the type discussed have been called "loans of convenience" (*emprunts de commodité,* Valkhoff, 1931: 9) since they are determined by affective associations connected with the transfer rather than any lexical inadequacy in the recipient language. A "loan of necessity" (*emprunt de nécessité,* Valkhoff, 1931: 9), on the other hand, is a transfer used when no precise equivalent exists in the recipient language. Generally, such transfers designate culture-tied phenomena and may move in either direction between more and less prestigious languages. A technically and economically more advanced language community tends to export more culture-tied terms than a less advanced community, primarily because newly developed concepts and objects are accompanied by their designation — loosely stated, "the word follows the thing". It is this phenomenon that explains the historical enrichment of a language by transfers, as when Welsh imported words of Latin origin when Roman influence on the British Isles brought with it such novel institutions as the church (Latin "ecclesia">Welsh "eglwys") or technical improvements like the bridge (Latin "pons">Welsh "bont"). More recent equivalents are such French transfers from English as "le marketing, le briefing", or the Luganda borrowing from English of a term to designate baptism, "bbatisimu", an activity not indigenous to Luganda society (Mosha, 1971: 292).

In cases where borrowing from another language leads to enrichment and reinforcement of the recipient language's lexical stock one might talk of *positive transfer* (as with the examples "eglwys, bont, bbatisimu"), whereas cases of borrowing which affect the norms of the recipient language might be examples of *negative transfer.* The value judgement implicit in these designations should be handled with care, however, if one is trying to establish what bilingual community norms may be independent of monoglot terms of reference.

Perhaps more important for the nature of bilingual speech than prestige, convenience and necessity in the explanation of lexical transfer or interference is the question of the amount of contact, or pressure from one linguistic group upon another. Many of the above examples can be found in what are traditionally considered as monoglot speech communities, though at some stage bilingual speakers must have acted as mediators to allow for the penetration of the term of foreign origin into general speech. It is of interest to capture this mediating phase by looking at the circumstances which determine the bilingual's use of transfers where the monoglot would not normally do so. This happens when there is frequent contact between two linguistic communities. Loans can potentially occur in any field of human activity but seem to be determined by the following criteria:-

a) The nature of the activity indulged in by the bilingual; if a subject which is normally and regularly handled in one language infrequently gets discussed in the other the speaker might find lexical availability in the other language impaired. Thus a scientist who normally conducts his research in English may readily use English terms in discussing the same subject in another language. (This might be one explanation why so many Dutch speakers use the English term "research" instead of its widespread Dutch equivalent "onderzoek".)

b) The frequency of contact between two language communities; the bilingual may well have terms readily available which are indigenous to either of his languages but more frequent contact with an area of activity in one language may lead to an automatic use of language A's terminology in language B settings. Thus although the Dutch term "zegel" should be familiar and widespread in the Brussels bilingual setting one will often hear the French term "timbre" ['tembər] used in the local spoken Dutch.

c) The frequency with which the individual bilingual uses his two languages can also affect transfer; the language used less frequently is more likely to reveal elements of interference or borrowing than that used more frequently as when long-term emigrants have temporary difficulty in re-adjusting their lexis when they are using their pre-emigration language. This may even lead to one or two startling examples of transfer, as noted in the case of a Dutch-English bilingual who spoke only Dutch for the first thirty years of her life and predominantly English for the subsequent thirty years; during the first few days of return to her community of origin she regularly introduced the conjunctions "and" and "but" into otherwise Dutch sentences.

It should be noted that these three criteria are closely inter-related but not quite the same. It would appear that social circumstances of the above type determine the quantity of transfer, though it is likely that structural forces within the two languages in question determine the nature and form of the transfer. To date there is little empirical evidence to bear out this assumption.

The different criteria alluded to may to a large extent determine whether a transferred element will take the form of a loanword, a loanblend or a loanshift, but this will also be tempered by individual characteristics of the speaker. Such things as degree of sensitivity to language in general and awareness of the norms in the two languages being manipulated come into play, as do level of education, literacy, and personality factors such as accommodation to the interlocutor's mode of speech.

Investigation into the semantic effects of interference is more difficult than the simple observation of lexical interference in cases where no formal features can be seized upon in the flow of utterances. It may often be only in the course of time that a listener may become aware of the fact that, as the dialogue proceeds, the semantics of the terms being used may differ from those monoglots would ascribe to the same terms. It is even possible that such differences may not be noticed at all, apart from some general feeling of misunderstanding or lack of communication between two speakers, in spite of apparent lexical clarity. This is particularly true if the divergences exist not on the denotative level but on the connotative level of meaning, leading to *connotative interference*.

The classical example of the way bilingualism can affect the semantics of a term is taken from an examination of the colour spectrum. It is a well-established fact that different languages identify the range of colours in the spectrum in different manners so that there is no necessary overlap in the cut-off points between one colour and the next when a given pair of languages are compared. Welsh, for example, has two terms for distinguishing shades of green which do not coincide with their English counterpart; *gwyrdd* = "green", and *glas* = 1) "blue", 2) "green", for natural objects like "grass, leaves, etc.", which is used with a transferred meaning of "young" in *glaslanc* = literally "green lad, youngster". A Welsh-speaker is likely to use two different terms to cover hues of green where his English-speaking neighbour will not distinguish between certain shades. The bilingual Welsh-English speaker, on the other hand, may use the English terms blue and green when using that language to coincide with the semantics of the equivalent Welsh terms. Differences of this nature have been illustrated in an experiment on *semantic shift* in bilingual speech (Ervin, 1961a) in which Navaho Indian bilinguals were tested to see to what extent their naming of colours differed from that of Navaho and English monoglots respectively. Interesting results showed that choices among the bilinguals were determined by their dominant language. Navaho-dominant speakers using English designated hues nearer to the Navaho range of classification while English-dominant speakers did so nearer to the English range. In cases where one language divided a range into two categories (e.g. blue and purple) and the other into three (e.g. violet, lavender, purple) it was found that bilingual speakers, in comparison with monoglots, tended to reduce the range of the middle category when speaking the language in which this was present.

The above illustrations show how differences in the denotative use of language can be detected in bilingual speech. Each linguistic community observes reality in terms of categories which are peculiar to the culture borne by the community's language. Things that play an important role in one cultural and linguistic community may have a far less significant place in another community, leading to a difference in the number of terms available to describe and talk about something. Wine plays an important part in the daily lives of the French whereas it plays a less significant role in the lives of the average American. One can therefore expect to find a far greater range of vocabulary in French to cover fields connected with wine than in English. The bilingual may restrict his range of terminology actively used to discuss wine as a function of his dominance configuration. It can also be assumed that when such clear-cut cultural divergences exist it is relatively easy to acquire the appropriate range of vocabulary, should the need arise, once one has been sufficiently acculturated. Where it is less easy to acquire a lexical usage comparable to that of a monoglot is in cases where the two cultures are more apparently similar in that they share analogous social patterns, standards of living, attitudinal dispositions, etc. Here, as with the hues in the colour spectrum, it is the apparent similarity that may lead the bilingual to ascribe semantic values to a particular lexical item differently from a monoglot. This is especially true on the connotative level of meaning.

The term "Bible" has the same denotative meanings in both English and French, but when one looks at the connotations associated with the term in each language noticeable differences arise. By means of word association tests (Lambert & Moore, 1966) it can be shown how North American English speakers tend to associate the term "Bible" with "God" whereas French speakers from both Canada and France tend to associate the French equivalent "bible" with "livre" (*book*) and not "Dieu" (*God*). Canadian French-English bilinguals tended to have different associations according to their dominant language (as did the Navahos in the colour experiment). In both languages the English-dominant speakers given the stimulus "bible" tended to have the associations "God/Dieu" whereas the French-dominant speakers gave the associations "livre/book" thereby revealing indices of connotative interference. Such divergent associations could, of course, be explained by cultural differences inherent in the two language reference groups, the majority of English speakers being influenced by a Protestant background and the majority of French speakers by a Catholic background, with the Bible assuming different relevance accordingly. Yet similar associative differences can be noted in areas where there is apparently no marked cultural link to explain them. Both the French and the English-speaking developed countries use doctors, nurses and medical equipment in similar contexts and where the medical structure would not differ as significantly as if comparisons were being made between a Western European model and a remote part of Africa. Nevertheless, the connotative associations attached to translation equivalents in this domain revealed different associations for each language. Lambert & Moore discovered that the concepts "child, sickness, doctor" elicited the associations "mother, health, nurse" for English-Canadians in English and the associations "baby, hospital, sickness" for the translated equivalents with French-Canadians in French. Bilingual Canadians tested on the same concepts in both their languages gave the associations "mother, bed, sick" in English and "baby, bed, sickness" in French. What we have then is partial correspondence in the bilingual associations with the respective monoglot norms and partial divergence, leading to a new set of bilingual associations which are probably accountable for in terms of connotative interference.

In cases where both denotative and connotative interference are in operation, misinterpretation of the bilingual's semantics can occur as in the following typical example of student error. At a very advanced examination session in English in which a highly competent Dutch mother-tongue student was asked what she intended to do after her studies she replied, "I'm going to solicit", on the assumption that the range of meanings covered by the English "solicit" coincided with those of the Dutch "solliciteren". The English range of meanings, covering "to apply for a job, to ask for something, to work as a prostitute" is wider than the Dutch range covering "to apply for a job, to ask for something", while the connotations associated with the English "to solicit" tend to evoke assumptions about prostitution as primary. As Pollitzer (1978) has noted, distinctly marked contrasts between two languages are often more easily acquired than less distinctly marked ones.

Bilinguals who are sensitive to language norms in their two languages and who are aware of potential problems with terms which have a formal similarity may also use strategies for minimizing interference which are not always successful. We have already seen how great similarity between two languages, as in cases like French "librairie" and English "library", can lead to interference. The bilingual who is aware of possible confusion in similar instances might make attempts to dissociate the parallelisms. An English-French bilingual was noted to have difficulties in clearly separating the English"esteem/estimation" from the French "estime/estimation"; in French a discussion about a friend led to the sentence "Il est monté dans mon estimation," which should have been "Il est monté dans mon estime" — questioning about the origin of the wrong use of "estimation" revealed that this was selected out of fear of momentary confusion that "estime" was an incorrect translation of "esteem". Perhaps this type of interference-based "error" could be called *second degree interference* since it is not directly attributable to a loan translation effect but more to a fear of using a loan translation (very similar to what Haugen, 1956: 54, calls negative interference, to be distinguished from our use of the term (see p. 46)). It is also a clear example of *strategic competence* (see p. 131) used by a bilingual to overcome problematic lexical gap-filling.

It is perhaps because of the effects of interference that have been discussed up till now that bilinguals are often considered as being imprecise in their lexical usage. This assumption of lexical inadequacy is given added weight in cases where a bilingual has lexical gaps in his knowledge, as is possible when one thinks of the wine terminology example, or where he might resort to transfers of some type. And yet, bilinguals who apply transfers in their speech, particularly if these belong to the group of positive transfers which are used in a community-shared fashion, may in some ways be equally as precise as, if not more precise than, a monoglot. When words are transferred from one language to another they may take on a specialized restricted meaning in the recipient language which causes a re-arrangement of semantic patternings to include both the indigenous and the transferred term. Thus the Luganda case referred to earlier of the borrowing of the English term for doctor, which is used side by side with the indigenous term, leads to a useful semantic distinction between the two items, with the loan from English designating a doctor trained in European-type medicine and the indigenous Luganda term designating a native doctor who deals in herbs and white magic (Mosha, 1971: 294).

Although the bilingual's semantics do not always coincide with those of monoglot speakers of his languages, care should be taken in making comparisons to examine the relevance of the monoglot measure of comparison in a given community. In situations of societal bilingualism it is possible that semantic patterns are the same for all speakers who regularly use the same pair of languages and that differences from monoglot patternings which are originally attributable to contact and interference phenomena have established themselves as a new set of bilingual norms.

Morphological Transfer

The classification of transferred lexical items into the categories of loanwords, loanblends and loanshifts highlights the significance of morphemic features in bilingually marked speech. This leads to the question whether there is any redistribution of morphemic patterns in the recipient language caused by the introduction of morphemes extraneous to that language's structure. It is generally felt that the effects of borrowing on structure are likely to be small (Haugen, 1973: 178) and that what most frequently happens is that transferred elements are re-aligned on the morphemic structure of the recipient language, particularly if the morpheme in question has a syntactic function. Thus although the English suffix -*ing* has been transferred into French in such loans as "le building, le footing, le smoking" it does not have any syntactic effects on French, is only marginally a productive morpheme in that language, and is assimilated into the regular morphemic structure of French for plural marking. Similarly, the many French nouns transferred into Dutch dialects in Belgium follow the recipient language morphemic patterns for plural formation. The regular French plural marker -*s,* rendered by /ø/ in spoken communication except in situations of liaison, is not applied to French loans used in Dutch but is replaced by one of the two regular Dutch plural markers, -*s* or -*en*, rendered as /s/ and /ə/ in spoken communication. Consequently the French loans "vélos, crayons, mutuelles" are re-aligned in the Dutch recipient dialects to become /'vlous/,/krə'jɔnə/ or /krəjɔns/, /myty'elə/. Similarly, past participles of verbs borrowed from French in the same dialects re-align their morphology on that of regular past participles in Dutch by addition of the prefix *ge-*, giving French "dérangé", Dutch dialect "gederangeerd", French "embêté", Dutch dialect "geambeteerd", French "retouché", Dutch dialect "geretoucheerd".

When lexical items are transferred into a language that has gender distinctions this process will bring in its wake morphological re-adjustments relating to the gender of the transferred elements. Transplanted nouns in such cases must have gender assigned to them and the way this is done may vary according to complex sociolinguistic factors coupled with purely internal structural factors. An examination of nouns transferred from Dutch dialect into spoken French in Brussels (Baetens Beardsmore, 1971b) showed a variety of possibilities dependent primarily on the level of acculturation of the speaker. A bilingual who manages to keep his two languages reasonably well apart will have recourse to relatively few loans and will tend to ascribe gender to whatever words he transfers on patterns close to the predominant norms of the recipient language. If, on the other hand, the speaker shows considerable signs of interference on the phonological, morphological and syntactic levels, then the way gender is ascribed to nouns, be they lexical transfers or indigenous, will show greater deviations from what other speakers do as well as a certain instability within his own speech. Some bilinguals of this type apparently reveal indifference as to what gender they opt for (hence leading to instability), others reveal variations due to an incomplete assimilation of lexical items in the non-dominant language (gender being learnt together with the noun), while still others will show variations due to subtle factors based on a systematization of criteria holding good for one or both of the languages in contact. Low levels of acculturation may give rise to all the above being applied, leading to seemingly arbitrary attribution of gender in the non-dominant language, whether referring to loans or not. Higher levels of acculturation lead to a greater systematization in the patterning of gender ascribed to transferred terms and less deviation from monoglot norms with indigenous items. As far as loans are concerned the patterning may take the form of sex-alignment for terms designating animate beings, as when the Dutch dialect "zeveraar" (*moaner, person who talks rubbish*) is re-aligned in lower-level Brussels French to produce "le zieveraire" in talking about a man and "la zieveresse" in referring to a woman. These particular loans happen to be sex-aligned in the donor language, which will reinforce the pattern of transfer. Others which are not sex-aligned in the donor language, even if designating animate beings, may follow two directions in the transfer operation to the recipient language. It has been noted that lower-level bilinguals in Brussels who borrow Dutch neuter forms into French may give these loans masculine gender, e.g. "mon crotje" = an endearing term addressed to a woman, whereas the linguistically more acclimatized user of French would give the same term feminine gender, "ma crotje" if he introduced the transfer. Examination of other similar cases of the transplant of Dutch neuters into Brussels French shows that speakers with low levels of acculturation tend to determine gender according to the source language (with Dutch neuters being assimilated to French masculines) whereas with more sophisticated speakers it is the recipient language, French, which determines gender re-alignments.

With transfers representing inanimate objects or abstract concepts other influences come into play. Here it may be the phonemic shape of the transfer that is of paramount importance in determining its gender in the recipient language. If we look again at illustrations of Dutch loans in popular Brussels French we can see how the French or Dutch aspect of the transfer can affect gender choice. The term that is almost a pure loanword maintaining its predominantly non-French aspect tends to get classified with the general pattern for assimilation of non-French loans to that language, i.e. the masculine group, as with the Brussels replacement for standard French "porte-manteau" (*coat hanger*) from the Dutch "kapstok" which becomes "le kapstok". If the transferred element has a morphological shape which gives it a more French aspect, in the form of a loanblend, then it does not necessarily follow the group of "foreign elements in standard French, i.e. masculine", but the morphologically determined gender categorizations of the recipient language. Thus the Dutch "kluts" (*dollop*) becomes "une clouche" in lower-level Brussels French, the Dutch "heilbot" (*halibut*) becomes "un elbot", following the major standard French distinction of nouns ending in consonant sounds being feminine, those ending in vowel sounds masculine. Finally, gender may also be ascribed not according to sound factors but under the influence of the original monoglot normative term that has been displaced by a loan for its particular expressivity or connotative associations. For example, the standard French "une tripotée" (*hiding*) may often be replaced in Brussels French by the Dutch-origin word "une rammeling", or the standard French "le remue-ménage" (*fuss and bother*) by the more onomatopoeic Dutch-origin "le rim-ram".

From all these examples of the handling of gender it seems clear that the most important factor in this particular type of cross-language interaction is the general level of acculturation of the speaker, which determines his degree of sensitivity to gender rules in the recipient language. From the Brussels evidence the less well-acclimatized bilingual either ascribes gender arbitrarily or is influenced by the source language, which is also the dominant language, in handling transfers. The more sophisticated and balanced bilingual will probably use fewer transfers in total and those he does use are likely more often to follow the patterns of the recipient language according to four sets of options: sex-alignment for terms designating animate beings, inclusion in the gender group of recognized foreign imports, alignment according to the morphological patterning of similar shaped words in the recipient language or alignment on the gender of the displaced word. In this way it is a combination of sociocultural and internal linguistic factors that determine the gender of transfers in languages that have gender categories.

Still in the field of morphology, an examination of morpheme structure in word formation shows that at least for Western European languages morphological transfer is not particularly productive in the recipient language. Weinreich (1953: 33) noted that the transfer of morphemes is facilitated between highly congruent structures. More specifically, when two grammatical patterns interfere it is ordinarily the one which uses relatively free and invariant morphemes in its paradigm, the more explicit pattern, which serves as the model for imitation. Readily identifiable morphemes lend themselves more easily to transfer and are more readily productive in the recipient language. In Brussels French, the Dutch dialectal diminutive suffixes -*je*, -*tje*, -*ke*, are not only easily transferred from Dutch into French by bilinguals but are also often used by unilingual French speakers for affective reasons, particularly with proper names, producing such regularly attested affectionate designations as "Jeanneke, Fonske, la Coupoleke" for "petite Jeanne, petit Fons, la petite Coupole". Weinreich (1953: 34) gives further examples of the transfer of endearment affixes and diminutives. The examples given reflect the congruence of structure between the recipient and donor languages since the Dutch dialectal diminutives coincide with the French endearment diminutives -*ette* (Jeannette), -*on* (Jeanon). For Haugen (1956: 46) such interlingually identified variants of morphemes could be described as *diamorphs*. Weinreich (1953: 34) has stated that other things being equal, and cultural considerations apart, morphemes with complex grammatical functions seem to be less likely to lend themselves to transfer than those with simpler functions and that morphemes which are as strongly bound as, for example, the inflectional endings are rarely transferred.

Syntactic Transfer

This leads us into the question of interference and its effects on syntax, though one should bear in mind that there is little uniformity in the drawing of boundaries between morphology, syntax and lexicon. Nevertheless there are cases where interference can be explained only by crossing the boundaries between different elements of linguistic analysis. In such circumstances one is confronted with what Bickerton (1971) has called *cross-level interference* or Weinreich (1953: 39) *interlingual equivalence*. This can be illustrated from Spanish-English bilinguals who have problems with the third person singular inflection -*s* in English, which they regularly omit. Spanish has six inflections in the present tense while English has only two for regular verbs but the omission of the English -*s* marker cannot be explained by a simple comparison of the two morphological systems. However, it can be explained by comparing the Spanish phonological system, which rejects syllable final consonant clusters, with the English morphological system where such clusters are functional.

Bearing in mind the need to investigate whether a distinctive syntactic feature in bilingual speech is due to morphological or other structuring in recipient and donor languages, we can now turn to the influence of language contact on syntax. The most obvious case of structural interference is that manifested by word order divergences from monoglot norms. Such divergences might range from the almost word-for-word super-imposition of elements in the weaker language onto the pattern of their equivalents in the dominant language to less complex interlingual re-alignment. The following example is taken from a Dutch-English functional bilingual

"I know what I did that with —
that pan putting on out of the oven" =
die pan daarop zetten uit de oven

(Baetens Beardsmore, 1979d)

where the second part of the utterance coincides almost exactly with Dutch word order. Similarly, the Dutch-French Brussels bilingual may often make his adjectives in French precede the noun they modify, as he would in Dutch, whereas French normally requires post-modification;

"Tu prends ton plus haut chiffre" = you take your highest figure = je neemt je hoogste cijfer.

Other readily detectable cases of syntactic interference occur when the structural attributes of elements in L1 are transferred to elements in L2 which do not share the same properties. Many examples of this kind can be found amongst second language learners, as when the Dutch adverb "goed", under the influence of partial homophony with English "good", causes the latter to function adverbially in Dutch speakers' English, producing sentences like "He did it very good". Note how in this case the re-alignment is reinforced by both partial homophony and partial similarity of function across the two languages. The Dutch "goed" regularly functions as both adjective and adverb, as in;

"Het kind is goed" = The child is good (adj.)
"Het kind deed het goed" = The child did it well (adv.)

whereas its English counterpart "good", which under specific circumstances can also function as either adverb or adjective, also has an adverbial counterpart "well". Compare:

"She doesn't look good"
"She doesn't look well"

Cases of reinforcement of this type might be classified under *double interference*, a different use of the label from that given by Weinreich (1953: 21) who relates it to the monoglot perception of, and adaptation to, foreign accents. It can often be seen when examining interference that the greater the points of similarity between two discrete linguistic systems the greater the likelihood of interference. If similarities are reinforced by convergence on several levels, as in our example of double interference, it is difficult for even highly proficient bilinguals to consistently avoid interlingual identification.

Foreign language teachers can provide countless examples of syntactic interference which coincide with those produced by bilinguals sharing the same languages. In the following examples the first language mentioned refers to the dominant or primary language. English-French bilinguals tend to neglect gender agreement of adjectives or past participles in French because of their absence in English, producing,

"les apparences sont *trompeurs*" (*appearances are deceptive*)
"les salades qu'elle a *cuit*" (*the salads she cooked*).

French-English bilinguals tend to replace the possessive by the definite article when referring to parts of the body in English, on the pattern of the equivalent French structure,

"I scratch the arm" = "Je me gratte *le* bras"

Dutch-English bilinguals may omit the preposition "of" in English because of its absence in Dutch, producing

"Was the one out your street absent?".

Contrastive analysis of the type used to facilitate teaching strategies can bring many such cases to light, but it must not be forgotten that contrastive analysis is more of a predictive technique which does not necessarily explain interference as it actually occurs. Quite often contrastive analysis will reveal likely areas of interference but not effects of negative or double interference. Error analysis, on the other hand, does tend to reveal interference as a consequence of contact between two languages.

Phonological Transfer

Perhaps the most difficult area of all for the avoidance of interference is that of phonology, though often the child or early bilingual has no problems here. The intriguing difference in phonological rendering in two languages can probably be explained with reference to standard theory on language acquisition as developed by Lenneberg (1967) which posits a critical age of 11± for the development of language ability, be it in monoglots or bilinguals. Asher & Garcia (1969/1982) and Oyama (1976/1982) prefer to talk of the "sensitive" period for the acquisition of an interference-free phonological system in young bilinguals and have produced experimental evidence to show that early childhood bilinguals attain native-like phonological systems in two languages whereas late bilinguals, irrespective of their length of usage of the second language in an L2 community, fail to do so after the onset of puberty. Beyond this age decreased plasticity of that area of the brain utilized in phonological processing leads the late bilingual to interpret and reproduce sounds of L2 according to relatively atrophied patterns developed for L1, hence bringing about *phonological interference* in L2. A schematized analysis of the effects of contacts between two distinct phonological systems within the bilingual individual has been produced by Weinreich (1953: 14–28). Examples from two Swiss languages, Romansch and Schwyzertütsch, illustrate how interference arises when a bilingual identifies a phoneme of his secondary system with one of his primary system, subjecting it to the phonetic rules of the primary language in speech. This can lead to four types of consequence.

Under-differentiation of phonemes can occur when two sounds of the secondary system are confused because their counterparts are not distinguished in the primary system, as when the French-English bilingual fails to distinguish between /i/ and /I/ in English. *Over-differentiation* of phonemes takes place when distinctions pertinent in the primary system are imposed on sounds in the secondary system where this is not necessary, as when the Romansch /'lɑdɑ/ is interpreted in Schwyzertütsch as /'lɑ'dɑ/ with extraneous phonemic length. *Re-interpretation* of distinctions takes place when the bilingual distinguishes phonemes of the secondary system by features which are relevant in the primary system but redundant in the secondary system, as when the Italian-English bilingual geminates reduplicated consonants in English on the Italian model, rendering English "fatty" as /fætti/ under the influence of Italian "fatto". Finally there is *phone substitution* when two phonemes are identified as identical across two languages but when in fact their production differs, as when the Dutch-English bilingual replaces the palatal /g/ of English by the Dutch fricative /ɣ/.

Both Weinreich (1953: 14) and Haugen (1954: 382) point out the difficulty of interpreting bilingual speech in functional or phonemic terms, since a list of phonemes in the contact languages is insufficient without the distribution and phonetic qualities of the allophones. Thus it is that familiar phonemes with unfamiliar allophones present more likelihood for interference than do completely distinct phonemes. Once again we see that greater similarity creates a greater likelihood of interference than does dissimilarity. The Dutch-English bilingual has greater difficulty in distinguishing between the so-called clear 1/l/ and the so-called dark 1/ɫ/ in English than he has between /ð/ and /θ/. Similarly the sequencing of phonemes in the non-dominant secondary language may lead to interference if no similar sequencing occurs in the primary language. The French-English bilingual is perfectly capable of rendering /z/ in initial or intervocalic position but often fails to do so in final position in English, since this rarely occurs in French as a plural marker and never after a consonant.

Haugen (1956: 45) indicates that the necessary information for analysing interference on this level is both the phonetic quality of the phonemes in the two languages concerned and their major allophones as well as their distributional sequences. Furthermore, he points out that for the sake of relevance the languages described must be the ones actually used by bilingual speakers and not some idealized standard norm which may be extraneous to the contact situation. The different cases of under- and over-differentiation alluded to earlier have been referred to as *diaphones* (Haugen, 1956: 45) by which are meant bilingually determined variants of a phoneme in the secondary language.

If we turn to the consequences of phonological interference on intelligibility, it appears that phone-substitution, although striking, is not all that prevalent and when it does occur it only slightly affects intelligibility. Re-interpretation, probably more frequent, is not a serious obstacle to monoglot interpretation either. Over-differentiation is often hardly noticed by the monoglot listener whereas under-differentiation, probably the most common form of interference on this level, often leads to misinterpretation on the part of the listener.

An intriguing feature which can affect the nature of phonological interference in the bilingual's weaker language is the degree of formality of the content of that language's usage. Hatch's (1983: 12–35) very clear overview of the different development stages in both the elimination and persistence of phonological interference features as competence in the second language progresses highlights studies which reveal how people articulate more accurately in formal rather than informal situations, with an increasing use of L1-determined phoneme substitutes as the speech situation grows more informal. The opposite was true, however, for Thai speakers learning English in the quality of r-sounds produced, as recorded by Beebe (1980). Because in Thai a trilled r is the most correct rendering in initial position in Royal usage its perceived high value was transferred to English in formal tasks but never occurred as such and was rendered by the correct English version in informal conversation. Hence the social value attached to particular forms in the dominant language can influence the presence of interference features.

Prosodic Transfer

The most insidious form of interference is that at the suprasegmental level, where even the highly accomplished bilingual with few traces of interference in other aspects of his speech may well betray the influence of the dominant or primary language on the secondary. This area is also the least well-documented in the literature. The subtle differences in stress and intonation patterns between two languages can account for the effects of contact on suprasegmentals; the fact that they are amongst the earliest patterns established in language acquisition and consequently probably most deeply anchored may also account for their effects on a weaker language, and in addition the fact that little conscious attention is directed to this level of speech.

Our investigation of Dutch-French bilinguals in Brussels has shown how accentuated strong stress typical of Dutch produces vowel reduction to centralized position in unstressed French syllables. Thus the standard French "téléphone" /telefɔn/ often becomes /'teləfɔn/ for the Brussels bilingual. Similar conditions explain the diphthongization of vowels in open position due to accentuated strong stress which is absent in standard French and leading to "coucher" /kuʃe/ being rendered as /ku'ʃei/. As for intonation patterns, these are often completely re-aligned in the secondary language on models appropriate for the primary language, producing cases like the following in which the Brussels French verbal element takes highest pitch on the model of the Brussels Dutch pattern:

Standard French	— "Il faut *pas* dire ça!" (*You mustn't say that!*)
Brussels French	— "Il faut pas *dire* ça!"
Brussels Dutch	— "Ge moogt dat niet *zeggen!*"

It is precisely in the suprasegmental features and their effects on the phonological system that one can often trace the effects of contact in communities that have switched from one language to another through some stage of transitional bilingualism which has led to a new monoglot community which uses a different language from that of its predecessors (i.e. residual bilingualism).

Gumperz (1977) gives a clear example of how interference, at the intonation level can create impressions of rudeness or indifference where none is intended. He noted how Indian and Pakistani women servers in a cafeteria in England enquired whether their customers wanted gravy on their meat by saying "gravy?" with a falling intonation, instead of the standard British rising intonation, and this was interpreted by the customers as indicating surliness. When the servers were taught the correct intonation the customers' negative impressions disappeared.

Following upon the overview of the major elements involved in the analysis of interference we should perhaps turn once again to the distinction between interference and code-switching. At the beginning of this chapter the potential difficulties were pointed out in identifying, on the one hand, the onset of code-switching, and on the other, the consequences of interference. In Chapter 4 the theoretical implications of the relationship between the two will be discussed, though at this stage it will be sufficient to note that neither interference nor code-switching is arbitrary, though the rules that govern their presence or absence may differ.

The determination of the nature and occurrence of interference is clearly due to the structure of the languages in contact, which affects the resistance and encouragement of transfer. Though not totally excluded, pronouns and articles show the greatest resistence to transfer in terms of interference. Extra-linguistic factors, such as the culture load borne by the two languages in contact, can determine the permeability of a recipient language to a lexical transfer. Sensitivity to language in general and the degree of cultural awareness, often coupled with educational levels, can reveal how interference may operate in such cases as the handling of gender. It is on the phonological level that interference can probably be most strongly felt, since, as Weinreich (1953: 24) points out,

> "it requires a relatively high degree of cultural sophistication in both languages for a speaker to afford the structural luxury of maintaining separate subphonemic habits in each".

Code-switching

Although there may be superficial similarities between interference and code-switching, particularly with respect to the lexis (cf. loanwords), in general it would seem that interference is determined by internal linguistic factors, whereas code-switching is determined by extra-linguistic factors. Bilingual speakers with more than one language at their disposal may *choose* to use the whole repertoire of linguistic elements available, where the monoglot might interpret the inclusion of elements extraneous to one of the languages as manifestations of interference. Whatever interpretation is given will depend on the norm one is using as a reference point. Fishman (1965a: 67) stresses the fact that the habitual language choice in multilingual speech communities or networks is far from being a random matter of momentary inclination or "inadequacy" (i.e. interference) and that "proper" usage in such communities indicates that only *one* of the theoretically co-available languages or varieties will be chosen by particular classes of *interlocutors* on particular kinds of *occasions* to discuss particular kinds of *topics*. Thus in bilingual communities certain elements extraneous to a particular language may be inserted by choice rather than unwittingly.

In a study of Malay-English bilinguals (Abdullah, 1979) it was noted that the following factors were decisive in determining whether "foreign" elements appeared in one of the languages available: whether the personal repertoires of the interlocutors were equal or not; whether certain personal characteristics were shared which led to the forming of a homogeneous group; the degree of intimacy or friendship; the setting or the locale, since formal situations tend to encourage linguistic purism; the topic, which determined whether certain subjects were better handled in one language rather than the other. Abdullah noted that in specific circumstances greetings, introductions, farewells and invitations tended to prevail in Malay while discussion concerning studies led to exchanges in English. In conversation in Malay, English was often used to refer to concepts that are specifically Western and the insertion of English elements in a Malay conversation demonstrated a certain degree of intimacy, on the basis of shared knowledge, between the participants. The following example from Abdullah shows this process in operation, where the English elements are not really questions of interference but of code-switching determined by extra-linguistic phenomena:

"Macam *I* tak tahu *the size of my clothes; I know it by heart...*".

Similarly, in a Malay context the word to indicate "wife" may be the English term replacing the Malay possibilities of "isteri", which has very formal connotations, or "bini" which may have crude connotations, to circumvent potential offending signals. One of the more interesting cases of transfer in the Malay-English bilingual context is the use of the English personal pronouns "I" and "you" in discourse between Malaysian bilinguals in a conversation conducted primarily in Malay. It has been noted earlier that pronouns tend to be highly resistant to interference effects and in this context the choice of a foreign pronoun is deliberate, not accidental, thereby not reflecting interference. Consider the following italicized pronoun usage:

"*You* ambil dua setengah gula"
"*I* suroh *dia* buat Masters, jadi *dia* buat Masters"

In the second quotation the English pronoun "I" is used alongside the Malay third person pronoun "dia" = he/she. Now the latter Malay pronoun is seldom replaced by its English equivalents so that the explanation for this complex case of mixed language usage has to be sought in terms of code-switching rather than interference. The Malay pronoun system is involved and is determined by rank or status; in face-to-face interaction a superior or senior may use personal pronouns when addressing an inferior or junior but the reverse is considered unacceptable. By inserting English pronouns for first and second person reference neutral implications are involved with respect to power, seniority or respect, something already present in the third person Malay pronoun "dia". This is an outstanding and popular feature of code-switching among Malay bilinguals.

The above examples show code-switching operating as a fairly conscious device and this is even more so when it is done for rhetorical purposes. Rayfeld (1970: 54) feels that this stylistic function is one of its most important traits. Literature has made ample use of this technique with such noteworthy examples as the insertion of French in Shakespeare's *Henry V* and Tolstoy's *War and Peace* (for a detailed account of code-switching in the latter, see Timm, 1978). In contemporary spoken language it has been noted as a device for emphasis through repetition in another language,

"Going so soon! Cepatnya!"
for emphasis by contrast,

"I know it by heart, tapi buat tak tahu"
or to make a parenthetic statement,

"I bought a rubber estate on credit.
Really? Pandai orang tua ni"

(The last three Malay-English examples are taken from Abdullah, 1979).

The above illustrations clearly contradict the statement made by Weinreich (1953: 73) that

"the ideal bilingual switches from one language to the other according to appropriate changes in the speech situation (interlocutors, topics, etc.), but not in an unchanged speech situation, and certainly not within a single sentence. If he does include expressions from another language, he may mark them off explicitly as 'quotations' by quotation marks in writing and by special voice modifications (slight pause, changes in tempo, and the like) in speech".

One of the more comprehensive overviews of the way code-switching operates within the speech act or the framework of discourse analysis is that produced by Gumperz (1982) who, by dint of examples from different language combinations, examines the nature of conversational code-switching. Contrary to the above statement by Weinreich, Gumperz (1982: 60) noted that no hesitation pauses, changes in sentence rhythm, pitch level or intonation contour mark shifts in code. He noted that most often, but not exclusively, the alternation between codes takes the form of two subsequent sentences, as when a speaker uses a second language either to reiterate his message or to reply to someone else's statement. From an analysis of his data Gumperz (1982: 75–82) noted six major functions of conversational code-switching, though he was not able to attempt setting up language usage rules which might predict or reliably account for the incidence of code-switching. The five major functions, clearly distinguishable from interference or borrowing, which he defines as the incorporation of single words or short, frozen, idiomatic phrases from one variety into another with morpho-syntactic adaptation, are given as follows:

i)   *Quotations* where the code-switched passages are clearly identifiable either as direct quotations or as reported speech;

ii)   *Addressee specification* where the switch in code serves to direct the message to single out one of several possible interlocutors;

iii) *Interjections* where the code-switch serves to mark an interjection or sentence filler;

iv)   *Reiteration* where a message in one code is repeated in the other code, either literally or in a somewhat modified form—in some cases such repetitions might serve to clarify what is said but often they merely amplify or emphasize a message;

v)   *Message qualification* where the switch in language serves to qualify constructions, as when sentence and verb complements or predicates follow a copula;

vi)   *Personalization versus objectivization* where code contrast seems to relate to such things as the distinction between talk about action and talk as action, the degree of speaker involvement in, or distance from, a message, whether a statement reflects personal opinion or knowledge, whether it refers to specific instances or has the authority of generally known fact.

Sanchez (1983) noted amongst Mexican American bilinguals that code-switching occurs most frequently amongst second generation bilingual immigrants, reflecting the transitional phase in language shift from Spanish dominance in the first generation to English dominance in the third generation. Like Gumperz she observed that the addressee and the nature of the speech act determined a code-switch, as when a bilingual girl used Spanish in talking to her grandmother but shifted from Spanish to English when insulting her younger sister, presumably because of stronger affective associations with English jibes reflecting teenager peer culture. She also explained how denotative and connotative factors can both affect the direction of code-switches in bilingual interactions. (For a similar classification of the function of code-switching, cf. Hatch, 1976.)

Gumperz (1982: 90) also looked into the syntactic aspects of code-switching, particularly noting how it is blocked where it violates the speaker's feelings for what on syntactic or semantic grounds must be regarded as a single unit. He noted that the ease with which a sequence can be switched was most closely related to the following factors:

a) the relative semantic independence of a phrase or perhaps its stressability or contrastability;

b) sequential unity whereby discontinuous sequences cannot be switched;

c) semantic or pragmatic unity—idiomatic units cannot be broken and conjunctions go with the phrase they conjoin, while pronoun-verb sequences are more unitary than noun-verb sequences; when a phrase has both an expanded and contracted form only the former appears as part of code-switched sequences; when a sentence is dominated by a performative verb unit the main clause acts as a single unit;

d) the total number of switches within any message sub-unit cannot be more than one.

It is the work of McClure (1981) on code-switching among children and Poplack (1980) among adults that deserves particular attention for the study of its formal linguistic aspects. Both these authors concentrated on Spanish-English bilingualism in the United States and the papers referred to build up on considerable earlier research by themselves and others in this field to provide in-depth analyses of not only its functional characteristics but also its linguistic determinants. Moreover, both come to the conclusion that the more bilingual the speaker is the more refined and complex the linguistic features of code-switching tend to become.

In her study of children McClure found that inappropriate choice of language when addressing a monolingual was rare and that the topic of discourse did not have as large an influence upon language selection as did who was present, while during interviews and narratives with adults code-switching was strongly inhibited, whereas in conversations it occurred freely. On the other hand she found that code-switching could be used stylistically to mark a desired change in topic, for example:

Chicana researcher: Dile que es una casa sin techo.
                            (*Tell her that it's a house without a roof.*)

Girl, 6:   We have a pretty, uh, Christmas tree.
                                                    (McClure, 1981: 85)

Saville-Troike (1982: 244–45) found that the age at which children could functionally differentiate codes depended to a great extent on the context of acquisition, but that most had developed this competence to switch appropriately according to the linguistic identity of the addressee by the age of three, and by situation or setting soon after. Switching by topic, or by the role-relationship between speakers other than the language of the addressee, comes at a later stage in development.

With her adult population Poplack, too, found that the most important factor to determine the actual occurrence of code-switching was the perceived norm of the speech situation, particularly the ethnicity of the interlocutor once other criteria such as appropriateness, the formality of the speech situation, were met. She also noted that speakers who learned both English and Spanish in early childhood showed the highest percentage of intra-sentential switching, while those who had learned English after the age of 13 showed a much lower percentage of intra-sentential switches, just as did those speakers who were Spanish dominant. This important observation shows up the inter-relationship between degree of bilingual ability and the occurrence of code-switching, particularly in stable bilingual communities of the type investigated by Poplack.

Poplack noted that the linguistic factors that determine the nature of code-switching involve the skilled manipulation of overlapping sections of two (or more) grammars and that there were virtually no instances in her corpus of ungrammatical combinations of L1 and L2, regardless of the bilingual ability of the speaker. This suggests that code-switching is itself a discrete mode of speaking emanating from a single code-switching grammar. Two major constraints have been posited as determining the structure of code-switches:

a)   *The free morpheme constraint.* Codes may be switched after any constituent in discourse provided that constituent is not a bound morpheme, except if the latter has been phonologically integrated, e.g. una buena exCUSE [eh′kjuws] (*a good excuse*) but not, * EAT – iendo (*eating*).

                                                    (Poplack, 1980: 586)

b)   *The equivalence constraint* states that code-switches tend to occur at points in discourse where juxtaposition of L1 and L2 elements does not violate a syntactic rule of either language, i.e. at points around which the surface structures of the two languages map on to each other. Poplack illustrates this constraint by the example below, where the dotted lines indicate possible switch points and the arrows indicate the ways in which constituents from the two languages map on to each other. The speaker's actual utterance is reproduced in C:

A.	Eng.	1	told him	that	so that	he	would bring it	fast
B.	Sp. (Yo)		le dije	eso	pa' que	(el)	la trajera	ligero
C.		I	told him	that	pa' que		la trajera	ligero

(Poplack, 1980: 586)

Further research on code-switching involving other pairs of languages is necessary to see whether the above two major constraints have some universal validity, particularly in cases where the languages involved have widely differing morphosyntactic structures.

Poplack further distinguished between *intra-sentential switching* of the type:

"Why make Carol SENTARSE ATRAS PA'QUE (*sit in the back so*) everybody has to move PA'QUE SE SALGA (*for her to get out*)?"

and *extra-sentential code-switching*, usually in the form of tags, or else single noun switches, of the type

"Vendia arroz (*he sold rice*) 'N SHIT."

and that the former typified speakers with the greatest degree of bilingual ability (Poplack, 1980: 589).

As will be seen in Chapter 4 the findings with reference to the nature and function of code-switching have important consequences of a theoretical nature, just as a clear distinction between code-switching and interference has.

Before turning definitively away from the question of interference we should stop to look at situations in which more than two languages may interact. Interference between the different codes available in these circumstances, although following the general principles outlined in this chapter, are not necessarily determined by the primary or dominant language. In complex multilingual societies as prevalent in South-East

Asia or Africa, the relative dominance of the different languages in a speaker's repertoire may not coincide with any chronological order of learning. The first language learnt may be restricted to intimate family life and be accompanied by a regionally more important second language at the onset of schooling. The effects of peer-group interaction and schooling may combine to outweigh the significance of the primary vernacular in the direction of interference and code-switching. If at the onset of secondary schooling a third language is introduced, producing a triglossic situation of the type described by T'Sou (1981), it may well be that the chronologically learnt second language is the source of interference in the third. This may even be the case when the chronological second language is less dominant than the primary language. As Chumbow (1978) has pointed out with illustrations from Nigeria and the Cameroon, although the determinants of transfer are the same irrespective of the number of languages involved, an interweaving of linguistic and extra-linguistic variables decide which of the languages serves as the source of transfer.

When only two languages are involved the most significant criterion specific to multilingual interference of the type under discussion is the degree of structural and phonological inter-relatedness between the languages under manipulation. West African students from Nigeria, who on top of their primary vernacular, Yoruba, learn Hausa, English and French at school, often show greater interference from English in their French than from Yoruba. The speaker's perception of cultural or ethnic relations between his different languages may be an extra factor in determining the direction of interference. Chumbow shows that the two genetically related African languages, Yoruba and Hausa, lead to greater interference from Yoruba in Hausa than from Yoruba in French, even though the medium for instruction of Hausa is English and not Yoruba. In Brussels, where French-dominant students had to learn Dutch via intensive methods, i.e. four hours per day, followed by intensive English instruction sources of interference in English were often from Dutch as well as from French. When the order of foreign language learning was reversed amongst a similar French-dominant population, i.e. intensive English followed by intensive Dutch, the English origin interference phenomena were equally significant. Here then, we have a case of classroom ascendancy of one language over another, together with genetic inter-relatedness, leading to a strong source of interference equal to that of the primary language.

One final point requires underlining before turning away from the present discussion. It would be a misapprehension if, because of the focus of this chapter, interference was felt to explain everything in bilingual speech.

Although different levels of interference may manifest themselves, at least in the weaker language of any type of bilingual, it is also true that many deviations from monoglot performance can be attributed to other causes. It would appear that interference is more prevalent with late bilinguals than it is with early childhood cases and with the former it tends to predominate in the early stages of second language acquisition. With childhood simultaneous bilinguals, however, it is surprising how few interference phenomena occur, while with both early and late bilinguals, as McLaughlin (1984: 67) points out, deviations from monoglot norms can be of three kinds, besides finding their origin in clear evidence of interference: (a) developmental errors, which do not reflect the user's first language, but are found among those who acquire the second language during childhood like a first language; (b) ambiguous errors which can be categorized as due either to interference or as developmental errors; (c) unique errors which cannot be categorized as due either to interference or as developmental errors. The emphasis given in this chapter to interference and code-switching should be seen from the perspective of the end-point of bilingualism, whereas if one were examining the development of bilingual proficiency one would have to be circumspect about over-hasty interpretations of striking features by using the classification we have provided as a possible but not exclusive frame of analysis.

To conclude it must be noted that bilingually marked speech patterns are determined by a complex set of factors, some of which are purely linguistic, others not, some of which lead to clear cases of interference, others leading to manifestations of code-switching, and that there may be apparent overlap in the formal properties of interference and code-switching.

Summary

This chapter has taken a close look at the observable features of bilingual linguistic performance by which the speakers of more than one language can be distinguished. Theoretical considerations on the nature of communicative competence provide the framework for the explanation of interference phenomena and the very similar, but distinct, operation of code-switching, showing how certain linguistic usage by bilinguals is comparable to monoglot behaviour. Different types of so-called interference have been examined on the phonological, morphological, lexical, semantic and syntactic levels, together with the notion of integration where this refers to specifically bilingual norms of language usage. Arguments have been provided to explain how and why interference occurs and to eliminate the presupposition that interference is necessarily a negative phenomenon. Certain cases of more subtle types of so-called interference have been illustrated, particularly those not normally detectable in the flow of speech, such as negative or connotative interference. The implications for interference of the presence of more than two languages in the individual have shown how the weakest language may often bear traces attributable not to the primary or dominant language but to the second best known. Closer investigation of the nature and occurrence of code-switching has shown how this, unlike interference, correlates closely with high-level bilingual ability. Situational switching determined by extra-linguistic factors has been linked to the linguistic factors involved, leading to an appraisal of code-switching as reflecting the overlapping sectors of the grammars of L1 and L2 to form a single code-switching grammar.

3 Measurement of Bilingualism and Biculturalism

The opening chapter, with its emphasis on the relative nature of bilingual abilities, should have made it clear that any attempt at measuring the phenomenon is hampered by the elasticity of what is covered. Yet it is also true that once the terms of reference for a particular type of bilingual case have been determined, one can hopefully measure with some degree of accuracy different aspects of specific linguistic behaviour which typify a particular bilingual situation. Chapter 2 has shown that one central focus of interest for the linguistic (as opposed to the social study of bilingualism) is interference, together with the incidence and functioning of code-switching, and the description and analysis of their different manifestations can be recognized as one type of bilingual measurement. However, at this stage one should not be led into the misapprehension that indices of interference can tell us all there is to know about bilingual behaviour. Indeed, to some extent they can tell us no more than that we are dealing with a bilingual situation worthy of investigation, bearing in mind that we have already classified perfect ambilingualism as a relatively uninteresting field of study. Although the amount, quality and frequency of interference phenomena, together with the type of code-switching operated, can provide some sort of measurement which allows for a partial classification of bilingual typologies, these by no means represent the only measurable features of relevance to a global understanding of how bilinguals behave.

To some extent it could be said that all second language testing represents an attempt at bilingual measurement, from the simple dictation exercise often given in early phases of foreign language learning, through carefully developed multiple choice and cloze techniques frequently used to measure certain receptive abilities, to the complex strategies designed to measure oral production abilities. Although all aspects of language testing play an important role in bilingual measurement, however, it is not this branch of applied linguistics that will be concentrated on in this chapter since it is felt that this would lead us astray into areas not specifically restricted to bilingualism but more relevant to foreign language learning. The two are intertwined, it is true, but foreign language testing is a vast domain which would lead into a very different type of book. Since nearly all foreign language testing techniques are based primarily on monoglot norms, revealing how near to unilingual behaviour a subject can perform, they tend to show up preconceptions of the tester's expectations on manipulating more than one language rather than the specificity of bilingual behaviour. Thus although we do not dismiss traditional language testing as irrelevant to our field of study we shall not be primarily concerned with an overview of this field. Many established second or foreign language tests provide the mainstay of a frame of reference for measuring differences between bilinguals and monoglots as will be seen from any publication on testing theory and practice from which useful ideas can be plundered (see for example, Carroll, 1980; Oller & Perkins, 1980; Oller, 1979).

Another field that will not be gone into is that of contrastive analysis (see Nickel, 1972) since it is felt that here again we shall discover little of practical relevance to the measurement of bilingual behaviour. Contrastive analysis, in which two languages are put side by side in order to discover the differences between them, should in theory provide information on problem areas for potential bilinguals. In practice, however, there may be no correlation between the degree of difference between two linguistic systems and the nature of the interference or deviation from monoglot norms in a bilingual's speech. At times, very wide divergences cause no problems, while slight differences cause many, while at other times the opposite is true (see Chapter 2, p. 64). More useful for bilingual studies is error analysis, which is based on the examination of production by bilinguals of one kind or another with an attempt at explanation of the errors (see Richards, 1974). Recent developments in interlanguage analysis (see p. 27) reveal the significance of both contrastive and error analysis in bilingual studies (Celce-Murcia & Hawkins, 1985).

Attention in this chapter will focus more upon experimental techniques designed to reveal how a bilingual behaves on the cognitive, affective, social and purely linguistic levels and on the problems involved in building up a composite picture of the different measurements which allow for a deeper understanding of the totality of what is involved in being bilingual. To this extent we shall disagree with Malherbe (1969: 50, quoted in Grosjean, 1982: 235) that,

> "It is doubtful whether bilingualism *per se* can be measured apart from the situation in which it is to function in the social context in which a particular individual operates linguistically. The only practical approach. . . is to assess bilingualism in terms of certain

social and occupational demands of a practical nature in a particular society. Here again the criterion is to be 'bilingualism for what?' Purpose and function are the main determinants."

On the contrary, it is felt that the specificity of bilingualism is an important dimension that can be measured, together with the function of bilingualism and its attributes.

One of the more intriguing areas of measurement is that which attempts to identify the mere presence of bilingual speakers in a given society and is concerned with language censuses. Here one is attempting to investigate dominance configurations at a societal level, or "who speaks what language to whom?" (Fishman, 1965b). Since the chapter on typologies and definitions has shown how many different interpretations can be given to answering the question "What is a bilingual?" or indeed to what is involved in knowing a second language, it is clear that the census gatherer is confronted with problems in formulating questions that can unambiguously be interpreted both by the respondent to a questionnaire and the statistical analyst. If one adds to these potential difficulties of interpretation that of the arbitrariness of deciding whether a given speech form should be classified as a language or a dialect the complexities are increased. Developing nations in Africa, Latin America and Asia have enough problems merely trying to establish how many languages are present, and the figures given for a sub-continent like India of 1652 languages (Ghosh, 1979) may well conceal a certain amount of arbitrariness, particularly if one is trying to produce statistics for speech varieties that have not been codified.

Some of the almost insuperable problems involved in trying to draw up census data on the incidence of bilingualism have been presented in the chapter devoted to this question in Kelly's *Description and Measurement of Bilingualism* (1969: 285-348). Several of the solutions proposed appear somewhat controversial. What is clear is that most facets of bilingualism cannot be handled in a general purpose census, particularly the more purely internal linguistic aspects such as interference, code-switching, diglossia, dialects, styles and registers. Even if these areas are omitted as not being necessary to the primary goals of census data gathering, the very nature of the determinants of census questions, dominated as they are by the requirements of ease of interpretation, leads to problems. The rapid survey of the types of questions used in different countries of the world as given in Kelly reveals how difficult it is even to discover the dominant language use of a multilingual population. A question asking what the respondent's mother tongue is may in no way reveal which language is best known, most used or still spoken. Questions asking which languages are known are open to ambiguity in the interpretation of what is to be understood by "known" — the ability to understand, read, write and speak more than one language or the ability to string together two words in a ritualistic formula such as "Bonjour, Madame". Even restricting the question to asking which languages are spoken is open to the same degree of ambiguity.

In situations where ethnic, political or prestige factors hinge on language questions considerable distortions in census responses can arise as a result of attitudinal dispositions. In Wales respondents have been known to deny any knowledge of Welsh, even though they were highly competent in the language, because of the emotional bond between Welsh nationalist politics and knowledge of Welsh (see covert bilingualism, p. 22). In Belgium respondents have claimed knowledge of French when in fact they could hardly manipulate the language because the census was interpreted as a referendum which would indicate the linguistic community the respondent would like to be identified with rather than his true knowledge of one or more languages.

The Belgian case is a prime example of the hazards of trying to identify the number of people who know one or more languages in a complex society. All questions pertaining to language were abolished from Belgian censuses after 1947 because of the political implications that could be interpreted from simple enquiries into knowledge of the three official languages, Dutch, French and German. Analysis of previous censuses in Belgium revealed that an increase in the number of bilinguals as registered over the years was accompanied by a switch in language most frequently employed to the advantage of French and the detriment of Dutch; in other words bilingualism on the societal level represented a transitional stage from unilingualism in Dutch to unilingualism in French. This pattern has been recorded in many countries (including Wales) where bilingualism pertains. The consequences of such shifts leading to highly charged emotional reactions determined by feelings of threats against cultural identity caused the Belgians to "freeze" their statistics after 1947 and officially divide the country up, for administrative purposes, into a monoglot Dutch-speaking north, a monoglot French-speaking south and certain bilingual areas scattered along the frontier between these two, the capital and in the German-speaking eastern areas. In other words, the last language census figures led to the re-alignment of the multilingual state on the "principle of territoriality" (Mackey, 1976: 83). Consequently one is in a somewhat anomalous situation where a country has officially demarcated monoglot and bilingual regions with no precise idea of the number of speakers of one type or the other present in any of them. A detailed analysis of the polemics surrounding the Belgian census questions on language makes interesting reading (see Baetens Beardsmore, 1971c: 23-25; Gubin, 1978) and begets the question how one can reasonably hope to assess the number of bilinguals present in a given society.

Suggestions have been put forward whereby questions could be posed about the most preferred language, the language most frequently used, the language first spoken, the language of instruction, the language used with peers, older and younger people, the language used in specific activities, and so on, all of which should then be ideally correlated with standard sociological data on age, sex, socio-economic status, etc. Subtle suggestions have also been put forward for trying to discover what is presumably the dominant language for a bilingual by enquiring what language is used for mental arithmetic, inner speech or meditation, and dreams. But here again the responses to such questions may not reveal as much as might be expected. A bilingual will probably do his mental arithmetic in the language he was taught to add, subtract and multiply in, even if this subsequently becomes a language of infrequent use. Inner speech and reflection may well be conducted in different languages dependent on the theme, and this may also be true of dreams (see Fitouri, 1983, for measurement of these dimensions). It is possible that the most frequently noted language in these contexts tends to be the dominant language but it may not be the only one used or the language first learnt. Informal questioning of bilinguals on these points tends to bear out the above assumptions. However, it is not clear what the position is with early childhood bilinguals who have kept up both languages in later life. According to Berman (1979: 169), dominance is determined by three inter-related factors: quantity of situational exposure and variety of contexts of use; linguistic knowledge and proficiency; cognitive processing and the nature of bilingual strategies.

It would seem that the only satisfactory manner of eliciting information of reliable validity would be by conducting small-scale in-depth investigations among a target population of known bilinguals based on standard sampling techniques. Detailed questionnaires could be drawn up based on the multiple typologies discussed earlier and administered by trained interviewers who would be sensitive to the potential ambiguities of responses which might engender misinterpretation. Such questionnaires, used widely in Wales (Sharp *et al.*, 1973), are usually known as *linguistic background scales*. In this way fairly reliable information can be gathered on ability in the different skills, together with that on the language most frequently used in specific circumstances, the order of learning, inter-generational language shifts and the relationship between bilingualism and its wider demographic and institutional context. It is possible that the results from such investigations would not necessarily be open to extrapolation to the whole population in a given bilingual community as is feasible with standard sampling techniques, given the extreme diversity of bilingual behaviour. Nor would the results necessarily indicate language dominance in the sense of primary grammatical functioning, though they would reveal the language most frequently used — the two need in no way be related. On the other hand they would provide clear indicators as to trends in bilingual usage amongst a given population and overcome the criticisms against the general vagueness of information provided in standard censuses which by their very nature cannot go beyond the limitations inherent in their overall design.

The measurement of *language dominance* in bilinguals represents a hazardous venture for which some intriguing solutions have been proposed. Previous chapters have shown how in certain cases it is easy to detect the relative dominance of a bilingual's two languages by such things as the nature and direction of interference. With the late bilingual, for instance, it is highly unlikely that the second language becomes dominant in the sense of the language of primary grammatical functioning, though this may well become dominant in the sense of most frequently used or preferred. Dodson (1981) uses the term *preferred language* rather than dominant language precisely to take this type of situation into account, since it reflects better the relative feeling of ease a bilingual may have in conducting certain activities in a particular language, even though this may not be the strongest language. In some cases standard test procedures used in many classroom situations will readily bear out intuitive assumptions on the dominant language for receptive or productive functioning. With certain types of functional specialization of language use it is fairly evident that the nature of the functional specialization brings in its wake feelings of preferred language which will coincide with dominant language for that set of activities.

Dominance configurations are less easily detected in cases of early childhood bilingualism which has led to apparent balanced proficiency. It might seem a contradiction to attempt to look for dominance in cases of balanced bilingualism, though this need not be the case if the sequence of early learning has been consecutive rather than simultaneous. It might be assumed that the language acquired first represents a greater likelihood for dominance but there is no certainty about this. With early bilinguals, too, preferred language for a particular domain of activity will also reflect dominance configurations that may differ over time.

Attempts to measure the linguistic dominance of bilinguals have been carried out by Lambert (1955) based on a technique which checks the speed of reaction to stimuli presented in two languages. In these experiments, three groups of French-English bilinguals were tested, natives of France who had lived in Canada for about seven years, English-speaking undergraduates studying French, and English-speaking postgraduate students of French. Results tended to show that the group with the least experience of French reacted most slowly to the presentation of stimuli in that language. It was also found that those subjects who revealed no difference in response time required for either language could be considered as balanced bilinguals, an assumption borne out by their case histories. Anomalous results, as when the subject's case history implied that the respondent should be dominant in one language when in fact reaction time responses indicated dominance in the other, were accounted for by favourable attitudinal dispositions towards the language and culture that came out best, with a negation of the cultural values implicit in the language which one would have expected to be dominant.

In a further experiment conducted by Lambert, Havelka & Gardner (1959) dominance was measured in three groups of French-English bilinguals, a French-dominant group, a balanced group and an English-dominant group, by using a whole series of tests designed to confirm case histories. These included a measure of facility with which word-completion tasks were carried out. Subjects were asked to give continuous free associations to French and English stimulus words within a sixty second time limit. In this test there was a strict correlation between degree of bilingualism and ability to carry out the task in a native-like manner. A second test was based on asking subjects to detect as many English and French words embedded in the nonsense neologism DANSONODEND. Results were scored on the number of different items given for each language and they showed that comparative ease of detection of possible words in either language corresponded closely to the degree of bilingualism of each subject. However attractive these two measures may appear at first sight, great care should be taken in the experimental conditions under which they are used. With a slightly different population the same two tests were used by ourselves and found to give strikingly different results. The same word association task and the neologism were presented to French students of English in Belgium who were studying English by intensive methods at the rate of four hours per day over a three month period. These subjects were manifestly dominant in French, given their presence on the intensive course. Nevertheless, within the context of the English-dominated classroom setting the subjects probably interpreted the exercise as a test of knowledge of English and produced consistently higher scores in English than in French. Thus here the context of the test situation could have been decisive in producing anomalous results.

Lambert, Havelka & Gardner also suggested a test to measure facility in reading as a measure of dominance where the materials used, consisting of twenty commonly-occurring English words, were intermixed with their French equivalents and the time taken to read aloud the total set measured. Again speed of response at this task correlated positively with degree of bilingualism. A further test consisted of stimulus words common to both French and English, such as "silence", "chance", "important", which subjects were asked to read aloud rapidly in order to discover whether a French or an English pronunciation would be ascribed to them most readily. As a distracting element the words open to ambiguous interpretation as being either English or French were randomly presented in the midst of either clearly English or clearly French words. It was found that degree of bilingualism on this test tended to reveal itself by the preponderance of pronunciation in one or the other language for the ambiguous words, while balanced bilinguals tended to achieve equal scores for both languages. The interest of these series of experiments lies in the fact that the type of bilingual dominance appears to have a pervasive influence throughout various aspects of verbal behaviour and that the directionality of the scores on one of the sub-tests correlates with that on others. It also appears that the nearer a subject approaches to balanced bilingualism the easier he is able to perceive and read words in both languages with similar speeds, to associate in both languages with similar fluency, and to make active use of vocabulary in both languages. If this pervasive nature of dominance in verbal behaviour is true then some of our assumptions about the changing nature of dominance according to the language of preferred domain of activity need reappraisal, though in the present stage of our knowledge it is not clear what the relationships may be.

Although the tests developed by Lambert and his colleagues and based on the reaction time of respondents tend to reveal that balanced bilingualism coincides with equivalent speeds of reaction in both languages, such measures have not been without criticism. Fishman (1968) regards speed as a very ethnocentric kind of measurement since if the culture in which the bilinguals live does not value speed highly, or if the culture embodied in one of the languages does not do so, then it is pointless to use speed as a measurement. Moreover, Skutnabb-Kangas (1984: 213) points out that it is common for the reaction of bilinguals to be slightly longer either in both or at least one of their languages than that for the equivalent monolingual, since the bilingual has more to choose between. This difference seems to apply above all to tests where the stimulus is ambiguous, in that it could belong to either language, or to tests in which the subject does not know in advance in which language the stimulus is going to be.

Ervin-Tripp (1973a) devised a different type of measure for dominance based on the learning and recall of pictorial material in two languages which showed that pictures were easier to name in the bilingual's more fluent language and were recalled more significantly in that language, regardless of the language of learning. Optimal circumstances for recall of such pictures were learning and recall in the dominant language while the worst condition for recall was learning in the dominant language and recall in the other.

Whatever intrinsic values the above tests may have, doubts as to their validity have been expressed (see Macnamara in Kelly, 1969: 84). Their major achievement seems to be the confirmation of what can be assumed from the bilingual subject's case history, namely the greater the contact with two languages the greater the likelihood of balance and the smaller the effect of dominance. (We should not forget the contradictory effects referred to earlier, however, determined by the context of the experimentation.) It should not be thought that dispensing with attempts at dominance measurement could be advocated in favour of language background questionnaires since these, too, have been shown as poor in predictive power (Macnamara, 1969: 89).

Bearing in mind the typological frame of reference given in Chapter 1 in discussions about bilingual dominance, one can perhaps turn most usefully to indices of interference and integration for measuring the language of primary grammatical functioning if it is present, together with reaction time techniques for balanced bilinguals where there is little or no interference. The latter group should then be measured in a series of domains of activity to discover what the overall dominance configuration may be. Even in cases where the skills of a balanced bilingual are extremely sophisticated it is often possible to trace elements of interference in part of his language use at least some of the time. Stress and fatigue can often reveal differences in the ease of use of two languages amongst such accomplished bilinguals as professionally trained interpreters, where the non-dominant language appears to suffer more. With the exception, perhaps, of the highly symbiotic type of bilingualism described in Asian contexts by Gumperz & Wilson (1971), it is noticeable that the majority of bilinguals predominantly manifest interference in a one-way direction, that is from the dominant to the less dominant language. Although interference can be bi-directional (particularly lexical interference) its incidence tends to be greater in one of the two languages involved.

Bilinguals in Brussels who show great ease in manipulating both French and Dutch nevertheless have a predominant interference pattern from one language into the other. Phonological systems in French may be strongly

marked by Dutch, or syntactic deviation from French monoglot norms may
be attributable to Dutch dialectal elements. However, in looking at this
purely internal linguistic evidence as a measure of dominance one must be
careful to take the totality of interference into account, since partial
measurements may produce skewed information. In the Brussels case, for
example, the local Dutch is heavily loaded with French lexical items but
shows almost no phonological or syntactic features attributable to French.
The local French, on the other hand, reveals relatively little lexical
interference in bilingual subjects' speech but many phonological and
syntactic elements attributable to Dutch. It is possible, moreover, that
lexical interference by itself is the weakest marker of language dominance,
since it may be accounted for by cultural and technological developments
which cannot be handled with ease in the importing language.

The above word of warning about lexical measures of language
dominance is given because so often apparent lexical inadequacies in a
bilingual's language performance are used to point at the detrimental effects
of bilingualism in general. Experimentation described by Doyle, Champagne & Segalowitz (1977) and based on the Peabody Picture Vocabulary
Test showed that very young bilingual children (mean age 60 months) did
have a relative lag in vocabulary development when compared with
monoglot peers (as well as a slight delay in the development of syntactic
rules). Here, lexis is used in one form of bilingual measurement for
comparison with unilingual language development. By means of other
measures designed to reveal the number of concepts expressed by the
children in question and based on showing children pictures depicting an
anecdote it was found that the bilinguals showed greater verbal fluency than
monoglots. Conclusions to be drawn from these experiments point to the
subtle complexities involved in measuring bilingual behaviour. The lower
vocabulary of bilinguals at certain stages of development may have nothing
to do with handicaps or dominance questions but probably more with a
smaller variety of linguistic input in each language taken separately.
Moreover, as Swain (1972) has suggested, when both languages of a
bilingual are examined separately the total conceptual vocabulary of the
speaker may exceed that of the monoglot.

Macnamara (1969: 91–97) provides a wide-ranging example of techniques designed to measure both degree of bilingualism and dominance
configurations, based on fairly traditional testing methodology used in
second language classrooms, together with elements of error analysis. In this
battery of tests aimed at measuring ability on the four basic skills of reading,
writing, understanding and speaking, attention is paid to the nature and
number of mistakes from monoglot norms recorded and these are then

statistically analysed to provide a dominance configuration. Particular attention in this indirect method for measuring degree of bilingualism is paid to the following criteria variables:

1. reading comprehension
2. reading vocabulary
3. spelling mistakes
4. grammar mistakes
5. syntactic interference from Lx
6. lexical interference from Lx
7. listening comprehension
8. phonetic mistakes
9. rating for rhythm
10. rating for intonation
11. intelligibility
12. word completion
13. word detection
14. reading speed
15. word naming
16. semantic richness

To this series are added further significant variables, such as the number of words used in the productive tests and the whole is then correlated with responses on questionnaires dealing with language background and self-assessment.

The complexity involved in the above measurement technique might be contested as superfluous overloading of the battery by those involved in classroom foreign language testing, since it has been found that many reliable tests correlate with others in a way which makes multiple techniques superfluous. Our earlier discussion of some of the tests produced by Lambert *et al.* show how certain restricted tests provide sufficiently reliable evidence for deductions of a more global nature. Moreover, some of these techniques are present in the above list (e.g. numbers 12, 13, 14 and 15). If we bear in mind, however, that many bilinguals have varying competence dependent on the nature of the skill involved, together with the fact that the varying skill may be tempered by time factors and input variables, a complex battery of measurement techniques may well be justified.

It might reasonably be assumed that the extent to which two languages differ from each other, or *language distance*, might also play an important role in determining the nature of dominance. This leads to the question whether language dominance, with its related implications affecting the amount and type of interference it may lead to, is in any way affected by the genetic disparity between two languages. In other words, do considerable genetic differences between a particular pair of languages lead to greater or smaller effects of dominance and interference?

An extremely detailed proposal for the measurement of language distance has been put forward by Mackey (1976: 281-307) in which translation equivalents of items in two languages are juxtaposed and analysed. The techniques developed measure divergences on the orthographic level of the written medium, phonetic and phonological comparisons, prosodic features, and syntactic distance. The measurement is based on the calculation of minimal equivalences and differences which are subsequently converted via mathematical formulae into a mean distance coefficient between the formal properties of two segments of discourse. For example, Mackey proposes a measure of distance at the graphemic level between the Canadian French and English expressions:

Le patron a subi un dur coup
The boss had a stroke of bad luck.

The procedure suggested goes through sixteen stages in which the equivalent segments are noted and counted then re-aligned to form parallels for equivalent items so that differences can be calculated between the number of elements and their position in the sequence. The individual letters in each sequence are then treated in the same manner to arrive at a sum total of equivalences and differences which are converted into a proportion or percentage. Finally, differences are calculated for the order of segments, their length, the length of the words and the number of elements in each word leading to results for each calculation expressed as a percentage. The sum total of this complex operation and the average difference between elements of the measurement can then be calculated, giving for the example in question a mean distance measurement for the formal characteristics of the two segments of discourse as 0.09 (Mackey, 1976: 283-85). Similar operations are likewise suggested for measuring relational and semantic distance as well as for other levels of discourse.

Although the complexity and detail of the analyses put forward are impressive, their practical usefulness may be more limited. Such techniques do provide one statistical measure for language distance but the results may not reveal the potential difficulty a speaker of L1 may encounter in attempting to become bilingual by adding an L2. Nor do they necessarily indicate whether there is any correlation between the statistical measure of language distance and the nature of interference.

Indeed one might be led to assume that language distance is related to questions of *mutual intelligibility* between languages or language varieties with, as a corollary, the greater the mutual intelligibility between two languages the less likelihood of learning difficulty and interference problems. It might equally be presumed that language dominance could be more easily overcome in cases of bilingualism involving genetically related languages. Karam (1979: 121-22) has pointed out that lexical similarity is more important than other linguistic similarity in determining mutual intelligibility and that phonological and grammatical similarity are important in reducing the exposure time needed for speakers of related language varieties to achieve a satisfactory level of mutual intelligibility. Geographical proximity seems to correlate well with mutual intelligibility for a group of fairly closely related language varieties, according to Karam. Nevertheless, easy mutual intelligibility between two language varieties may not necessarily help in attaining balanced bilingualism of the type that will eliminate dominance of the one over the other; in our earlier examination of interference it was noted that the more similar two features in distinct languages are the more difficult it may prove to render them discrete. Nor may linguistic similarity and mutual intelligibility necessarily promote bilingualism. Sociocultural factors, such as the perceived functional value of each language or dialect and the prevailing intercultural and inter-ethnic trends and relationships between two groups, can render mutual learning of the other group's language more inhibited, thereby minimizing the effects of internal language distance. If two individuals from different linguistic communities do not want to communicate or feel that they may have to do so under duress then the degree of inter-relatedness and mutual intelligibility between the languages concerned may in no way enhance bilingual ability. In other words, the effects of dominance of L1 may be exaggerated in production in L2 as a token of resistance to bilingual communication, thereby maintaining interference features which might otherwise not be manifested. Such is sometimes the case in the Belgian situation where bilingual ability is minimized and dominance traits exaggerated as a sign of allegiance to a particular language community.

Further measures of language dominance have been suggested in a variety of techniques surveyed and compiled by Jakobovits (1970: 149-221). The more interesting measures proposed are particularly relevant for second-language learners, especially the *semantic congruity test* in which subjects are required to make judgements about the acceptability of, for example, verb/adverb combinations of the type:

to attack violently/stupidly/meekly.

The *metaphor sensitivity test* proposed, similar to the previous one, should give an indication of the degree of sensitivity to a particular language, while a semantic range test can provide information on a subject's power of definition, inclusion, extension and combination with respect to the lexis. Jakobovits (1970: 181–82) elaborates on the usefulness of word association tests already alluded to (see p. 63) in which words are presented in the two languages involved while the subject is required to supply as many words as possible within a restricted time period. Jakobovits then suggests the following procedure for measuring degree of bilingualism:

1. counting the number of responses to stimuli in L1
2. counting the number of responses to stimuli in L2
3. measuring the different totals between (1) and (2)
4. counting the number of responses in L1 to stimuli in L1
5. counting the number of responses in L2 to stimuli in L2
6. counting the number of responses in L2 to stimuli in L1
7. counting the number of responses in L1 to stimuli in L2
8. the number of translation responses to stimuli in L1 and the number of translation responses for stimuli in L2
9. the results expressed in percentages for the above measures
10. the number of "bilingual" responses for L1 and L2 stimuli if applicable (i.e. cognates or homographs).

A further measure proposed is that for obtaining an insight into the appreciation of code-switching by means of a *language alternation test* where subjects are required to indicate comprehension of the global message by answering detailed comprehension questions on a message of the type:

> "A complex appareil used in deux ou plus parts de la world suggests un rapport between eux in very measure to leur complexité" (Jakobovits, 1970: 184-85).

Although the idea for this test is an intriguing one, it appears to us that the example provided does not correspond with standard code-switching strategies operated by Franco-English bilinguals (e.g. the switch across determiner and noun in "la world" or from preposition to pronoun in "to leur complexité"). Grosjean (1982: 252–57) criticizes similar tests used for measuring code-switching abilities and questions the artificiality of measuring a highly spontaneous productive ability, naturally carried out by bilinguals in appropriate circumstances, by means of highly unnatural receptive measures occurring in abnormal test circumstances. A properly designed test might perhaps be more useful for measuring productive code-switching abilities than for comprehension purposes. To do this subjects could be asked to read aloud a mixed language text which has been taken from natural code-switching samples while recording hesitations, stumbles, erroneous renderings and blendings. The results should then reveal to what extent the operation which is so frequently carried out by functional bilinguals in spontaneous speech can be perceived as disturbing when more consciously carried out. They might incidentally lead to a confirmation of the difference between code-switching and interference discussed in the preceding chapter.

The reservations made earlier in this chapter about dominance measurement are in part determined by the importance of attitudinal factors and their relationship to bilingual ability. Much investigation has been conducted into the role played by attitude and motivation in the acquisition of bilingualism. Jakobovits (1970: 260-317) gives an accessible model of *attitude questionnaires* which could serve as a starting point for a beginner seeking information on this aspect of measurement. Samples are provided which cover attitude scales in general, measures of ethnocentrism, cultural allegiance scales, an orientation index, a measure of the desire to learn other languages, a motivational intensity scale, etc. Pedagogues in general are convinced of the relationship between skill in a second language and positive attitudes coupled with strong motivation towards the language group in question. The implications are clear for the promotion of bilingualism and justify the amount of attention paid to attitudinal measurements. However, knowledge gained from attitudinal measurement does not always lead to the production of successful strategies for language promotion. Kjolseth (1973: 4) points out that there need be no necessary invariable or universal correlation between attitudes towards a language (ethnolinguistics) and actual patterns of language usage (dominance configurations) within a speech community. He quotes a case of a study of Yiddish where negative attitudes to the language co-occurred with increasing use and *vice versa*. Investigations into contemporary attitudes towards dialects and standard language in Flemish Belgium (Geerts *et al.*, 1978) reveal that although the majority of persons investigated admired the standard language and encouraged their children to use it they did not themselves wish to speak the standard model.

The intriguing nature of such contradictions can be explained by the complex intertwining of political, sociological and psychological factors which combine to make up subtle attitudinal dispositions not always perceived by the persons under investigation. The status and function of the languages involved play a primordial role in determining attitudes, enhancing or reducing feelings of loyalty to a linguistic group. We have already seen (p. 88) how a high prestige language which is perceived as having functional utility when in contact with a less prestigious language can lead to rapid language switch in mixed bilingual communities of the type found in

Belgium. Resentment towards a particular language community can also lead to antipathy towards its language and impede the learning of that language; a perception of low status accorded to the primary language can, on the other hand, lead to a minimization of its usage and receptivity to language switch. The consequences of such attitudinal dispositions are often held responsible for the decline in numbers of certain language communities (as in Wales with Welsh speakers) and at the same time for ethnic and political conflicts between communities in which groups are involved in arresting language switch through transitional bilingualism.

The majority of attitudinal measurements are based primarily on direct interviews which subsequently lead to the design of questionnaires which provide open-ended answers. The disadvantage here is the difficulty of coherent analysis beyond the tabulation of anecdotal comments. On the other hand, information culled from open-ended questionnaires can provide the necessary background information in a pilot study from which a set of more restricted closed question items can be selected for standardized analysis across a larger population.

To take an example. It might be considered desirable to discover what self-styled bilinguals' attitudes towards their own bilingualism are in an attempt to shed light on the positive or negative consequences of using more than one language in daily life. In the pilot study a restricted number of bilinguals would be interviewed in order to gain an overall impression of the range of sentiments expressed. From this the designer would extract both recurrent sentiments expressed impressionistically in a variety of ways as well as a few striking extreme opinions; the latter could possibly be idiosyncratic amongst the pilot group or else reflect sentiments subconsciously shared by others but which the hazard of circumstance had not brought to the fore. The next stage would be to draw up a list of points based on the items selected from the open-ended interviews and submit them, together with a restricted range of answer possibilities, to a broad range of bilinguals.

Of the several techniques widely used for measuring attitudes the following are representative (for further details, see Fishbein & Ajzen, 1975: 61–84). Thurstone (1931) developed a technique which was based on the assumption that responses to questions about a person's beliefs express his attitudes. In what has since become known as the *Thurstone scale* judges are requested to indicate the amount of implicit agreement or disagreement with a stimulus item according to eleven categories ranging from total agreement, through a neutral position, to total disagreement, with finely graded intermediary positions. Thus, if one wished to enquire of bird lovers whether they felt that teaching their parrots or budgerigars to express themselves bilingually had beneficial effects, they could be asked to express their degree of agreement or not in finely shaded opinions. Likert (1932) developed a simplified technique subsequently known as the *Likert scale* which allows for measurement of agreement with an item, disagreement or a neutral opinion in cases where the stimulus appears ambiguous or irrelevant. Here a five point scale is used, as in the following example;

Stimulus: "Teaching parrots/budgerigars to speak two languages is cruel" Strongly agree: slightly agree: don't know: slightly disagree: strongly disagree

Osgood, Suci & Tannenbaum (1957), developed what is known as the *semantic differential technique* in which a large number of bipolar adjective scales are submitted to subjects in an attempt to obtain a representative sample of the possible dimensions along which concepts can be judged. Here subjects fill in responses on a five or seven point scale with a neutral median possibility which allows for a profile of judgements to be obtained. Thus with our example of bilingual birds the adjective scale used to elicit attitudes could possibly contain items like: intelligent/stupid; handsome/ugly; bad/ good, to find out what bird lovers thought about bilingual parrots or budgerigars.

The advantages of these different techniques lie in the fact that they enable the tester to direct his subject to express nuanced opinions while at the same time combining features of ease of analysis, statistical relevance and applicability to large groups. The significance of the answers provided will depend, of course, on the nature of the questions used. A concrete example of the use of attitude scales in bilingual investigations can be found in Sharp, *et al.* (1973) with reference to Welsh and English.

The Canadian social psychologist, W.E. Lambert and his collaborators have together developed an adapted form of the semantic differential technique known as the *matched guise technique* which has clearly shown correlations between degree of bilingual ability and attitudinal dispositions. This consists of presenting subjects with the same text translated into different languages or different varieties of a language (e.g. a variety spoken with a strong foreign accent) and asking respondents who hear the translated versions to indicate their reactions on a scale. The scale consists of polarized adjectives expressing personality features such as friendly/unfriendly, intelligent/unintelligent. Subjects responding are unaware of the fact that the different extracts are read by one and the same person and the texts selected as a basis for recording are as neutral as possible in content so as not to betray any cultural bias to one language or social group. In this way a subtle means of measuring attitude towards a language and its speakers is available, since the only factor that is likely to have determined the respondents' opinions is the language in which the recording has been delivered. As can be inferred, the matched guise technique is particularly useful in measuring ethnocentricity or degree of receptivity towards another language and its community. It reveals to what extent subjects perceive speakers of a particular language as having desirable or undesirable traits with which they may or may not wish to identify. The degree of identification can subsequently be seen to correlate in some way with ability in a particular language.

When attitude measures are combined with standard language tests for degree of competence in a given language it is remarkable how well they correlate. In a review article covering this aspect of bilingualism Lambert (1969a) has clearly demonstrated how the nature of the testee's motivation determines the quality of his bilingual ability. Subjects who learn a second language merely for utilitarian purposes, e.g. because it is necessary for their career, are said to have an *instrumental motivation*, while those who do so because they wish to learn more about another linguistic community and perhaps become a potential member of this group of speakers are said to have an *integrative motivation*. Integrative motivation generally, but not always, leads to better language ability results in the non-primary language than does instrumental motivation, and this on all levels of linguistic competence. Gardner (1973) made some very pertinent observations on the role played by parents in developing children's attitudes about other ethnic groups. He noted that in contrast with pupils who professed an instrumental orientation, integratively oriented pupils tended to come from homes where the parents had definitely marked attitudes in favour of the group whose language their children were learning, although there was no apparent relationship between the pupils' orientation and parental proficiency in the other language or the number of friends parents had made in the other language community. Gardner also made a subtle, but, it is felt, important distinction between the parents' active and passive roles in contributing to their children's motivational patterns in acquiring a further language. An active role is where the parent actively and consciously encourages the child to learn the language. The passive role, felt to be more significant, is when the parents' subconscious attitudes towards the community whose language the child is learning are transmitted. The parent who encourages a child to learn a second language by stressing its importance is playing an active motivational role but if at the same time this parent holds negative attitudes towards the second language community he may undermine the active by the passive role and reduce the motivation to learn the language.

Whether motivation to acquire another language is instrumental or integrative can be decisive in determining community-based language maintenance or language shift in different parts of the world. In communities where a second language is learnt for instrumental purposes there is less likelihood of assimilation and language shift to the second language than if an integrative attitudinal pattern lies behind the motivation. The Act of Union with Wales in 1535, for example, which banned the use of Welsh in all official transactions, has often been designated as the trigger which led to the switch from Welsh to English in the Principality. Yet Welsh maintained its numerical predominance until the beginning of the twentieth century, when it was more the desire to identify with English-borne cultural values, coupled with sociological factors largely determined by the English language, that led to the contraction in numbers of Welsh speakers. It is likewise this integrative motivation which accounts for the language switch in Brussels from a predominantly Dutch speaking city in the last century to a predominantly French speaking city at present. For although socio-economic factors which link one particular language to certain advantages represent a kernel factor behind mass language switch, they are not alone responsible. It is also true that the speakers of a less prestigious language in contact with a more prestigious one are the group which feel the greater need to become bilingual and who subsequently hope to achieve upward social mobility by identifying with the other language group. Thus in the Brussels case it is not the unwillingness of French monoglots to learn Dutch which is solely responsible for mass language switch, though this is a contributory factor, but the readiness of the Dutch speakers to integrate with the other group.

It should not be felt, however, that integrative motivation which brings in its wake greater fluency in a second language necessarily leads to language loss via transitional bilingualism. This tends to occur when integrative motivation is coupled with deprecatory feelings towards the primary linguistic-cultural community. Again, socio-economic factors can play a decisive role in situations like these, though there are other factors to be taken into account. Immigrant communities in countries like Australia may have either integrative or instrumental motivation in learning English, though whether this leads to loss of the primary language depends on the role that language plays in the immigrant community's life. Smolicz (1979) has shown how Polish and Greek immigrants in Australia tend to maintain their original language while still wishing to be fully integrated into Australian society, whereas Dutch immigrants tend to lose their original language by the second generation. This is explained by the fact that language represents one of the *core values* which typify Poles or Greeks, whereas language is not a core value for Dutch immigrants. According to

Smolicz a core value is a fundamental component by which a group indicates its cohesion and its identity, other examples being Roman Catholicism for Poles and the extended family network with close ties for Italians. It is significant, too, that whatever the motivation in becoming bilingual, speakers from communities where language represents a core value often maintain a marked foreign accent in the second language whereas this is less the case with others. This might be explained by the desire to identify the core value to outsiders (to show one's colours as it were) if the foreign accent remains marked, while at the same time indicating one's readiness to meet the other linguistic group on its terms. It is a sort of defence mechanism against total assimilation into the dominant group; perhaps it even represents some half-way stage between instrumental and integrative orientations.

A comprehensive case study of measurements used to identify bilinguals' language attitudes and to correlate them with biculturalism is that produced by Bentahila (1983) on French-Arabic bilinguals in Morocco. He showed how Moroccan bilinguals' attitudes to the world varied, depending on which language was being used, with the outlook tending to be more westernized if French was used and more traditional and bound by Islamic doctrines if Arabic was used. Bentahila is careful to point out that his results did not show that language controls thought or determines culture but that language, as one aspect of a society's culture, becomes naturally linked with other aspects of that culture. Several measurements were used to tap both conscious attitudes about Classical Arabic, Moroccan Arabic and French, and less consciously held dispositions which clearly revealed the bicultural component of the subjects' language knowledge. The first was a classical questionnaire eliciting responses to questions such as: What language do you find the most beautiful/the richest? What language do you find the most modern, the most useful for studies? To these questions subjects were requested to select one of the three language alternatives available and give reasons for their choices. A second test consisted of selecting from a list of ten epithets, such as "practical, versatile, useless, rich" and applying them to the three languages under investigation. Results from both these tests of conscious language attitudes revealed similar patterns of responses with clear contrasts in the attitudes towards the three languages.

The third list used by Bentahila brought out the bicultural element in his subjects in a more subtle fashion than the elicitation of overt attitudinal dispositions. This consisted of a sentence completion task based on a technique developed by Ervin-Tripp (1964) in which subjects were given thirty incomplete sentences in one language and asked to complete them as they wished; six weeks later they were given the corresponding incomplete sentences in the other language and carried out the same task. Results on both sets of sentences revealed striking differences which showed a relationship between the language of the sentence and its cultural attributes, as for example:

French: One needs a good job to live happily.

Arabic: One needs a good job to be able to spend one's last days praying in the mosque.

(Bentahila, 1983: 41)

French: When my wife disobeys me, I try to understand her.

Arabic: When my wife disobeys me, the only solution is divorce.

(Bentahila, 1983: 44)

The above, highly integrated study, only part of which has been discussed here, shows how the differences between bilinguals' views of their languages are paralleled by differences in the way they use them.

In an attempt to join the linguistic and cultural elements of bilingual behaviour in some overall theoretical framework Oksaar (1983) shows how a person manifests parallelisms to L1 and L2 language usage by C1 and C2 cultural attributes (where C = culture). Just as the bilingual speaker often reveals linguistic interference in at least one of his languages, so he may reveal cultural interference at times when using the second or weaker language with the behavioural patterns associated with the first. Moreover, Oksaar shows how the bilingual/bicultural person represents elements of C1 and C2 as well as Cx, where the latter contains cultural elements of both C1 and C2 as well as autonomous ones. Investigators are beginning to be ever more aware of the role of cultural interference and Cx features in bilingual behaviour, though few measures other than those of a descriptive nature appear to have been developed to date. This is because of the extreme difficulty of circumscribing culture in general and more specifically in isolating it from language. Oksaar points out that quite often one notices what cultural norms are and what margin of difference is allowed in various situations only when somebody acts against them. She does, however, make a useful distinction between *cultural interference* and linguistic interference, with illustrations, which heighten our awareness of the different phenomena.

The preceding illustrations lead us into the question of the interdependence of the bilingual's two languages and the consequences for the measurement of interference features. In Chapter 1 it was pointed out how the compound-coordinate dichotomy was a theoretical explanation of how some bilinguals successfully manage to keep their two languages free from influences of the other, although techniques designed to test this hypothesis have been inconclusive. One way of measuring this aspect has been the *stroop procedure*, named after its inventor, R. Stroop (1935), and considerably developed by Lambert (1969a). By this method words printed in different colours are presented on cards while subjects are requested to ignore the words themselves but to name the different colours in which they have been printed as rapidly as possible. When the words themselves are the names of colours which do not coincide with the colour of the print the task becomes difficult for literate speakers, since the name of the colour interferes with the task of deciding which colour ink has been used. If the words used are respectively "Red, Green, Blue" but the inks used are respectively orange, yellow, brown, it is difficult to give the colour "brown" while reading a word that says "Blue". This clear manifestation of interference potentiality led Lambert to add words in French like "maison, garçon, printemps" which were printed in different colours and subjects were asked to indicate in English what colour the words had been printed in. Colour words were also used in both French and English and the subjects were asked to indicate the ink hue used in the opposite language from that of the printed item. The object here was to measure the amount of time taken to carry out the task of filtering out the interfering element caused by decoding in one language and encoding in another. Results showed that bilinguals had some difficulty in separating the language of response from the stimulus language, particularly when the stimuli consisted of words designating colours that had been printed in a different coloured ink. This was less the case if the word was a non-colour word in one language and the task was to name the ink used in another language.

The significance of this type of experiment is twofold. Firstly, measures of this type tend to confirm our assumptions about the rarity of ambilingualism and the unlikelihood of bilinguals producing interference-free speech in both of their languages. They therefore show how the total separation of the two languages cannot always be maintained. Secondly, they tend to indicate that rapid translation from one language to another need not come spontaneously to the bilingual. Indeed many bilinguals who can function extremely well in two languages in clearly demarcated situational contexts often find it difficult to translate spontaneously between their languages without heavy interference. This is one reason why professional interpreters require special training for a task that does not necessarily come naturally, even if they were childhood bilinguals.

If we now collate the evidence that has been accumulating in the first three chapters of this book with reference to the presence or absence of features which identify bilingual speech, we arrive at the question, "How bilingual must a bilingual be to be a bilingual?". In other words, is there any way of going beyond impressionistic evaluations by which one can establish a cut-off point between incipient bilingualism and the higher ranges of functional bilingualism? There is no clear answer to this question, for if there were Chapter 1 would have been much shorter. Nevertheless, a tentative step can be taken towards measuring the tolerance and recognition level of interference-marked bilingual speech (Baetens Beardsmore, 1977c, 1979d).

Much research into listeners' reactions towards marked bilingual speech has been concerned with attitudinal dispositions towards the bilingual's personal attributes (d'Anglejan & Tucker, 1973; Giles, 1970; Lambert, Frankel & Tucker, 1966) revealing how interference-marked bilingual speech can lead to positive or negative personality evaluations which are determined by prestige factors associated with the speakers from a particular cultural community. Similar positive or negative personality judgements have been elicited with respect to native-speakers who use a non-prestige variety of a language (Tucker & Lambert, 1969). These experiments have been based generally on the matched-guise technique and have concentrated on revealing how speech can trigger communally shared stereotyped images of a linguistic community. Incidentally, they also reveal the degree of tolerance of deviation from monoglot norms or standard varieties of a given language. Apart from providing information on the nature of stereotyped reactions to accented or interference-marked speech, such techniques can also be adapted to indicate just how well such speech is understood or tolerated in a given community. According to Mackey (1976: 312) certain communities tolerate interference better than others and this tolerance is probably linked to the amount of contact between two linguistic communities, with bilingual communities that are regularly confronted with interference-marked speech being probably more ready to be tolerant than homogeneous monoglot communities. To measure this hypothesis isolated utterances as well as connected speech culled from a variety of speakers who reveal different levels of deviation from monoglot norms could be submitted to different groups of respondents for evaluation on a series of scales. Our own experiments concentrated on the speech of a functional bilingual who spoke both English and Dutch, while other extracts used as distractors in the task were taken from a highly proficient balanced bilingual (English-Dutch), a Dutch learner of English as a foreign language and a monoglot native-speaker of English. Judges of the extracts were native-speaker English monoglots, self-styled bilinguals and learners of English as a foreign language. These three groups were asked to indicate whether they thought the speech extracts presented were comprehensible or not, acceptable or not, whether they indicated bilingual ability or not and whether they indicated native-speaker ability. The questions were presented in the form of semantic differential scales on which respondents indicated degrees of agreement with one of the adjectives. The choice of the functional bilingual on whom the test concentrated was made on the assumption that she represented a widely prevalent case. She was an adult immigrant to Britain who had exclusively used her L1 (Dutch) for the first thirty years of her life and almost exclusively L2 (English) for the next thirty years. The external case history of the subject indicated that by any token she must be a functional bilingual of advanced ability since she could adequately accomplish all activities in either language, though not without traces of interference in both.

As was predicted by Mackey (*vide supra*) the three groups of judges rated the speech extracts in different fashions, even though general trends for all judges went in similar directions. For instance, all three groups of judges rated the person being investigated fairly negatively on the bilingual scale (i.e. tending to consider her as non-bilingual), though the self-styled bilinguals were more ready to accept the speaker as a bilingual than the native-speakers who in turn were more positive than the learners. In other words, degree of sensitivity towards bilingually marked speech was reflected by greater tolerance of interference among the self-styled bilinguals. On acceptability the native-speaker judges were more severe than the self-styled bilinguals and learners but on comprehension it was the group of native-speakers that appeared most tolerant and positive. This last result might be explained by the native-speakers' greater ability to compensate for inadequacies in comprehensibility by the reconstruction of intended meaning. This, however, should also have been true for the self-styled bilinguals. When the scores for the functional bilingual subject were compared with those of the other non-native-speaker extracts serving as distractors it was found that the highly competent balanced bilingual rated highest on the three measures of comprehension, acceptability and degree of bilingualism, followed by the learner of English as a foreign language, with the functional bilingual who was central to the investigation coming off worst. On the other hand, a small proportion of judges did consider this functional bilingual to be a native-speaker of English, which was not the case with the distractors.

Measures of this kind may be useful, even though they perhaps throw up as many problems as they attempt to resolve. On the other hand they tend to provide some community-based, statistically-determined scale by which tolerance to bilingual speech can be measured. For surely it is the community in which the bilingual is supposed to function that is most apt to judge whether he comes up to their criteria of satisfaction or not? On the other hand, one of the problems that came to light was that all judges tended to consider the native-speaker and bilingual scales as mutually exclusive; thus judges considered the extracts presented as either native-speaker and not bilingual or bilingual and not native-speaker, though they knew that native-speaker ability and bilingualism were possibly present. Moreover, most judges gave as their subjective definition of bilingualism the equivalent of native-speaker competence in two languages. The inconsequence brought out by these results which forced judges to take a standpoint on the relationship between bilingualism and linguistic competence shows to what extent the lay definition of bilingual ability so widely held is not supported by any tangible evidence.

An incidental piece of information this type of measure reveals is connected with teacher-determined evaluation of a foreign learner's accomplishments. It has been noted in different parts of the world where expatriates teach their native language to foreigners that they judge their pupils' efforts with far less severity than do the indigenous teachers. It might well be that the expatriate teachers are impressed by the extent of progress achieved by the learner, whereas the indigenous teacher uses absolute native-speaker norms as his yardstick; the native-speaker judges' score on our experiment for comprehension was highly positive, which would seem to reflect this assumption.

The question of bilingual measurement cannot be left without some examination of those measurements that have been applied to look into the relationship between bilingualism and intelligence, if only because of the widespread emotional involvement in discussions on this point. The debate around semilingualism (see p. 12) has revealed how certain circumstances in which bilingual education is provided can possibly have negative consequences. This is particularly true with respect to cognitive and psychological development of children, leading some to fear that learning two languages can have disturbing effects on the intellect. Parents faced with the choice of moving to a foreign country are often worried about the linguistic problems this may bring with it in their child's upbringing. Moreover, ever more people are being confronted with the need to become bilingual to some extent, whether as a matter of choice or not, and many developing countries are consciously applying programmes of bilingual education. Thus the question of the relationship between bilingualism and intelligence is important.

A detailed overview of experiments designed to measure the positive or negative effects bilingualism may have on cognitive development has been produced by Balkan (1970), in which information published since the 1920's on the scholastic development of children receiving instruction in a language other than that of the home was carefully sifted through. It was noted that results based on verbal tests purported to show that bilingual children suffered from a linguistic handicap, from mental confusion or from intellectual development diminished by half (Balkan, 1970: 9). However, many of the tests which produced such disturbing results were found to be inadequate in design, since they had not been appropriately modified to deal with specific bilingual populations. The verbal components of many test batteries were designed for monoglot populations (used as controls) and then merely translated for bilingual subjects without taking into account the cultural bias which was inherently built in against the bilinguals. Some bilinguals were tested only in their L2 (e.g. English for Welsh first language children). Other significant factors often neglected were careful matching of IQ ratings, socio-economic backgrounds of the bilinguals and the control monoglots as well as a clear definition of the type of bilingualism that was under investigation. Investigators attempting to measure the relationship between bilingualism and cognitive development on the basis of verbal tests should also take into account the tendency to compartmentalize activities according to language specialization and experience so that a particular range of behaviour might well reveal certain shortcomings in a verbal test concentrating on the language not normally used for specific activities. For a subject who normally conducts the more intimate, home-tied, activities in language A and the more public and communal activities in language B, a verbal test containing items relevant to both should reflect a certain compartmentalization by way of different types of response.

Not all early tests in this field contained inadequacies, since Spoerl produced a battery in 1944 which included measures of mental ability, a questionnaire on social adaptability and a word association test to overcome certain problems. With these it was shown that if there were negative results which appeared to coincide with bilingualism these were not so much attributable to linguistic or psychological problems connected with learning two languages simultaneously but to social pressures in the environment (which were often at the source of the very need to become bilingual). Frequent change of residence, insecurity in home and social life, ghetto-like isolation coupled with socio-economic disadvantages were seen as far more likely to be the origin of the intellectual handicap that the bilinguals manifested in comparison with monoglots. In any discussion about bilingualism it is often the fact that the language element brings certain problems more acutely to the observer's awareness to the detriment of more fundamental issues; this leads to language and bilingualism *per se* often being blamed for problems which have merely surfaced more clearly through the fact of bilingualism.

One of the major arguments Balkan (1970: 29ff) puts forward against the detractors of bilingual education is the absurdity of using verbal tests in measurements of intelligence among groups using different languages. No one would seriously consider testing a monoglot by means of a foreign language for intelligence measures yet many bilinguals have been subjected to tests in their weaker language which have led to conclusions about their intellectual abilities. It is not sufficient to assume that, because a bilingual has received all his education in a given language which differs from the home language, this compensates for not taking into account the potential compartmentalization of language behaviour. If compared with a monoglot whose totality of linguistic experience is enjoyed in one language, the bilingual may well reveal differentiated behaviour on verbal tests, since his total linguistic experience is spread over two languages. This does not imply that unilingualism automatically leads to advantages but should lead to the more cautious supposition that bilingualism will lead to differentiated reactions to verbal stimuli tempered by the amount of contact and experience with a particular language.

Peal & Lambert (1962) attempted to overcome the obstacles in comparing bilinguals to unilinguals in tests designed to measure intelligence by analysing as many features as possible that were known or suspected to correlate with intelligence and discovering what, if any, differences between the two types of person could be attributed to linguality itself. Their experiments were based on a threefold overview of the studies that supported the detrimental effects of bilingualism on intelligence, those that showed favourable effects and those which showed no correlation. The contradictory evidence was compared to siphon off the possible effects of interlingual interference as a possible indicator of language handicap in bilinguals, on the assumption that interference is a regular feature of "normal" bilingual behaviour and that its possible incidence on intelligence tests should be eliminated or carefully controlled. To this end a whole battery of measures were used after carefully matching the groups under comparison for age, sex and socio-economic background, and where possible taking children from the same school system or even the same school (thereby standardizing a further environmental influence). Subjects were French-Canadian 10-year-old balanced bilinguals in English and French who were compared with English and French speaking monoglots respectively. The bilingual group had been selected on the basis of a word association test in which words were presented alternately in French and English and the children asked to write down as many words as possible in the language of the stimulus word in a 60 second time limit per item. From a sum total of all the associations to the French stimuli and the English stimuli counted separately, a simple formula was used to produce a balance score which revealed whether either of the two languages was dominant. This formula was;

$$\frac{\text{Total French responses} - \text{Total English Responses}}{\text{Total French responses} + \text{Total English Responses}} \times 100$$

By this formula a zero score was considered to indicate that the subject was a balanced bilingual while a plus score implied French dominance and a minus score English dominance.

Subsequently a word detection test was used based on the DANSO-NODEND experiment already referred to (see p. 91). The Peabody Picture Vocabulary Test was also administered, whereby four pictures are displayed together with one oral stimulus word while the subject has to indicate which of the four pictures corresponds to the stimulus word. Finally, subjective self-assessment was incorporated whereby the subjects were asked to indicate how well they felt they could speak, read, write and understand a given language along a four point scale. These combined selection procedures allowed for a fairly precise grouping of subjects into balanced bilinguals, speakers dominant in one or the other of the languages concerned, and, of course, monoglots.

After this group selection, standardized intelligence tests were applied in which great care had been taken to use materials that had been standardized in each language separately if they depended on verbal measures, rather than merely translating a test. Attitude measures towards each linguistic community were used to discover whether positive or negative attitudes towards a particular group might not play a certain role in the results. The semantic differential technique was brought in to assess the subjects' evaluation of themselves and members of the two language communities represented by the bilinguals' two languages, and certain minor tests were included to further control any potential anomalies (Peal & Lambert, 1962, reprinted in Lambert, 1972a: 124–30).

Highly significant results were obtained by these controlled measures, which tended to come out to the advantage of the bilingual children. The bilingual group performed significantly better than the monolinguals on non-verbal IQ measures and also on the verbal sub-tests, a striking contradiction with previous findings and hypotheses. The monolinguals did not surpass the bilinguals on any of the sub-tests and the bilinguals were often rated better in general school accomplishments. Attitude measurements revealed that the bilinguals were more favourable to English Canadians than to French Canadians; the French Canadian group, on the other hand, was more favourable to French Canadians. The conclusions from this investigation merit quotation;

> "The picture that emerges of the French-English bilingual in Montreal is that of a youngster whose wider experience in two cultures has given him an advantage which a monolingual does not enjoy. Intellectually his experience with two language systems seems to have left him with a mental flexibility, a superiority in concept formation, and a more diversified set of mental abilities, in the sense that the patterns of abilities developed by bilinguals were more heterogeneous. It is not possible to state from the present study whether the more intelligent child became bilingual or whether bilingualism aided his intellectual development, but there is no question about the fact that he is superior intellectually. In contrast, the monolingual appears to have a more unitary structure of intelligence which he must use for all types of intellectual tasks."
>
>   (Peal & Lambert, reprinted in Lambert, 1972a: 152)

Perhaps it should be pointed out that these very positive results, which contrast so strikingly with those given by Skutnabb-Kangas & Toukomaa (1976) in cases of semilingualism, may be attributable to a variety of felicitous circumstances. Firstly, the bilinguals all came from favoured socio-economic backgrounds where parents encouraged bilingual ability and positive attitudes towards the two communities represented by the languages in question. Secondly, they originated from an environment where many external stimuli together with both French and English cultural indices were a natural part of the setting, providing rich external back-up material to enhance the relevance of becoming bilingual. The positive attitudes the successful bilingual group held towards the two cultural communities around them may be accounted for, perhaps, by the fact that the children had not been uprooted from a particular culture and thrown into another (as is often the case with migrants), and did not have antagonistic cultural values thrown at them which were exacerbated through linguistic mediation.

Seeking to corroborate Peal & Lambert's findings, Balkan (1970) went one step further by trying to discover whether the favourable results found in the Canadian setting led to specific scholastic advantages in bilinguals. Again, subjects were taken from upper middle-class socio-economic brackets with comparable general intelligence level ratings. Balkan chose balanced bilinguals with high levels of accomplishment in French and English who were at school in Switzerland, and compared them with Swiss

French-speaking monoglots, all between the ages of 11 and 16. The sample here was larger than in the Canadian experiment but based on similar selection criteria.

Apart from the word association test, Balkan used self-evaluation and the teacher's appreciation of the pupils for inclusion in the bilingual group, particularly whether the teachers felt the child was accentless in both languages, (i.e. free of traces of phonological interference) and grammatically accurate and fluent. Slightly different scholastic aptitude tests were administered to take the Swiss context into account; these had been developed by Cardinet & Rousson (1965) and consisted of two verbal aptitude tests for measuring comprehension, two reasoning tests, a numeracy test, a test of verbal plasticity and a test of perceptual plasticity. What is significant in the results from this experiment is that the positive findings which corroborated the Canadian cases were in no way attributable to selection procedures established in forming the bilingual group. In Balkan's case even the less intellectually gifted bilinguals, when matched with comparable less gifted monoglots, on average scored higher on certain dimensions of the intelligence measures, notably on verbal and perceptual plasticity (by which is meant the capacity to restructure given elements, to discover new organization in elements structured in a different manner).

In the more serious studies since the sixties several measurements have brought to light the fact that bilinguals perform better than monolinguals on different aspects of cognitive and linguistic development provided the socio-affective background was normal. Bilinguals do better than monolinguals on measures of divergent thinking which represent an ability to reorganize material, provided that the level of proficiency in both languages is high. Similarly, bilinguals apparently do better on measures designed to bring to the fore metalinguistic awareness and capacity for linguistic awareness. In other words, bilinguals seem more sensitive to the semantic properties of words, more aware of the arbitrary nature of words and have greater ease in analysing language. Further, bilinguals seem to show greater ability at reacting to feed-back cues and non-linguistic communication, i.e. an ability to react to misunderstanding, disapproval or amazement, to interpret facial expressions, gestures, etc. Most explanations for these abilities are based on the need bilinguals have to learn to switch codes and to know when to do so:

> "The bilingual speaker needs to notice and take account of very
> small often not verbalized cues and to modify her behaviour
> accordingly . . . Various very small changes in a social situation
> may be observed more closely if their effect is to require a code

switch; and so the bilingual gets more practise than the monolingual at paying attention to the fine detail of a social situation and at
reacting in various ways."

(Skutnabb-Kangas, 1984: 232–33)

Results of the type discussed in the above measurements should not
lead to triumphant generalizations about bilingualism and its effects on
scholastic achievement, even though they are encouraging. Nevertheless,
there is ever-growing evidence that bilingual education need not necessarily
have any deleterious effects on either intelligence, general levels of
education or emotional development. Further information on this subject
can be found by looking at Swain's (1980) review of Canadian models of
immersion programmes (i.e. a home-school language switch) which is based
on earlier documentation by Swain (1978a; 1978b; 1978c; 1976b). Swain
recognizes some early retardation in the development of language skills
when compared with monoglots in children following early total immersion
programmes in which the break between home language and school
language is complete. However, as the programme continues the bilingually
educated children gradually outpace their monoglot peers on several levels
of the home language skills (i.e. the one not initially used in school
instruction), particularly in reading comprehension and knowledge of
vocabulary. On the tests which measured skills in the language of
instruction, pupils were not necessarily as good as unilinguals in that
language but they gradually approached native-like levels after about six
years in the programme. Moreover, almost without exception the bilingual
children performed as well as their monoglot counterparts on both
computational and problem-solving tasks in mathematics and equally well in
science and social studies.

Again it should not be forgotten that the immersion programmes
described by Swain involve middle-class children from backgrounds where
there is much positive supportive action for the success of the language
learning task. The children from such backgrounds join those throughout
the ages who have been in a position to select the type of education they felt
most appropriate to their needs. From the time of the ancient Egyptians as
far back as 3000 B.C. to the present day the upper classes of widely diverging
societies have consistently encouraged their children to become bi- or
multi-lingual, as has been illuminatingly documented by Lewis (1976) and
Mackey (1976). This fact should give food for thought to the detractors of
bilingual development in children who base their arguments on fears of
mental deficiency or intellectual retardation. For why should the powerful
have tried across the ages so consistently to promote something in their

children which could lead to consequences susceptible of diminishing their power advantage?

Certain riders should be borne in mind, however. Almost all successful bilingual education programmes recorded (see Baetens Beardsmore, 1980; Fishman, 1976; Mackey, 1972a), like the experiments referred to above, record advantages noted in children suffering from no extra-linguistic handicaps such as socio-economic, psychological or affective disadvantages. There are also other records of similar success with less favoured groups (Lim Kiat Boey, 1980; Andersson & Boyer, 1970) but we should not forget the unsuccessful cases, particularly with reference to migrant populations and certain minority groups. What does appear clearly from the literature is that successful bilingualism appears in contexts where the environment allows for the full and harmonious development of the individual and where tension and conflict are not exacerbated by linguistic oppositions. Also, most, though not all, the evidence on successful bilingual education arises in cases where the bilingual element is introduced early in the child's development and continuously promoted in an uninterrupted and coherent programme (Titone, 1972: 331–44; Balkan, 1970: 99).

> "Désormais, se demander si le bilinguisme est nuisible à l'enfant n'a plus de sens. Il faut d'emblée définir les termes en précisant le concept du bilinguisme... On a pu constater que tout apprentissage laissé au hasard des circonstances est d'emblée voué à l'échec."
>
> (*Hence, it is pointless to wonder whether bilingualism is harmful for children. From the outset one has to define one's terms by making the concept of bilingualism clear. . . It has been noted that any learning left to chance is destined to failure from the beginning.*)
>
> (Balkan, 1970: 98)

More detailed development of the arguments around the effects of bilingual education will be dealt with in Chapter 5.

Summary

Given the insistence in earlier chapters on the relative nature of bilingual ability, any question of measurement is determined by the type of bilingualism under investigation as well as the particular aspect to be considered. This chapter has deliberately ignored standard second language testing techniques designed to measure achievement, though without minimizing their significance. Instead it has concentrated on questions more directly pertinent to bilingual studies by beginning with a discussion of the difficulties involved in merely establishing the presence of bilinguals in a given population. In this way there is a link with the criteria used for defining types of bilingualism in Chapter 1. Techniques for measuring language dominance have been described, based on speed of response to certain stimuli, semantic associations or indices of interference. Language distance measurements have cautiously illustrated the effects of mutual intelligibility between languages on the purity of a bilingual's performance. Attitudinal dispositions have been discussed in some detail, given their influence on language ability, not only to reveal the distinctive results that can possibly arise from integrative or instrumental motivation but also to illustrate the recognition and tolerance level of interference-marked speech. Indications of some of the ways in which biculturalism can be measured have been given. A final section has dealt with measurements of the cognitive consequences of bilingualism, particularly in education, presenting a review of the contradictory evidence from experimentation over the years.

4 Theoretical Considerations

Although there has been much empirical work on different aspects of bilingual behaviour, as is clear from the preceding chapters, there is to date no cohesive theory of bilingualism as a linguistic phenomenon. The definition of bilingualism in Crystal (1980) is telling, in that it is given as "a pre-theoretical frame of reference for linguistic study". This can partly be explained by the wide range of abilities and types of linguistic behaviour that are gathered together under the umbrella term of bilingualism. Chapter 1 has shown that an ambilingual is a very different type of person from a receptive bilingual, that dominance configurations can clearly affect the input and output of the languages involved, that age and mode of acquisition can lead to highly differentiated degrees of competence, all of which make it difficult to produce an all-pervading theoretical frame of reference capable of clarifying bilingual behaviour. For any linguistic theory used in monoglot analysis is not likely to be confronted with such a variety of highly diverging real-life cases that have to be accounted for in bilingualism. Whatever the language involved, certain fundamental principles will hold good for monoglot analysis, if the theory is adequate. In bilingual cases it would seem that some of the fundamental principles appear blurred just because of the need to account for phenomena that do not appear pertinent to one-language studies and are likewise not present in some two-language situations. A glance at a few of the major differences between monoglots and many bilinguals should reveal some of the problems which illustrate the greater complexity involved in studying the latter. At a later stage we will also look at the points of similarity between monolingual and bilingual language usage in spite of apparently striking differences.

All normally constituted monoglots are capable of acquiring the total range of linguistic features necessary to the perfect realization of linguistic competence in a particular language, be it a highly prestigious one or a non-codified dialect of some obscure tribal language. By adolescence all normally constituted monoglots can manipulate perfectly whatever ver-nacular they may have been brought up in. This statement, of course, has nothing to do with codified standards but refers to the internal rules of a particular language, dialect or vernacular. With bilinguals things are not quite the same. Only some bilinguals, and more specifically the rare case of the ambilingual, acquire a competence in two languages comparable to that of two separate monoglots of the respective languages. Most equilinguals with high mastery of two languages will at times betray features which distinguish them from monoglots. Thus even the highly competent bilingual when he uses his language A may well make himself identifiable as a bilingual who is different from a monoglot of that language A. If there is anything that is bilingually marked as distinctive, peculiar, striking, and this feature is not present in other bilinguals who share the same set of languages, just as it is absent in the monoglot, then bilingual theory has to take this distinctiveness into account, explain its presence in certain speakers and its absence in others.

One could try to simplify the problem of a theoretical approach to bilingual questions by separating early from late bilinguals, since the former, having acquired their two languages in the formative years of speech development, are more likely to be indistinguishable from monoglots most of the time. One would still have to try to explain how this feat has been achieved in terms which coincide with those used for monoglot behaviour but which can also account for the late bilingual, far more likely to be identifiable by distinctive features, but who will have certain features in common with both the early bilingual and the monoglot. Hence a coherent theory of bilingualism would have to bring the early and late bilingual together at some point in the discussion and equally try to link both up in some way to features of monolingual behaviour. It is at this point that the second difficulty arises.

The normally constituted monoglot child attains complete competence in his language because he cannot help it. He has to learn his L1, not because he has been pre-programmed to learn a given language but because it is a biological necessity, and this even in the most unfavourable psychological and sociological circumstances. Whether the monoglot child comes from a stable, middle-class background with constant child-parent interaction in its formative years or from a deprived poverty-stricken community with few intellectually stimulating accessories it will still attain complete mastery of the language of the specific community in which it grows up. However, this does not hold good for the majority of bilinguals unless they are of the early childhood type. Indeed, the majority of late, consecutive bilinguals never attain ultimate achievement or complete competence in two languages, though they do in L1; moreover, successful bilingualism for those who do attain it depends on favourable environmental circumstances of a psychological and sociological nature. Hence, any comparison that will be made between monoglots, early and late bilinguals will have to take into account a cut-off point beyond which many, if not most, bilinguals never get, which would allow them to melt into the anonymous monoglot mass of speakers of both languages, if not just one of them.

A further significant difference between monoglots and bilinguals concerns the relationship between receptive and productive abilities. The normal monoglot who can understand the language of his community can also speak it (even though he may not be able to read or write it), whereas many receptive bilinguals can understand (and perhaps read) a particular language without being able to speak (or write) it. It may be true that many monoglots appear to understand far more complex syntax and lexis than their productive abilities would tend to indicate, though this does not necessarily imply that the receptive bilingual is a more striking case of a similar phenomenon. For many bilinguals of the receptive type are totally incapable of activating their receptive ability into a productive one that comes anywhere near to matching the two sets of skills; in some cases the mismatch between reception and production may lead to a total breakdown of interaction between a receptive bilingual and a monoglot, something which does not happen with two monoglots possessing a diversified range of productive flair. The reasons for the receptive bilingual's inability to activate his weaker language may be purely affective, such as the fear of ridicule, a sensitivity towards personal linguistic inadequacies, and so on, but these do not normally occur with monolinguals.

The third important feature to be taken into consideration in the comparison between bilinguals and monoglots is the significance of interference and code-switching in the formers' speech. The question is whether features similar to interference and code-switching manifest themselves in the unilingual.

But whatever the type of speaker we are dealing with, certain fundamental issues remain constant. No matter what the degree of bilingualism involved it is important to bear in mind that being bilingual is as normal an occurrence as being unilingual and that in this field we are not dealing with anomalies. Hence the core principles that determine the nature of human speech must be the same for both types of speaker. The brain of the bilingual will in essence operate in the same fashion as that of the monoglot, determining the organization of linguistic capacities on the same biologically determined criteria. Thus any striking difference in bilingual behaviour of the type already mentioned could in principle be accounted for by processes that underlie syntactic or phonological operations in general.

The major problem in trying to clarify bilingual investigation is the significant number of unknown complexities that are not even clearly understood by the bilingual specialist, e.g. language loss, recessive bilingualism.Thus it is likely that the coherent theory of bilingualism implicitly called for so far is still likely to be some way away from elaboration. Nevertheless, much recent investigation into what is involved in knowing and using two languages provides indications as to possible solutions.

It should perhaps be noted at this stage that a surprisingly small amount of work connected with bilingualism has been developed within the framework of the transformational generative debate which has dominated linguistic theory over the last few decades. To some extent this can be explained by the primary concern of transformational generative linguistics to account for the "ideal native-speaker/hearer" whereas the ideal native-speaker bilingual is far more difficult to circumscribe. Students of bilingualism tend to do the opposite by not looking at ideal states of bilingual competence but at differentiated degrees of bilingual ability without positing any ideal case beyond that of the marginally representative ambilingual.This has led the majority of workers in our field to ignore a strict adherence to transformational generative principles as irrelevant to their preoccupations. Weinreich's seminal *Languages in Contact*, based on structuralist principles, has been the cornerstone of much thinking in the field of bilingualism and yet most investigators, like their colleagues in mainstream linguistics, are aware of the inadequacies of structuralism in accounting for human language. Consequently much of the work on bilingualism has been conducted in some limbo which, while ignoring transformational generative grammar and paying lip-service to its rejection of structuralism, plunges into pragmatic investigation, picking up inspiration on the way from divers language orientated disciplines, including sociology, ethnography, anthropology, and insights from teaching practice. Many studies have concentrated on the output resulting from the contact of two languages, i.e. on performance features, trying to reconcile widely disparate observations noted in different bilingual cases. Yet there should be some basic common ground whereby theories applicable to monoglot cases and bilingual facts can find some meeting ground. After all, both situations will evolve round competence as an instance of the universal conditions that limit the form and organization of rules in the grammar of human language. It is perhaps the well-deserved prestige of Weinreich's work, coupled with an earlier narrow interpretation of some of Chomsky's basic principles, that has led to the downgrading of transformational generative approaches in bilingual studies in favour of more pragmatically orientated investigation that can cope with extra-linguistic parameters.

Nevertheless transformational-generative lines of thinking have not been entirely excluded from bilingual studies since there is no *a-priori* reason to suggest that the Chomskyan frame of reference cannot mirror the linguistic competence of a speaker/hearer who is not a monoglot. The major theoretical debate for students of bilingualism would seem to centre on the question of whether bilingual competence is in any way distinct from monoglot competence and how one can account for any potential distinction. In this preliminary stage of theory building we will concentrate on linguistic competence as opposed to communicative competence and decide on the significance of the latter at some later stage according to our interpretation of priorities in theoretical linguistics.

In the past it has been felt that the most central feature around the argument of bilingual competence has been the question of interference, its presence or absence in the speech of different types of bilingual. Yet not all differences between bilingual speech and that of monoglots can be accounted for by interference, as we shall see later. It has already been pointed out that the early childhood bilingual is less prone to interference manifestations at the end point of acquisition than the late bilingual, so that it might be wise at this stage to distinguish between these two major categories of speakers of more than one language.

McLaughlin (1984: 61–62) strongly argues against the pre-eminence of interference in second language production, based on an overview of several empirical investigations. His conclusions are that, in general, adult second language learners and children make the same *kinds* of mistakes and appear to go through essentially the same *stages*. He further defines interference as

> "those errors that occur in the learning of the second language (B) that reflect the acquisition of a previous language (A) and that are not found in the normal development of those who acquire that language (B) as a first language." (McLaughlin, 1984: 66–67)

He also found that only about a third of errors was attributable to first language structure while the rest were potentially of three kinds:

> *developmental errors*, which do not reflect the first language but are found amongst children acquiring a second language simultaneously to another, i.e. early simultaneous bilinguals;
> *ambiguous errors*, which could either be due to interference or be developmental errors;
> *unique errors*, which do not fit into either above category.

A further important observation was the sparse occurrence of interference in early childhood acquirers, indeed its minimal appearance. McLaughlin (1984: 128) believes that interference is greatest in situations where languages are learned in a classroom setting and where there is no daily contact with native speakers. Although it is probably true that early childhood acquirers manifest remarkably few traces of interference, its prevalence among older bilinguals is not restricted to classroom learners. Many adult immigrants who have undergone no formal training but who do have frequent contacts with native speakers of the L2 show heavy traces of interference at all levels of linguistic analysis. Moreover, Gass & Selinker (1983) feel that there is overwhelming evidence that language transfer is a real and central phenomenon in the second language acquisition process and we tend to share their view that for late consecutive bilingualism at least both the developmental and the interference elements play an equally significant part in accounting for differences from monoglot output. Andersen (1983) gives some detailed argumentation for both the significance of interference and its directionality, providing a set of constraints which tend to indicate the way it operates.

We should not lose sight of the fact that there are recorded instances of stable multilingual communities in the Far East and Latin America where everyone's speech, be they young or adult bilinguals, is by monoglot norms heavily larded with interference traces attributable to the presence of more than one language. Gumperz & Wilson (1971) showed how in these cases the bilingual competence of the polyglot speaker reflected similar underlying features to those found in monoglots. In their examination of interference features in the gender systems of the languages along the Indo-Aryan/Dravidian border they revealed a tendency towards isomorphism in the polyglot informants with evidence to indicate that, in the polyglot context concerned, the same rules — a single set of rules — can account for different syntactic surface structures reflecting two separate language families and that the difference in such structures was attributable to variations in morphophonemic rules (Gumperz & Wilson, 1971: 155).

As long ago as 1941, Swadesh put forward the idea that phonemes belonging to the phonological system of Russian-English bilinguals are merged into one complex system in which [t] [t'] [tʰ] all occur in identical environments so that,

> "the two sets of sounds... from the standpoint of phoneme theory, can be regarded as a single system." (Swadesh, 1941: 65)

Weinreich (1953: 8-9) expressed doubts about this conclusion, preferring to restate the facts in terms of two co-existent systems. However, in an often overlooked footnote Weinreich indicated that his doubts applied to interference in the *speech* of bilinguals, which should be distinguished from the language(s) as a system. He also went on to indicate that in describing the more or less established "borrowings" in a *language*, a single phonemic system was often to be preferred. By this token Weinreich did not exclude the possibility of considering bilingual competence in terms of a single system, even if bilingual performance may not always reflect this in a clear and self-evident fashion.

Most bilinguals would seem to have a tendency to exploit any points of resemblance between their two or more languages to the fullest (Graham, 1956). In most recorded cases it has been shown to be almost impossible for the bilingual to keep his output in two languages totally free from influences which mark it off from monoglot production. As Diebold (1962: 59) has put it,

> "...even with a speaker's conscious efforts to offset interference... Greek-English co-ordinate bilinguals cannot switch to one language in the context of the other without incurring phonemic interference... This suggests to me that we need to review our still imperfect notions of what is involved in the separability of two language codes in the same speaker."

Given this tendency to coalescence, so-called interference features could possibly be seen as a reflection of the bilingual's unified language system which falls outside the related two or more L1 systems. Strong evidence to support this argument, as suggested by Weinreich, is provided in the integration of loanwords and their possible effects on the phonemic and morphemic systems of both languages used by the bilingual (Vogt, 1954). Therefore, in order to discover a bilingual's linguistic competence his code must be defined and described in terms of its internal consistency rather than by reference to monoglot behaviour. If this is done, then of course bilingualism can be analysed in transformational-generative terms without any difficulty. It is also possible this implies that the two distinct language realizations of competence are in some way comparable with stylistic variation in the monoglot, as will be seen further.

Observational evidence of childhood bilingual acquisition would tend to corroborate the assumptions connected with a unified underlying system serving two distinct languages. Rūke-Draviņa (1967: 19), who studied the Swedish-Latvian development of her children, noted that before the age of about 3 they were not aware of the existence of two languages in their speech and that later awareness only gradually emerged. Kessler (1971) used a transformational-generative frame of reference to study the sequencing of syntactic structures acquired by children bilingual in Italian and English, on the assumption that languages evidence certain shared rules as well as language-specific characteristics, and that the shared elements or processes are to be found in the deep or underlying structures. Kessler used Fillmore's case grammar adaptation of the transformational approach, considering this as more amenable to application to two languages which are in the process of being concurrently acquired. From this study it was concluded that the deep structure was manifested in the underlying similarities or "sames" in the abstract set of relationships accounting for the semantic interpretation of sentences from the two languages concerned, while the observable, linearly ordered, pronounceable constructions constituted the surface structure manifestations in the particular language. According to Kessler (1971: 97) this supports the theory of language universals and language uniqueness in terms of specifiable rules. She also found that similar structures in Italian and English were developed in approximately the same sequential pattern and at approximately the same rate; deviations in the ordering of acquisitions were traceable to structural differences in the two languages, differences which could be stated in terms of language-specific rules. Swain (1977) reached a similar conclusion in her study of pre-school children learning French and English bilingually. In the progression from deep to surface structure a specific set of rules must be applied to each language, this line of argument meeting that put forward by Gumperz & Wilson (see p. 123). Thus in the case of the early bilingual it is suggested that the two languages are not encoded separately and that the rate at which young children acquire two languages simultaneously suggests that the same set of rules are being brought into play to a large extent.

It should be of little surprise that the theoretical frame of reference originating in Chomsky's ideas should be applied to early bilinguals without much difficulty since the nature of the performance in the two languages and the processes of acquisition (if the extra-linguistic circumstances have been favourable) have much in common with circumstances of children learning only one language. However, a similar theoretical approach has been taken by Hasselmo (1972) to investigate the grammar of adult bilinguals whose speech distinctively differs from that of monoglot production by traces of other language elements. The investigation of Swedish-American bilinguals and the attempt to explain code-switching led to the assumption that code-switching, from the point of view of one of the languages involved, could be seen as the resolution of linguistic tension by the use of elements from the other language. The bilingual who does not strictly follow the extreme set of norms represented by each of the original separate languages may reduce language distance through the introduction of lexis, syntactic, morphological and phonological features from the one to the other. Hasselmo set up a model for American-Swedish which took into account lexical conversion rules, conversion formulae involving the substitution of a surface unit from one language to another, a repertoire model based on vertical and intralinguistic rules (on the assumption that the totality of the bilingual's behaviour is a manifestation of an overall code, a single American-Swedish grammar), notions of grammaticality and ungrammaticality, productivity and restrictions.

If relatively few students of bilingualism have followed these transformational-generative paths this may be accounted for by the general focus of interest in the field of research. Students of bilingualism in general have been more interested in describing what identifies the bilingual as such rather than explaining his grammar. Moreover, on a misinterpretation of the tenets of transformational approaches they have often over-emphasized the disparities in individual bilingual cases compared with others, thereby claiming the futility of attempts to codify bilingual grammar. Yet as Goyvaerts (1982) has pointed out, generativists do not in essence work in any different way since it is perfectly normal for individual grammars to manifest idiosyncracies which exclude consensus agreement on their grammaticality. Hence, it is perfectly acceptable within this approach to discuss constructions which are considered as grammatical for speaker A but ungrammatical for speaker B. For the transformational generative approach always places the individual central to its enquiry and produces a grammar for the individual native speaker by looking into the systematicity of the individual's use of a particular structure.

However, late bilinguals are not "native-speakers" of their L2, even if early bilinguals might be considered as such, and although it would be perfectly feasible to write a generativist grammar for the former it would still be difficult to reconcile the different bilingual grammars produced into some overall frame of reference that draws together early bilinguals with potential ultimate achievement, monolinguals of the two languages in question, and late bilinguals with perhaps only partial competence in their weaker language.

This situation has perhaps led students of bilinguals to being rebutted by a further stumbling block in the Chomskyan interpretation of linguistic competence which is difficult to reconcile with bilingual reality. Chomsky (1965: 577) claims that the ideal speaker/hearer is in a position to distinguish sentences from non-sentences and to detect ambiguities irrespective of his level of intelligence. Although the highly competent bilingual may well be able to do this for the two languages he regularly manipulates, many less proficient bilinguals, particularly the late case, are not able to do so for the non-dominant language. This type of bilingual, who may regularly use both his languages, perhaps with manifest traces of interference in one or both, is not necessarily able to detect what to monoglot speakers appears as bilingually marked or even ambiguous in his output. Even when his attention is directed towards an anomaly that has been pointed out, say, in the non-dominant language, he may be unable to see what is unclear, ambiguous, even incomprehensible about a particular structure in the eyes of the monoglot; he is totally incapable of realizing what it is that may disturb his interlocutor and is often incapable of disambiguating the particular feature or of making it more acceptable.

Structural inadequacies, and the inability to detect ambiguity in the case of the late bilingual particularly, could be accounted for by the hypothesis put forward by Selinker (1972) for explaining second language learners' marked speech. Basing his approach on the ideas implicit in Chomsky's account of linguistic competence, Selinker proposed an *interlanguage hypothesis* to explain the inadequacies (by monoglot standards) present in the weaker language of the non-fluent bilingual and which tended to show that not everything which distinguished bilingual speech could be explained by interference or by referring to the first language. Certainly, some of the distinctive features could be accounted for by *fossilization* of linguistic items, rules and sub-systems which speakers of a particular L1 will tend to keep when they are attempting to operate in L2, their weaker language. Selinker gives an example from the phonological system, as when a French-dominant bilingual maintains the use of his French uvular r while speaking in English. Such fossilization is explained by taking into account the speaker's L1 or dominant language, the L2 or non-dominant language as used by its native-speakers, and the separate linguistic system based on the observable output which results from the attempted production of the L2 norm — in other words, the interlanguage. The fossilized items, rules and sub-systems observable in the non-fluent bilingual's weaker language which can be attributed to the influence of the dominant L1 represent the process of language transfer. These are cases of over-generalization of L1 rules in L2 and account for a large part of interference in bilingual performance. On the other hand, certain bilingual utterances tend to show over-generalization of rules specific to the L2 which lead to an inadequate awareness of restrictions to a particular rule. Observations of this phenomenon have led some researchers to use the basis of the interlanguage hypothesis to see it as a universal series of interim grammars which all learners would systematically work through as they acquired the new language. Hatch (1983: 91–106) reviews the research which minimizes the interference component of

Selinker's original theory by examining the similarities and differences between L1 acquisition and the progressive stages of L2 development in both children and adults. The conclusions of her overview of studies looking into, for example, the auxiliary system of negation, show that the data reveal similarities with L1 progression but differences as well. Felix (1982: 78–86) is of a similar opinion that acquiring an L1 followed by an L2 at some later stage manifests points of comparison and divergences, but that the L1 speaker, in the early stages, possesses an astonishing variety of structures, whereas the early stages of L2 acquisition are characterized by relative structural poverty. Felix also felt that L1 knowledge definitely influences L2 acquisition but not exclusively in terms of interference. Hatch (1983: 97) gives an example of this from a study of adult English speakers learning negation in Swedish by going through several phases; first they placed negative markers before the verb, whereas in Swedish this should follow the main verb in main clauses but precede it in subordinate clauses. Later the learners realized that the equivalent of *no* + V constructions are not the way native speakers of either Swedish or English formed negatives, so they proceeded to place the negative markers after auxiliary verbs. Swedes, however, do not go through this phase with their L1 acquisition but learn to differentiate main clause negation from subordinate clause negation. In a third phase the English learners of Swedish put their negative particles after main verbs.

The interlanguage hypothesis has revealed that in passing from early to more advanced stages of proficiency speakers follow a sequence which is not random. Although progression into L2 shows systematic changes the system is not invariant for all learners and there may be backsliding with correct and incorrect forms overlapping as the learner sorts out the rules for each part of the system (Hatch, 1983:, 105). Moreover, different learners progress in different ways. Whether the incipient bilingual is a child or an adult the sequence of interlanguage stages develops with the same systematicity and the same variability, though the extent to which transfer or interference plays a significant role might not be the same.

Other marked or anomalous patterns in the non-fluent bilingual's performance may be accounted for by the fact that the bilingual is achieving satisfactory communication with the L2 native-speaker so that his strategy of communication becomes fossilized at the stage where he no longer needs to progress any further in the weaker language. Harley & Swain (1977: 75-76) show how this happens with English-Canadian children learning French. Their communicative needs in the classroom are orientated towards the conveyance of cognitive meaning, and once the children have reached a point in their cognitive development where they can make themselves understood to the teacher and their classmates there is no strong social incentive to develop further towards native-speaker norms. Selinker also suggests that the speaker's strategies of second-language learning, together with the transfer of training procedures utilized in becoming familiar with the L2, should be taken into account when formulating the interlanguage competence of the non-fluent bilingual.

The attractive element in Selinker's argument is that it draws a link between the highly accomplished early bilingual and the non-fluent late bilingual in terms of common reference. Indeed, Selinker, Swain & Dumas (1975) explicitly extend the interlanguage hypothesis to young children learning an L2. It is suggested that the type of bilingual who does not attain native-like standards in the weaker language reaches a plateau of ability through the intuition of a set of rules culled from different sources. The new set of rules, partly determined by teaching strategies and learning processes, and originating in the contact situation, lies somewhere in between monoglot competence of the type acquired by the highly successful bilingual and the original competence in only one language. Many speakers of more than one language might never go beyond a specific plateau which they have attained, thereby accounting for the inability to appreciate grammaticality or ambiguity when confronted with a native-speaker in their weaker language. The interlanguage theory also explains the great range and variety of abilities encountered in different degrees of bilingualism, since the component factors which determine them will vary from case to case. (For the most recent developments in interlanguage theory, see the volume edited by Davies, Criper & Howatt, 1984.)

Although the interlanguage hypothesis accounts for certain similarities between L1 and L2 development as well as certain differences based on ideas of fossilization, transfer or interference, sequencing of rule acquisition, and input or teaching strategies, it still does not give any clear explanation for the fact that late bilinguals rarely attain complete competence in an L2, whereas early bilinguals often do so. As has been pointed out earlier (see p. 28) the idea of a critical age period beyond which it is difficult to obtain native-like mastery of a second language has been called into question. Yet it is also true that few late bilinguals achieve as well as their early counterparts, though there are exceptions. Ekstrand (1979) took a close look at all theories purporting to prove that the onset of puberty represents a decisive factor in the attainment of ultimate achievement. After a careful examination of the data he came to the conclusion that general cognitive development, native language learning, second language learning, learning ability and memory, perception, imitation and social learning all improve with age and are all positively inter-related (Ekstrand, 1979: 37). His conclusions were that the older person learns more rapidly than the young child and that there may possibly be an optimal age round about 4 or 5, but that this does not contradict the overall observation. He does concede, however, that pronunciation does seem to be affected by the age at which the L2 is begun, with late bilinguals rarely achieving native-like proficiency. Hatch (1983: 196) feels that the research to date does not support an optimal age hypothesis that says "the younger the better". Nor does it support a contrary hypothesis, "the older the better". She states another hypothesis, "the older *child* the better," but even that is not clear from the data. She further concludes cautiously that there is a difference between initial learning in favour of the older person on the one hand, and long-term attainment in favour of the younger beginner on the other, if only because of the greater exposure to language and the opportunity for more practice. Hence we cannot lightly dismiss the popular belief that early bilinguals end up by and large with greater L2 proficiency than late bilinguals. (For detailed discussion see Krashen, Scarcella & Long, 1982.)

Krashen (1981a, 1981b) has addressed himself to this question by developing a theory which distinguishes between language *acquisition* and language *learning*. For him acquisition develops in a sub-conscious fashion both in L1 and in L2 by dint of natural communication and meaningful interaction in which concentration is directed towards message-orientated communication. Learning, on the other hand, is a more conscious process (what Dodson (1981) refers to as medium-orientated communication) in which one concentrates on form, on rules and on error correction. According to Krashen successful bilingual development depends primarily on acquisition, be it with children or adults, but with the onset of puberty learning begins to take on importance and this may have an inhibitory effect on achieving ultimate attainment. He further speculates that any observed differences between child and adult second language development may be due to the fact that from about the age of 12 onwards the language learning potential is boosted while the language acquisition potential is weakened. This is because the adolescent becomes an abstract thinker who is able to reflect on the rules he possesses and on his thoughts (Krashen, 1981a: 76). He also felt that the older learner makes use of a *monitor* which is not available to the young acquirer or the older performer following acquisition principles. In language learning the monitor functions as an editor by which we make corrections, change the output before we speak or write or sometimes afterwards, as in self-correction. For the monitor to operate usefully there are three conditions: the performer must have enough time in order to use conscious rules; the performer must also be focussed on form or correctness; the performer must know the rule, that is, have a correct mental representation of the rule to apply it correctly (Krashen, 1981a: 3; 1981b: 58). Given these three conditions it is difficult to apply conscious learning to performance successfully.

Although not to be discarded out of hand, it is felt that the monitor theory does little to explain the inhibited progress of second language development in the older speaker.

In a further development of his thinking Krashen (1981b: 61–62; 1982: 202–26) posited the notion of the *affective filter* to account for differences in ultimate attainment between early and late bilinguals. This is based on changes in attitude and personality which occur around puberty and which affect progress in second language acquisition but which are not relevant for the language learning component of Krashen's original dichotomy. Three elements make up the affective filter, anxiety, motivation and self-confidence, determining whether the speaker has a low affective filter and is permeable to input in the L2 or a high affective filter, leading to sub-conscious resistance. Subjects who have low levels of anxiety about manipulating a weaker language are more willing to communicate and more likely to make better progress. People with higher motivation are equally more likely to take chances in using the weaker language and maximize opportunities for interaction. In a review of the literature on integrative and instrumental motivation, Krashen (1982: 213–14) noted that both could lead to high levels of competence, depending on the circumstances of the acquisition process, but that with integrative motivation the affective filter was probably lower than with instrumental motivation. Also, integrative motivation led to better aural-oral skills, possibly because of the desire to socialize with members of the target language group. Finally, people with more self-confidence, an outgoing personality and who are not shy about using unaccustomed speech patterns tend to have a lower affective filter, leading to higher achievement potential.

Thus, according to Krashen, the fact that the affective filter is strengthened at puberty accounts for a difference in the amount of "intake", irrespective of the amount of input provided, which may also help to explain the difference between early and most (but not all) late bilinguals in ultimate attainment.

Krashen's monitor could well form part of *strategic competence*, which refers to a part of the ability to use the linguistic resources available in order to achieve one's communicative goals (Canale & Swain, 1980a). However, strategic competence comes into play both in L1 acquisition and in L2 acquisition or learning, irrespective of age. In L1 circumstances this can be illustrated when children use already identified question words with an extended significance, leading to semantic over-extension. With L2 speakers it includes such things as over-generalizations, simplifications, a preference for a fixed word order, and avoidance strategies (Felix, 1982: 63–64; Selinker, Swain & Dumas, 1975: 147–49). It is perhaps the notion of strategic competence which best encompasses the effects of both interference and other features of L2 development independent of L1 influences. Here we tend to agree with Krashen (1981a: 67) who maintains that second language markedness is not merely due to structural influences from L1 but simply the result of the speaker being called on to perform before he has learned the new behaviour—the result is "padding", using old knowledge, supplying what is known to make up for what is not known.

In an examination of lexical knowledge and usage among young adults in intensive English courses whose first languages were either Dutch or French, Lee (1983) analysed strategies used to achieve communicative goals which he broke down into the following classification (all examples are from Lee, 1983: 120–38):

1° reformulation—where the speaker goes back and starts again, e.g. "Some plastics don't burn they. . .the form can change (=melt)";
2° prime skipping—where words semantically simpler than the complex words they replace are used, e.g. "So that they can't take you (arrest)";
3° analytic rebundling—the redistribution of semantic information into smaller units, e.g. "You begin to take off the clothes of the potatoes (= peel)";
4° synonym seeking—as when the learner who is unsure of the distinction between "much" and "many" opts for "a lot of" to resolve the difficulty;
5° gap stopping—where the learner falls back on his known language(s) to fill what would otherwise be a gap in the message structure, e.g. "My parents were more er *streng* (= stricter)";
6° updating—where the learner uses a known language lexeme as a temporary gap-stopper while search is in progress, e.g. "I mean there's a. . .*allez niemandsland* nobody's land";
7° appeal to authority—where the learner abandons the attempt to find a solution to his lexical difficulties and appeals to the authority of his interlocutor, e.g. "They come to have a . . . I don't know the word, a *gamma*";
8° message abandonment.

It could be said that all the above phenomena are different manifestations of avoidance strategies and that although their features are different the processes are very similar to what monoglots do. Reformulation, prime-skipping, analytic rebundling and synonym seeking all occur in some shape or form when a native speaker is at a loss for the precise term; gap-stopping and updating do not appear in monoglots in the forms illustrated, since there is no other language to fall back on and consequently no code-switching but they seem to be similar to the use of formulae like "You know, the what's its name, etc.," i.e. there is a functional similarity; both updating and appeal to authority form part of what Stubbs (1983: 48ff) calls metacommunicative acts, particularly prevalent in classroom talk; message abandonment is the least likely to occur in monoglot speech, unless one puts it on a par with the situation when the speaker "dries up".

Applying Lee's categories to a 13 year old pupil in a bilingual education programme on an interview in his L2, French, we noted how the speaker overcame structural and lexical inadequacies by reformulation, prime skipping and synonym seeking. The following transcription of the French utterances on the left are accompanied by our interpretation of the intended message on the right, based on Stubbs' (1983: 91–97) arguments about intuitions, predictability and idealization of discourse sequences to justify our bilingual interpretation. The question put to the pupil was whether he had ever been afraid when out sailing.

"Un peu, oui. Quand c'est. . . euh. . .très. . . (reformulation, leading to prime skipping as a lexeme is sought for to indicate rough weather)	"A little, yes, when it's . . . er. . .very. . .er
. . . le vent est très fort. Mais maintenant, ç'est. . . j'ai plus peur, parce que je sais nager et je sais que je peux. . . (reformulation, leading to a synonymic expression). . .je dois faire si je tombe."	. . . the wind is very strong. But now it's . . . I'm not frightened any more, because I can swim and I know that I can. . . . . . what to do if I fall (in)

The following extract from the same pupil's interview reveals similar operations in reply to a question about where he had lodged during a school trip to Amsterdam and where he was trying to describe a youth hostel. Although the pupil has no strategy for overcoming confusion between personal pronouns "tu/vous" (or no awareness of it) and other structural inadequacies, he does apply a strategy for getting the content element of the utterance across by reformulation to lead to prime skipping or analytic rebundling while using the metacommunicative "*si tu veux*" to justify "*refuge*" instead of (presumably) "*auberge de jeunesse*"; Question: "C'était pas à l'hôtel?"

Reply: "Non, non. C'est une chose de. . .refuge, si tu veux, il y a. . .euh . . .lits, et il y a. . .le . . .le. . .tu peux manger là, et tu peux faire votre sandwiche. . .et. ..tu restes là toute une nuit."

"No, no. It's a thing. . .refuge, if you like, there are. . .er . . .beds, and there are. . . the. . .the. . .you can eat there; and you can make your sandwich. . .and. . .you stay there for the night."

The above examples of strategic competence are felt to be of greater explanatory power of what goes on in performance in the weaker language than the monitor theory, since whether one considers that the illustrations reflect either acquisition or learning it is clear that there is a certain level of conscious effort (imprecise though this may be) to effect the lexical element of production, whereas the phonological or morpho-syntactic elements are totally neglected by conscious effort. The examples also illustrate the feeling held by Canale & Swain (1980a: 42) that communicative strategies are of two sorts: those that relate mainly to the grammatical code (e.g. how to avoid certain forms that one has not mastered or cannot recall) and those that relate more to the communicative interaction (e.g. how to indicate that one intends to continue or stop speaking).

An alternative theory to explain the apparent difference between ultimate achievement in early and late bilinguals has been developed by Felix (1982). He feels that the crucial difference between child and adult L2 development is to be explained by the fact that different cognitive systems operate on the input data. While children acquire the language they are exposed to through a system of cognitive structures whose innate principles are specifically geared to the acquisition of language, in adults this language-specific cognitive system competes with another largely autonomous cognitive system which operates in general problem-solving tasks and is fundamentally inadequate for the purpose of language acquisition. Felix believes that these two systems compete with each other in what he has called the "competition model". This assumes that the human mind consists of a number of independent cognitive sub-systems, some of which are geared to process only highly specific mental tasks. With the onset of puberty it is felt that the *language-specific cognitive sub-system* enters into competition with the *problem-solving cognitive sub-system* with respect to the processing of linguistic input for the purposes of acquisition. Problem-solving cognitive sub-systems are felt to be essentially inferior to the linguistic-specific cognitive sub-system for the purposes of acquisition; young children rely exclusively on the linguistic specific cognitive sub-system, whereas beyond puberty the older person uses both to handle abstract information. The problem-solving cognitive sub-system is thought to be the wrong tool for processing linguistic input but the older person has no control over which tool to use and therefore is unable to acquire a native-like command in the target language.

Felix's theory introduces a new version of the critical age hypothesis, based not on the physiology of the adolescent but on age-determined changes in the cognitive system. Although some supporting evidence has been provided by Felix to back up this intriguing hypothesis it still requires a considerable body of research in order to lend it convincing proof.

What does seem to be emerging from the different types of argument put forward by various scholars is that bilingual ability, by and large, seems to be affected by the age of initial *prolonged* contact with the second language, that in the process of becoming bilingual the speaker goes through several stages of interlanguage in the L2, that these are partially determined by factors like the nature of the input, interference effects from L1 and other effects independent of the L1, that the acquisition of bilingual proficiency partially follows that of native-language acquisition but not completely, that strategic competence seems to play a significant role in the achievement of linguistic goals in the weaker language and that fossilization may set in at different stages of bilingual development, leading to only partial attainment in the L2.

The type of fossilization present in individual cases can equally apply to whole groups of bilinguals, which may well result in the emergence of a new *contact dialect* (Haugen, 1977: 94), where fossilized interlingual competences may be the normal situation. In such circumstances we are dealing with communities using new bilingual norms of the type found in immigrant circles or in stable multilingual societies. Since such societies tend to be composed of bilinguals with different levels of ability in their two languages which are characterized by bilingually-marked speech as well as code-switching, any theoretical explanation of their behaviour must be able to take such circumstances into account. It was observation of just such mixed language communities that led Hymes (1972) to reject the concentration on purely linguistic competence as inadequate as an explanation of the complexity of perfectly normal but highly variegated bilingual behaviour of individuals placed in a community where more than one language is in operation. Hymes further went on to reject those theories that concentrated solely on linguistic competence as equally inadequate for explaining monoglot language behaviour.

Hymes' ideas on communicative competence provide a wider frame of reference than the purely grammatical notion of linguistic competence in the quest for a theory of bilingualism, since they allow for the integration of much sociolinguistically relevant data into the explanatory model. The communicative competence model in effect accommodates the highly fluent bilingual who is virtually interference-free in both languages, and the non-fluent bilingual who successfully operates in two languages thanks to his interlanguage, and incorporates both into an overall descriptive context determined by the nature of the circumstances. It is particularly helpful in clarifying the operation of code-switching which, as was noted in Chapter 2, is not arbitrary, is not necessarily determined by inadequacies in a given language, but is contextually determined. The presence or absence of code-switching, varying as it does according to the role of the interlocutor, the domain of activity, the setting, as well as purely linguistic constraints, can be accounted for by physical and community constrained criteria of possibility, feasibility, appropriateness and actual performance. The theory gives an explanation why a bilingual may attempt to produce interference-free speech in both of his languages and eliminate code-switching, or why neither of these may occur. It can explain why the non-fluent bilingual who has gone beyond the incipient stage to the functional level can stop at some interlingual stage of ability that satisfies his communicative needs. It can go a considerable way to drawing together the two different types of bilingual behaviour so often noticed within one and the same speaker, the type which consists of correctly generating output in two distinct languages without extraneous elements from either, and the type which consists of switching between the two in the same context, of interlarding elements borrowed from one in the use of the other. The theory of communicative competence allows the analyst to use similar terms of reference for successful balanced bilingualism and the individualized interlingual competence of the non-fluent bilingual, where in the latter case the anomalous linguistic competence is revealed by the presence of ambiguity and ungrammaticality.

At this stage we should perhaps look more closely at the similarities between bilingual and unilingual behaviour to see whether the above line of thinking holds good. For the implications of what has been discussed so far are that variation in performance output is not necessarily linked to great underlying divergences. Hence we shall here try to present arguments on more convergent lines of approach.

Sociolinguistic investigations into the relationship between style-shift and degrees of formality in the speech of monoglots have revealed the non-monolithic nature of monoglot output which has many parallelisms with cross-language, contextually-determined code-switching. Code-switching has not only been accepted as a useful concept in bilingual studies but has also been called upon to describe the use of two or more varieties of a language or even speech styles within one language (Swain, 1972; Hymes, 1974; Scotton & Ury, 1977). The speech of most individuals is marked by numerous oscillations, contradictions and alternations which are inexplicable in terms of a single idiolect, as has been emphasized by Labov (1972/1978: 208) in monoglot cases, who claims:

> "As far as we can see there are no single-style speakers. Some informants show a much wider range of style shifting than others, but every speaker we have encountered shows a shift of some linguistic variables as the social context and topic change... We find that styles can be ranged along a single dimension, measured by the amount of attention paid to speech. The most important way in which this attention is exerted is in audio-monitoring one's own speech, though other forms of monitoring also take place."

Gumperz (1972) has likewise shown for bilinguals how they alternate between two languages for much the same reason that monolinguals select among styles of a single language and that the social pressures which would make a monolingual change from colloquial to formal or technical styles may lead a bilingual to shift from one language to another:

> "Where this is the case, the difference between monolingual and bilingual behaviour thus lies in the choice of linguistic symbols for socially equivalent processes." (Gumperz, 1967: 48).

With monoglot speakers style-shift may be far less easily perceived than is cross-language code-switching, thereby accounting for a widely held belief in an apparent dissimilarity between the two phenomena. Style-shift with monolinguals may reveal itself only in phonetic changes or in morphological variation, such as the alternation between final -*in* or -*ing* in polysyllabic words in English, depending on the degree of formality (Labov, 1972/1978: 239–42), though syntactic and lexical usage often co-varies with such changes. In bilingual speech, however, any deviation from the monoglot norm is more readily perceptible, leading to the impression that bilingual behaviour is somehow different. Yet Gumperz (1972) has shown that in bilingual communities speech behaviour can be described in terms of a single grammatical system and that in such cases "it seems reasonable to assume that two genetically distinct languages have in fact nearly identical grammars. On the other hand the grammatical differences between the dialects of the same language seem in some respects greater than the differences between the two local dialects (of genetically distinct languages)."   (Gumperz, 1972: 150)

Perhaps the extent to which this is true can be assessed only by appraising the difference between interference and code-switching which was touched upon in Chapter 2. It would appear that the distinction is not as clear-cut as was originally assumed in earlier works on bilingualism. Interference used to be considered as any features in a bilingual's L2 which differed from features found in unilingual speech and were attributable to the linguistic structure of L1. Bilingual code-switching is very similar in that it consists of using elements of a second language in contexts where a monoglot speaker would not do so. Since bilingual code-switching may range minimally from the introduction of a single sound not normally present in monoglot speech to a complete change of language over large chunks of discourse, it is not always evident where the difference lies. However, observation of how the bilingual behaves allows for a clarification of the distinction between code-switching and interference. For the triggering mechanism for either phenomenon is different. Whereas interference phenomena tend to operate at the subconscious level, and are intrusive in that the speaker is not aware that he is producing features alien to monoglot norms, code-switching operates nearer the surface of consciousness in that it tends to manifest itself only in situations where it is meaningful to the interlocutor. A bilingual speaker will maximize avoidance of code-switching when speaking to a monoglot whereas if he is speaking to another bilingual who shares the same codes he will not do so and may even deliberately choose to code-switch for the sake of nuanced expressivity.

On the other hand he may not be able to avoid revealing a substratum feature from L1 while using L2, whoever the interlocutor may be. The distinction can best be illustrated from the speech of the Brussels bilingual in the following example who used a preposition in French that could only be attributed to Dutch and where the difference from standard French was not perceived:

Standard French: "Les mouettes sont venues nous manger *dans la* main."
Brussels French: "Les mouettes sont venues manger *sur notre* main."
Dutch: "De meeuwen zijn *op onze* handen komen eten." =
                         The seagulls came and ate from our hands.

Note in the example how the bilingually marked elements in the Brussels French sentence coincide with the Dutch syntax (standard French "*dans la main*" = in the hand, Brussels French "*sur notre main*" = Dutch "*op onze handen*" = on our hand(s)). This differs considerably from the type of code-switching equally found in Brussels in situations where the interlocutor shares the same two codes:

"Tu dois être grand, un petit/geraakt er niet bij"
= You have to be big, a little one/won't get in.

If we think back to the interlanguage hypothesis with respect to these two examples it is most likely that the speaker in the first utterance was blithely unaware of the deviation from standard French and would probably have been unable to do much about it even if this had been pointed out. In the second case the speaker was most likely more conscious of the change in language and would have been able to "correct" the utterance to fit the patterns of one language if requested to do so.

The parallelism with monoglot behaviour is clear when one thinks of the efficiency of style-shifting dependent on degree of formality, which is also primarily determined by the nature of the interlocutor. A lower-level native-speaker of English who attempts to articulate in a normative fashion in careful speech is still likely to use stigmatized forms roughly four times more frequently than speakers of a higher socio-economic status (Labov, 1972/1978: 239). In this way he manifests a trait very similar to that of interference in a bilingual, if one accepts the following equation for the lower-level monoglot:

monoglot stigmatized form   = bilingual's L1
monoglot non-stigmatized form = bilingual's L2

Similarly, the norm-conscious monoglot who, for example, relates a joke may well vary his style to render his anecdote more authentic, on the assumption that his interlocutor appreciates the expressivity indicated by style-shift. In this case he is operating on the more conscious level in the same way that the bilingual does in code-switching. It should not be thought that bilingual code-switching is determined by such things as lack of lexical availability in the weaker language since code-switching is possible even when two variants are readily available (Lipski, 1978b: 263). This fact is strictly parallel to the unilingual case where several variants may be available for selection, the choice of style depending on the social role. Compare the following variants of the same request possible for the native unilingual English-speaker:

formal   : May I borrow a cigarette?
informal   : Could you lend us a fag?

with the examples from a Dutch-French bilingual in Brussels:

formal   : Un cornet de frites avec une magnifique *motte*
                    de mayonnaise
informal   : Un cornet de frites avec une magnifique *clotte*
                    de mayonnaise (where "clotte" comes from the
                    Dutch "kluit". Baetens Beardsmore, 1971c:
                    358). = A bag of chips with a magnificent dollop
                    of mayonnaise.

The similarity in the operations pointed out above has been discussed by Oksaar (1972a: 492), who notes that the only difference between the unilingual who switches to entities from other registers and the bilingual who switches to the second language in similar circumstances is that the latter has a possibility that is not open to the former. There is ever more evidence available to show how the same social pressures which would lead the monoglot to change from one style to another may lead the bilingual to shift from one language to another (Gumperz, 1967: 48). The points of similarity between the two operations become more clearly underlined when one realizes that the distance between certain varieties of recognized standard languages, e.g. Hindi and Urdu, is grammatically less distinct than between some forms of upper and lower-class English in New York (Gumperz, 1967: 49).

While accepting the classificatory usefulness of distinguishing between interference and code-switching in bilinguals, based on triggering mechanisms that are not the same, we should not forget that in those bilingual communities where there are large numbers of speakers who share the same pair of languages, bilingually determined phenomena should perhaps no longer be considered as peculiar or different from what monoglots would do in other circumstances. As Mackey (1976: 310-12) has indicated for such cases, if the bilingually marked feature is the only one used by a particular community, whatever that feature's shape, it cannot be considered as interference (or even fossilization or interlanguage) since no alternative or more standard form is either known or used.

There are a large number of studies that have been produced which tend to minimize the difference between bilingualism and unilingualism. Evidence from brain-damaged bilinguals show that generally all the patient's languages are similarly represented in the brain in the same manner as in a monolingual speaker (Whittaker, 1978: 21), although refined experimentation by Genesee, Hamers *et al.* (1978) has shown a difference in the neurophysiological processes of early compared to late bilinguals. The former appear less inclined to keep their two linguistic systems functionally distinct or segregated than the latter, which evidence corroborates the supposition of different operational processes involved in acquiring two languages in pre-adolescence as distinct from learning an L2 on top of an acquired L1 after puberty. The significance of these differences has already been discussed earlier in this chapter and their role in determining easier interference-free output with the early bilingual. Yet they pose a problem in that there is no explanation as to why early bilinguals often show less interference than late bilinguals, when one would expect the opposite from these findings. Perhaps the early bilingual theoretically possesses an integrated language sub-system with two clearly distinguished output channels, where the late bilingual has to reconcile learned L2 patterns with acquired L1 patterns that may lead to interference. The directionality of the operations in both the early and the late cases is probably the same, i.e. towards integration, though the consequences may be different in that the former are more able to avoid interference. Both, however, may well carry out code-switching.

Other parallelisms between unilinguals and late bilinguals can be found, in spite of apparent differences. A monoglot speaker whose speech habits are originally marked by region of origin or socio-economic class during pre-adolescence may at times have difficulty in concealing traces of his original speech forms if at some later stage in life he feels obliged to use speech not so marked. If so, his behaviour will be very similar to that of interference-marked speech in late bilinguals. A native-speaker lecturer of English who originated from an h-less regional speech area, Coventry in the United Kingdom, was observed to use standard English pronunciation in his professional adult life. However, in rapid speech and under circumstances of stress traces of his original stigmatized h-less pronunciation would creep in as well as hypercorrection in the insertion of initial h where not required, giving sentences of the type:

I 'ope he hasked him.

This is a case of a bidialectal monoglot showing traces of his regionally-marked speech patterns in his use of standard English. The moot question is whether an early bidialectal monoglot accustomed to using two varieties of the same language from early childhood would be able to avoid confusions of the type illustrated in the same way that the early bilingual can usually keep his two languages successfully apart.

If we now take up the question of interference and code-switching again, bearing in mind the earlier distinction made, together with their apparent parallel manifestations in bilingual and monoglot speech, we can now see that what appears superficially as deviant in both cases is relatable to normal speech production. Lattey (1978, 1981) considers that speech-error substitution in unilinguals and code-switching substitution in bilinguals both occur on a kind of continuum ranging from polar positions of unattended (or unaware) substitution — what we have been calling interference throughout — to fully attended (or intended) substitution, i.e. what we have been calling code-switching. Lattey shows how the same type of mental processes are involved in non-linguistic substitutions, the single variety and the multiple variety linguistic substitutions or confusions. She gives examples of motor confusion (non-linguistic substitution) where one gesture is subconsciously substituted for another, as when the driver who is approaching a toll gate on a fee-paying road throws a biscuit into the machine and places a coin in the mouth. Examples of monoglot slips of the tongue illustrate single-variety substitution as when a speaker says:

> I'm not under the alfluence of incohol,
> instead of:
> I'm not under the influence of alcohol,
> or asks for:
> a fifty-pound dog of bag-food
> instead of:
> a fifty-pound bag of dog-food.

Here "the wires have been crossed", according to Lattey (1981), in a way similar to what happens when bilingual confusions are attributable to interference. Lattey also gives an example of a monoglot code-switch similar to bilingual cross-language switching in the case of the speaker of standard English who put the sign

> Bell don't work!

on her door in a non-standard English-speaking neighbourhood so as to achieve more successful communication.

Drawing the comparison between unilinguals and bilinguals even further, Lattey quotes the example of a monoglot speaker who says:

> Second Hungarian Restaurant
> instead of
> Second Hungarian Rhapsody

perhaps prompted by the sign across the street or a memory of a meal the night before; this is an externally motivated slip which is related to the momentary social situation, but it is very similar to the bilingual who switches from English into German because of the external stimulus of the presence of another bilingual:

A: What line is it?
B: Sechs und fünfzig.
A: Sechs und fünfzig. Here we are.

According to Lattey, in both monoglot and bilingual speech, attended and unattended slips, interference or switches are determined by their *utterance potential*. This means, given a possibility of choice between two types of output the element with the strongest internally or externally motivated association is likely to be most readily available for insertion in discourse. If one looks at language as a code system with a pairing of signal and meaning, then the phenomenon noted in the bilingual speaker can readily be related to those in the multiple-variety unilingual speaker. The monoglot has in his inventory signal-meaning combinations which differ in form depending on style, register, etc. The bilingual has these plus additional signal-meaning pairs which belong to the second language. The choice among the available ways of expressing the message to be communicated under given circumstances is controlled by the social setting and by other contributing factors such as utterance potential, ease of expression or the availability of a succinct way of saying something in one language (or variety), speed of recall, etc. For unilinguals the constraints of a formal setting rule out elements of a casual register; for bilinguals, the constraints of a monolingual communication setting rule out linguistic switching. For both types of speaker the slip of the tongue or interference feature is due to inadequate screening of the available material in a given social setting.

The similarity between the bilingual and the monoglot is that neither of their linguistic repertoires is one-track. The major difference is that with the monoglot this repertoire includes several available varieties of a single language, while for the bilingual the multiple system includes the available varieties of two languages. Degree of bilingualism may well determine whether the bilingual has at his disposal all the varieties of two languages that two separate monoglots would have, though it is likely that functional specialization would make this superfluous in most cases. It is indeed rare for a bilingual (apart from the professional interpreter) to need to reduplicate all activities in both languages so that the total range of varieties available, at least for production, might not be the equivalent of 2 × L1 ranges, though receptively this might well be the case.

Oksaar (1972a: 1979; 1983) claims that the analysis of bilingual behaviour has shown that the bilingual uses elements from L1 and L2 in his speech but has also constituted an Lx or L3 which accounts for speech patterns marked by interference and code-switching. In terms of repertoire one could posit that the bilingual's Lx or L3 represents a unified repertoire made up of elements of L1 and L2 which in their totality equate with the complete repertoire of an L1 speaker, though do not necessarily coincide with it.

Diagrammatically the two types of speaker under comparison might be envisaged as shown in Figure 1.

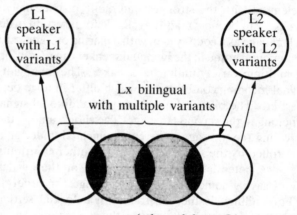

FIGURE 1   (adapted from Oksaar, 1979)

The complex picture above shows how elements from both the L1 and the L2 speakers' repertoires form part of the composite language repertoire of the bilingual which may partly or totally match what is found in each separate monoglot (depending on degree of bilingualism); there are also elements in the bilingual which are not present in the repertoires of either monoglot. The single shaded areas represent the features caused by the presence of a contact language in the bilingual speaker, such as interference and code-switching. The double shaded areas represent those features which are independent of any reference to the respective L1 and L2 of the monoglots but arise from the fact that the two are present and available for re-alignment within the total frame of reference of being bilingual.

Lipski (1978b) considers that bilingual competence in its totality is more integral than two separate grammars and accounts for the use of elements from both languages by stating:

"... it is clear that, despite superficial appearances of random and unprincipled behaviour, bilingual code-switching does seem to obey a rather stringent set of sentential constraints. These constraints are of two fundamental types, intralinguistic constraints and interlinguistic constraints." (Lipski, 1978c: 274).

Lipski considers that the interlinguistic constraints are difficult to isolate since there is no clear picture of the quantity of code shifts that may be accommodated in a stretch of discourse, nor how many words or syllables must intervene between switches. It is extremely rare, however, to find certain switches in specific combinations of languages and he gives Spanish-English examples where crosses of language in combinations Det.+Adj.+Noun or Det.+Noun+Adj. were considered as rare or unacceptable, e.g.:

Spanish-English   "su favorito spot" (Spanish+Spanish+English)
                     "su favorite lugar" (Spanish+English+Spanish)
                     "his favorito spot" (English+Spanish+English)

but where "his favorite lugar" (English+English+Spanish) was accepted (Lipski, 1978c: 265). For the intralinguistic constraints it seems that immediately preceding a code-switch there occurs a brief moment of anticipation, in which, at some subliminal level, the basic syntactic structures of the remaining portions of the sentence in the two languages are compared and tested for congruence. The overall motivation behind such a comparison seems to be the achievement of a unified superficial syntactic pattern, regardless of the linguistic code in which the individual elements are represented. Code-switches which would in effect combine incompatible syntactic structures are normally avoided (Lipski, 1978c: 275). Oksaar, Lipski and Poplack (1980) all conclude that bilingual competence is more integral than two separate grammars and that it lies somewhere between the two diametrically opposite poles, being neither two completely distinct language systems nor one homogeneous amalgam. Poplack illustrates with the following diagram (Figure 2) how different degrees of bilingual ability are reflections of expanding grammars, with the least fluent bilingual being illustrated by a), and the most fluent operating in a bilingual community by c), as illustrated by different frequencies of characteristic code-switching operations.

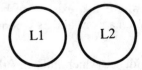 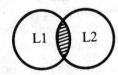 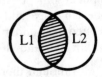

a) Inter-sentential switching   b) Tag-switching   c) Intra-sentential switching
FIGURE 2 (From Poplack, 1980: 615)

If we have concentrated so much on interference and code-switching in this section of our discussion it is because these two features appear to present the biggest, but not the only, stumbling block in attempts at distinguishing bilingual speech. The arguments we have presented have tried to show how any distinctiveness that may be present can be discussed in terms of reference that link up the two. There is another side to the question that needs to be examined, however, namely, how interference and code-switching are avoided by bilinguals. In this respect we are heavily indebted to the synthetic overview of linguistic, psychological and neurophysiological studies of bilingualism produced by Albert & Obler in *The Bilingual Brain* (1978).

These authors were particularly interested in how the bilingual successfully or unsuccessfully encodes and decodes messages in two distinct languages, separating the receptive and productive abilities and examining their inter-relationship. We have already seen in Chapter 1 that reception and production need in no way match in bilinguals and after sifting through the evidence Albert & Obler (1978: 41) came to the conclusion that for bilinguals at least language production and language perception are to some degree independent of each other. This conclusion was arrived at from examples like the detailed longitudinal study of childhood bilingual acquisition produced by Leopold's *Speech Development of a Bilingual Child* (1939-49); in this it appeared that although a different language became dominant for production across time, depending on the child's environment, both languages were equally well comprehended after the third year of life. Leopold's daughter, Hildegard, had a fluctuating productive ability in her two languages as she grew older, whereas her comprehension ability appeared to develop smoothly in both languages. Albert & Obler came to the conclusion from all the evidence they had looked at that the bilingual builds up a unitary system for perception which has some similarities with the perception systems of two respective monoglots and some differences. On the phonological level it appears that the bilingual's unitary system for perception is distinct from that of two separate monoglots with L1 phonemic categories influencing L2 in certain cases and L2 influencing the perception of L1 in others. On the lexical level it seems that bilinguals process language input at some semantic level beyond the language-specific and that a word in one language and its translation equivalent, where this exists, are both related in a similar way to the relationship between a word and its synonym within one and the same language.

Although there is a certain amount of evidence which indicates that there is a unifying process for receptive abilities, and this whatever the age of onset of bilingualism, this is less apparent in production processes. Indeed,

Albert & Obler (1978: 220-21) feel that language production and language perception systems are to some extent independent of each other. Evidence from neurolinguistics and studies of aphasia has shown that the part of the brain known as Broca's area controls language production and if this gets damaged speech production may be severely impaired. Slightly posterior in the brain is a different area, known as Wernicke's area, which seems to control comprehension, and patients who have suffered damage to this part of the brain tend to be fluent, with grammatically organized speech, though they often have great difficulty in understanding what is said to them. (For a clear outline of the relationship between neurolinguistics and bilingualism, see Hatch, 1983: 198–218.)

Although the identification of these different parts of the brain does not give any clear explanation, it represents a line of enquiry for accounting for the greater facility in acquiring and retaining comprehension and reading abilities in two languages, as opposed to productive abilities.

The case of the professional interpreter who needs to be trained in the specific skill of producing material in a different language from that in which he is receiving it tends to corroborate the supposition that a different process is involved. If one can accept that something extra is involved in productive skills, then it is easier to understand how certain receptive bilinguals may never develop the skills necessary to speaking and writing in more than one language. Thus although it may be argued that with receptive bilinguals the inability to activate their second language may be due to personality factors (inhibition) and social circumstances (no pressing need to communicate orally in the second language), the fact that where productive abilities are activated they tend to lag behind the receptive ones seems attributable to the distinction in processes.

Whether we are dealing with receptive or productive bilinguals, we still need some explanation for the way in which they can filter the linguistic input as pertaining to one language or the other. Albert & Obler (1978: 213ff) reject the notion of an input switch, as proposed by some specialists, which is somehow turned on in the brain in order to channel information into appropriate L1 or L2 directions. Instead they prefer to posit that a continuously operating monitor system controls the processing of input in the bilingual as much as in the monolingual:

"All incoming stimuli are processed at the phonetic level and assigned to potential phonemes, which are then assigned to potential words, which are then interpreted syntactically; and in the light of linguistic and extra-linguistic context, decisions are made about the likely meaning of the incoming speech. Such a monitor would work most efficiently by assigning priorities in interpretation. We suggest, for example, that if one were in France, the tendency would be to interpret incoming data as if they were French. Nevertheless, should stimuli from another known language enter the ear, the monitor system would soon realize that its processing strategies were not optimal, and it would reassign priorities so that the stimuli would be checked against the other language systems."

(Albert & Obler, 1978: 213)

As far as output is concerned, it is not necessary to posit the idea of a special output switch either as something which triggers off production in one of the two available languages, since:

"The decision to switch from one language to another, just like the decision to speak in a particular language in the first place, is more economically explained by the functioning of a general neural mechanism than by a special mechanism for that specific purpose alone. There is no need to postulate an anatomical localization or even a specific functional organization, other than that which every speaker already possesses and which allows him, among other things, to switch registers within the same language."   (Paradis, 1977a: 91)

Perhaps one should go a little further, however, than trying to explain the bilingual's ability to manipulate more than one language as a simple extension of the monoglot's ability to select from a wide range of speech styles in his language and attempt to discover if there are any more significant differences.

Research conducted over a long period of time has convincingly demonstrated that in most people the left cerebral hemisphere is dominant for language. Albert & Obler (1978: 238-42), after reviewing many studies, came to the conclusion that in most bilinguals there is some distinctive type of cerebral organization. Unlike the majority of monoglots it appears that the average bilingual is less strongly lateralized for language and that the right cerebral hemisphere is also called into play. In other words, the language organization of the average bilingual is more ambilateral, though this does not mean that either language is necessarily distributed equally. It appears that different languages may have different anatomical representation in the bilingual, determined by such factors as the age of acquisition of the second language, the manner of acquisition, the order of learning, and factors specific to each language. Nuanced evidence from the overview of experiments supports the notion that the right hemisphere plays a significant role in bilinguals, while this does not seem to be involved in most cases where only one language has been learnt. In certain studies it was noted that early childhood bilinguals had left cerebral dominance while the later adolescent bilinguals appeared to rely on the right hemisphere for language processing. In others it appeared that those who seemed to rely on deductive methods for learning a second language tended to be left-dominant, whereas those who relied more on inductive methods were less clearly left-dominant. Further studies of English-Hebrew bilinguals showed the involvement of the right cerebral hemisphere, but that the order of learning determined whether both languages were left-dominant or whether English was left-dominant and Hebrew more balanced. The conclusions are that in bilinguals both hemispheres come more into play than is the case with monoglots but that the two languages involved may reflect different cerebral dominance patterns according to some of the factors mentioned above. The major point to be borne in mind is there is greater right hemisphere participation in language processing in bilinguals than in unilinguals:

> "Thus the learning of a second language can alter the 'standard' lateralization pattern which we have come to expect in right-handed monolingual adults. Moreover, we have seen that the circumstances of the language learning may affect the neural organization of that language. Since it is unlikely that one individual will learn all of her languages at precisely the same age, in precisely the same manner, with precisely the same affective considerations, it then seems likely that certain bilinguals have asymmetrical or different dominance patterns for their several languages."
>
> (Albert & Obler, 1978: 242)

At this point we can attempt to suggest tentative answers to the questions raised at the beginning of this chapter, namely, to what extent bilingualism is different from or similar to unilingualism and what accounts for the distinctive levels of ability in more than one language that characterize specific types of bilingualism.

From the purely linguistic point of view we have underlined certain similarities between bilingual and unilingual speech behaviour and stressed that they should both be amenable to explanation in terms that are applicable to either. There is the proviso, however, that those factors which are peculiar to certain types of bilingualism have to be worked into the overall framework as factors to be considered apart, particularly late onset of bilingualism, unequal input of the two languages and role specialization in the way they are put to use. It has been argued that interference and

code-switching should be seen in terms of the bilingual's overall competence, which bridges two languages, rather than with reference to two sets of
distinct, idealized monoglot native-speaker norms and that this method of
approach will reveal more of what is common between bilingual and
monoglot performance than what is different. Particular emphasis has been
given to the similarities between early childhood bilingualism and monoglot
cases, while attempts have been made to show how late bilinguals, who often
manifest striking discrepancies in their weaker language, can be accounted
for in terms of reference that hold good for monoglots. The distinction
between early and late bilingualism is perhaps the most significant factor in
any theoretical discussion of the presence of more than one language in the
same speaker. Although there are many recorded cases of late bilinguals
attaining remarkable levels of accomplishment in their second language, it
still remains true that the vast majority of late bilinguals do not succeed in
passing off as native speakers of both their languages. Other late bilinguals
reach a cut-off point in ability in their second language which may range
from an inability to speak or write it, even though they can understand
perfectly well, to the ability to satisfy most of their requirements by the use
of the second language without approximating native-like fluency or
accuracy. Three explanations can be given for the late bilingual's more
restricted set of abilities. The first is the proven distinction between
receptive and productive capacities witnessed in unilinguals and bilinguals
alike, where input faculties seem to develop earlier and with greater facility
than output potential. The second is that with the late bilingual who is of the
receptive type the output faculty has either not been activated because of
affective and social inhibitions or with the productive type the output faculty
has not been developed to the same extent as the input ability. The third
is the apparent turning point in linguistic development represented by the
onset of puberty, even though the exact nature of this change is not clear
to us.

The explanation for dominance configurations with respect to relative
ease of ability in the bilingual's two languages given by Albert &
Obler may well also account for the mismatch in abilities across two
languages. These authors do not dwell on the more obvious sociolinguistic
explanations for this mismatch, concentrating their attention on how it is
that language x may be more readily available for general purposes than
language y. Their conclusions about cerebral lateralization are more
concerned with explaining the fact that both x and y are *available* for
discrete or to some extent mixed usage, but the inferences reveal
interesting sidelights which may account for differentiated ability among
varied degrees of bilingualism. If one re-interprets the findings connected
with lateralization and preferred learning strategy it is noted that both the

late adolescent bilingual and the person who relies on deductive methods in second-language learning tend to use the right hemisphere more readily. The early childhood bilingual and the person who prefers an inductive approach rely more on the left cerebral hemisphere, even though in all cases of bilingualism both the left and the right hemisphere seem to be called into play. When we bear in mind that natural childhood language acquisition is inductive rather than deductive and that left cerebral dominance appears more standard in monoglots, too, it is not a very big step to question whether the greater proficiency in two languages manifested by early bilinguals, who presumably also acquire both their languages via induction, is not connected with this dominance configuration. If so, then the greater difficulty in learning a second language after the onset of puberty, as witnessed in most late bilinguals, may be connected with spheric lateralization'and may in part be accounted for by some inability to harmonize right cerebral hemisphere operations with left. This is a highly hypothetical question but it might represent an intriguing line of investigation.

Summary

This chapter has attempted to draw together different theoretical questions pertinent to bilingual ability as well as arguments generally applicable to monoglot cases. The aim has been to show what is peculiar to bilingualism and then to attempt to explain any distinctiveness in terms that are relevant to mainstream linguistics dealing with one language. First the difference between early and late bilingualism has been analysed, followed by a separation of receptive and productive abilities in order to explain certain differences which distinguish the bilingual from the monoglot. At the same time the basic determinants of all human language have been underlined as applicable to speakers of any number of languages. The place of transformational generative approaches in bilingual investigation has been discussed, with an emphasis on the highly important need to explain interference and code-switching as both normal in bilingualism and peculiar to it. The fact that many bilinguals are not in a position to detect ambiguity or ungrammaticality in their production, unlike monoglots, has been explained by the interlanguage hypothesis and linked to the theory of communicative competence to allow for an explanation of varying degrees of bilingual ability. The discussion has also gone into the question of how interference and code-switching are avoided, as well as the apparently distinctive cerebral lateralization patterns which seem to characterize most bilinguals.

5 Problems of the Bilingual Speaker

The preceding chapters have already revealed a large number of difficulties in connection with different aspects of bilingual investigation and, indeed, if one were to attempt to be exhaustive the number of problems to be discussed could not be contained in one chapter but would lead to a new book. This is particularly true in cases of societal bilingualism where the relationship between different linguistic communities has often led to conflict and compromise tempered by official policies and language planning. The variety of publications on this subject is overwhelming. The International Centre for Research on Bilingualism at Laval University in Quebec has published a series of volumes which could provide a starting point for those interested in these questions, including Savard & Vigneault's *Les états multilingues: problèmes et solutions* (1975), the anonymous *Minorités linguistiques et interventions* (1978), Touret's *L'Aménagement constitutionnel des états de peuplement composite* (1973). Much of Fishman's production given in the bibliography at the end of this book is highly significant to the question of societal multilingual problems, while Nelde's *Sprachkontakt und Sprachkonflikt* (1980) provides further broad overviews which can be completed by consulting such specialized reviews as *The International Journal of the Sociology of Language, The Journal of Multilingual and Multicultural Development,* or *Language in Society.*

Since the major focus of this book is on the bilingual individual, and up to this point more specifically on the purely linguistic characteristics of bilinguals, the problems that will be dealt with in this chapter deal more with the effect that the presence of two languages can have on an individual's development, though the societal element will never be far from mind given that the majority of problems encountered by bilinguals are societally determined. The very fact that a person is a bilingual is usually a reflection of the society in which he lives, originating in such things as migration, exogamy, social mobility, job requirements, and so forth, and often the individual bilingual has had little choice in deciding his status. Whatever the causes, this status often leads the individual bilingual to question the rôle that languages play in his life. This is particularly true when bilinguals represent a minority and are confronted with members from a monolingual majority who tend to perceive bilingualism as abnormal, as has been most refreshingly illustrated by Haugen in his article, *The Stigmata of Bilingualism* (1972c). Yet for many people in the world where bilingualism is widespread there is either no choice between unilingualism and bilingualism, or else little hesitancy about becoming bilingual. Moreover, on a purely statistical basis it is highly likely that unilingualism is abnormal in that there are probably more bilinguals in the world than speakers of only one language, as has been pointed out by Lewis (1976: 151), Mackey (1976: 73) and Oksaar (1983), among others. To those encountering bilingualism for the first time because they come from communities where it is not prevalent, this may lead to heart-searching, worry and even hostility, particularly among middle-class, articulate persons who attribute a problem factor to dual language usage. On the other hand, in cases where bilingualism has come about by force of circumstances among groups of people who suffer from social disadvantages, as is often the case with minority migrant populations, problems associated with minority status may well be compounded by the bilingual factor. Indeed, much of the hostility manifested towards the phenomenon of bilingualism appears to mask sentiments more akin to class-related'or racialist prejudices conveniently hidden behind a rationale of unilingual superiority. This leads to the intriguing questions: who's afraid of bilingualism? And why?

For many, particularly parents, the major worry connected with becoming bilingual is its effects on personality development and intellectual capacities. Thus the rôle of language in education has often been the centre of debate, as has already been seen in the discussion on semilingualism in Chapter 1. In the early years up to about the 1950s when investigators began to look into the effects of the presence of two languages on an individual's educational progress, many negative characteristics were isolated, some justifiably attributable to the bilingual element in the question, others not so. Since the 1960s, however, much serious research has unravelled the purely linguistic from the pedagogic, social and psychological elements involved in bilingual development, leading on the one hand to far more positive appreciations of the effects of bilingualism in general, and on the other to a greater understanding of why bilingualism is not successful in certain cases.

One of the more important problems involved in becoming or being bilingual is that connected with *anomie* (alternatively spelled *anomy*), which can be defined as a feeling of personal disorientation, anxiety and social isolation. The role of anomie in the lives of bilinguals, particularly adolescents, was brought home in a study by Child (1943) in *Italian or American? The Second Generation in Conflict.* Child had observed that the children of Italian immigrants to New York often revealed symptoms of bewilderment and frustration brought about by the conflict of loyalties and aspirations generated between the home language and culture, which was Italian orientated, and the language and culture of the outside world, overwhelmingly orientated towards the values of American culture. For many Italo-American adolescents the conflict could not be resolved without making a choice, either to withdraw from the all-pervading outside environment into that of the Italian-centred home community, or to manifest an open preference for the American set of cultural values (and language), thereby causing upset and often severance from the family unit. A third alternative was withdrawal in a rather apathetic way from thinking in ethnic terms of any sort. All of these solutions could be beset by hazards for the individual's psychological development, since they implied rejection of an important component of these adolescents' life-pattern. In short, they led to a confusion of identity.

The reaction noted by Child arises from an inability to resolve the conflicting demands made upon the bilingual individual by the two linguistic-cultural communities in which he finds himself. Such conflicting demands are forever present in the bilingual but can be more acute for the adolescent trying to develop a complete set of personality traits along two different channels.

The very nature of the average bilingual's development implies that the goals after which he is striving will be inaccessible, since the acquisition of perfectly balanced ambilingualism is exceptional. Thus it is that the bilingual who tries to reconcile two widely divergent linguistic and cultural patterns may find the inaccessible goals presented to him by his two environments leading to feelings of frustration. This is more so when the cultural norms of the two communities are highly differentiated, as for example, those of Western European and Arab communities. Moreover, since cultural communities tend to be exacting in their demands on the individual, and particularly the young person who is expected to develop along patterns laid down by the community, the stresses imposed can be very great. As Sharp (1973: 77) has put it;

> "The bilingual's two languages give him access, consciously or unconsciously, to two cultures, which may in general be very similar or very different, though however similar they may be there will be differences which in many cases will cause conflicts

of loyalties. Learning a language involves acquiring the values and attitudes of the community using the language, learning two languages which have or gain equal or near equal status in the individual's life presents him with many moments of choice or confusion."

The phenomenon of anomie does not tend to present itself in the early stages of the move up the cline towards bilingualism, i.e. in the pre-bilingual stage of the foreign-language learner who is looking into the new linguistic environment from the secure reaches of his own culture, accepted value-judgements and unquestioned, shared, standard behaviour patterns. It tends to show up more when the individual has moved a considerable way towards becoming a bilingual, at the point where he begins to move out of one linguistic cultural group and into another. This may force him to adjust his accepted set of behaviour norms in the light of new, totally different norms accepted in the other group. The difficulty inherent in this situation is created by the fact that both the cultural group one originates from and the one being entered will not fail to notice any potential lack of total assimilation. Both are likely to sanction this in a multitude of subtle ways, thereby underlining the individual's "difference" or even inadequacies in group reference terms:

> "... it is difficult to be both Jewish and Russian, or Algerian and French, and this is so because the person involved realises that two separate networks of valued people expect him to show unambiguous signs of allegiance to one group or the other. It is extremely painful to be caught in the influence systems of two or more ethnic groups and to be 'tested' by members of one group or the other who demand evidence of one's true colours."
>
> (Lambert, Giles & Picard, 1975: 127)

The problem is rendered acute from two directions. The individual, as he progresses in the second language, becomes potentially more aware of his linguistic inadequacies and more conscious of their cultural implications. The "new" community, on the other hand, raises its expectations for the individual to conform as he progresses towards greater proficiency in the second language. It is here that the relevance of the learner's communicative as opposed to his linguistic competence is brought home. The speaker of a second language with an acceptable accent and accurate syntax who is not aware of the cultural implications of what he is saying may provoke astonishment or even hostility if the message does not coincide with the assumptions the native-speaker interlocutor associates with the particular code.

A similar duality exists with reference to the first language. Greater acceptance of the values of the "new" linguistic-cultural community may cause a re-appraisal of those of the original linguistic-cultural community as bilingualism develops. The original community, on the other hand, still expects this bilingual individual to react towards this community as though he had not assimilated any of the values of another community.

Anomie can be less prevalent, though not necessarily absent, amongst young children than it is among adolescents and adults who have greater difficulty in reconciling new behaviour patterns with older acquired ones. Potentially disturbing for the psychological and social development of the individual, anomie is the result of an inability to work out some solution to the conflicting demands imposed by the presence of two languages and cultures. In a pilot study we have carried out amongst adults brought up as bilinguals from early childhood onwards, it was noted that although they were extremely satisfied with their adult bilingual status they confessed to a period of unease and confusion about the values of the bilingual element in their lives during adolescence. The subjects questioned all considered that this was a temporary stage, lasting for about two years, but that subsequently it left no scars behind and they were happy to be bilingual and bicultural. On a purely linguistic level, Haugen (1962) calls an awareness of individual inadequacies *schizoglossia*, where the bilingual worries about elements of his speech which are non-normative or non-native-like. He goes further to suggest that this is particularly prevalent amongst foreign-language teachers and leads to purism and a rejection of bilingual norms.

It would seem that anomie is inversely related to socio-economic status:

> "... anomy is highest among certain sectors of the population: old
> people, the widowed, the divorced and separated, persons of low
> education, those with low incomes and low prestige occupations,
> people experiencing downward social mobility, negroes,
> foreignborn, farmers and other rural residents."
>
> (McCloskey & Schaar, 1965: 19)

In other words, persons who do not share in the articulate and active community and who are prone to confusion about the norms.

Lambert, Just & Segalowitz (1970) were particularly interested in the avoidance of anomie amongst second-language learners and noted how the attitude of the person involved was crucial. If the bilingual experience was of the additive type, leading to biculturality, it could be viewed as a broadening experience. If it was of the subtractive type, however, it could well engender anomie. The successful second-language learner gradually adopts aspects of behaviour which characterize members of another linguistic-cultural group, particularly if the learner's ethnocentric tendencies are not over-strong and if the motivation is *integrative* (i.e. wishing to become an insider in the community of the language that is being learnt) rather than *instrumental* (i.e. learning the language out of necessity, for job requirements, examination criteria, and so on, without wishing to participate in the culture borne by that language). However, it must be remembered that anxiety to learn another language for integrative purposes may perhaps be based on feelings of dissatisfaction with one's own linguistic-cultural group. If this is the case it is still likely that anomie will manifest itself since total severance of the bonds that link the learner to his original group is unlikely, while total integration into the new group may be hard to realize. This is more likely to be true if the two cultural communities involved are widely divergent. Even when two cultures are as compatible as those of French and English, success, in the widest sense of the term, is not at all guaranteed:

> "Depending on the compatibility of the two cultures, he (the bilingual) may experience feelings of chagrin or regret as he loses ties in one group, mixed with the fearful anticipation of entering a relatively new group."
> (Lambert, Just & Segalowitz, 1970: 274)

The assumption that anomie can be present in the highly motivated learner is based on an experiment carried out by Lambert (1972) where it was noted that advanced college and postgraduate students who were learning French showed signs of anomie which were markedly high when they thought and even dreamed in French:

> "At the same time they began to seek out occasions to use English even though they had solemnly pledged to use only French for a six-week period."
> (Lambert, 1972a: 227)

An explanation for this behaviour is that the students in question felt a strong dose of anomie at the point where they became so skilled as to begin to feel like Frenchmen, and the resulting unease led to the development of strategies to minimize such feelings.

In a further study Lambert & Aellen (1972) tried to discover whether adolescents from mixed language-background marriages were faced with conflicts because of the demands made upon them to learn the distinctive social characteristics of the two cultures represented in their families. Tests were developed to measure ethnic identification, social distance (i.e. identification with or rejection of one or the other ethnic group involved), self-esteem and stability, the child's perception of its parents, peer relationships, attitudes and values. Results showed that by comparison with children from homogeneous monoglot backgrounds the mixed or bicultural adolescents appeared to have no problem in identifying with their parents, nor with self-esteem or stability. In peer relationships it appeared that the minority language group, whether from mixed or homogeneous marriages, required more warmth and affection than the similar majority language group. In attitudinal dispositions the mixed group showed no bias towards either major cultural reference group, whereas homogeneous subjects clearly favoured their own ethnic group over others. It is worth quoting at some length from this study of the effects of bilingually mixed marriages on children:

> "In conclusion, the profile of characteristics of the subjects with mixed ethnic parentage is a healthy one in every respect when comparisons are made with groups with homogeneous ethnic backgrounds; ... they show no signs of personality disturbances, social disorientation, or anxiety, nor do their self-concepts deviate from those of the comparison subjects; they see their parents as giving them relatively more attention and personal interest, and their attitudes towards parents are as favourable as those of the comparison groups; ...the values they receive from their parents show the influence of both ethnic backgrounds as do their achievement orientations which are less extreme than those of comparison groups. Rather than developing a divided allegiance or representing one of both aspects of their backgrounds, as has been noted in the offspring of immigrants to America ...they apparently have developed a dual allegiance that permits them to identify with both their parents and to feel that they are wanted as family members."
>
> (Lambert & Aellen, 1972:, 284-85)

Now this somewhat rosy picture should not be over-generalized, since the study in question dealt with Canadian middle-class children from stable backgrounds; it does point out, however, that anomie does not necessarily arise out of the mere fact of a mixed marriage presenting a child with potentially divisive cultural allegiances. In other words, it is not essential for parents in mixed marriages to opt out of bringing their children up bilingually out of fear of conflicting developmental consequences.

In a further study of a linguistic minority group (Louisiana Franco-Americans) by Lambert, Just & Segalowitz (1970), it was found that students who had problems in learning the majority language, English, strived to dissociate themselves from their background of origin so as, they hoped, to make a more satisfactory adjustment to American culture and the English language. Here we see how specific socio-economic factors and minority status affect the development of anomie. The children faced a cultural conflict of allegiances which affected their skill in both their languages, together with sentiments of reserve and comparative embarrassment about their particular variety of French. The children who expressed a preference for American over Louisiana French cultural values and who negated the desirability of knowing French were more proficient in English than in Louisiana French and were anxious about their ability in English. Those who identified themselves as Louisiana French showed greater skill with French than English, while those with conflicting allegiances had relatively poor performances in both languages. Only those who were above average in intelligence and unprejudiced towards foreign peoples profited totally from their experience and became fully bilingual.

Studies on anomie amongst bilinguals tend to show the significance of cultural equilibrium. If there is no balance then the individual, as he progresses towards bilingualism, encounters pressures that can affect his self-concept, his sense of belonging and his relations to the two linguistic-cultural groups, the one he may be slowly leaving and the one he is entering. This appears to be particularly true of adolescents. On the other hand, bilinguals who are bicultural, particularly from early childhood onwards, appear to enjoy certain fundamental advantages which can counterbalance the different pulls of allegiance they might be subjected to. Many studies have shown that minority group youngsters learn the majority group language better and adjust more comfortably to their bilingual environment if their linguistic and cultural ties with the minority group of origin are kept alive and active from infancy onwards.

Anomie can become more prevalent and more problematic with the older learner, even among the strongly motivated, intelligent pupils. Outside cultural pressures produced by the environment can provoke anomie even when motivation to learn a second language well is positive. The Louisiana Franco-American case illustrates how a positive attitude towards the overwhelmingly monoglot environmental culture may well be determined by a negation of the minority language of origin, engendering rejection of the home culture without any necessary satisfying or satisfactory assimilation to the outside culture. The integrative motivation noted in this case was based on a rejection of one of the aspects of the bilingual's make-up, resulting in no more global satisfaction than if that motivation were not present. However, it should not be thought that integrative motivation necessarily implies deprecatory feelings towards the linguistic-cultural community of origin.

The notion of equilibrium is the all-important factor which runs through any discussion on the avoidance of anomie. This equilibrium should be fostered not only in the linguistic achievement of the learner but also in his cultural awareness. It cannot be referred to solely in terms of calculable teaching hours devoted to one or the other languages, or in the make-up of the sub-components of a curriculum, since it is probably undesirable and impossible to duplicate all activities conducted in the two languages for the sake of equivalence. The equilibrium to be aimed at is on the personality level, by means of a bilingual programme designed to avoid negative transfer of stereotypes and cultural attributes from one language and culture into another.

The appearance of anomie is determined by many variables, some of which belong to the domain of the educational psychologist. It cannot be dissociated from the normal psychological problems to be encountered in any learning situation — personality problems, retardation, insecurity, etc. Test data from a study on the psychological dimensions of anomie (McCloskey & Schaar, 1965: 14) revealed that cognitive and personality factors (e.g. hostility, anxiety, inflexible defensiveness) play important rôles in the appearance of anomie which often resulted from psychological impediments to interaction, communication and learning, and that these revealed impaired socialization. The most difficult variable to manipulate in an attempt to mitigate the effects of anomie is that of the all-pervading outside community's cultural environment. The attainment of satisfaction in the majority group setting is largely determined by social factors. For example, complete acculturation on the part of an immigrant child may well be unattainable (even if considered desirable, which it may not be) because of racialist tendencies prevalent in a given society. The balanced bilingual adolescent of Arab origins in a West European country might have anomie forced upon him in spite of intellectual abilities no different from those of other children in the majority community if he becomes aware of discrimination. Indeed, his heightened acculturation brought about by bilingualism may well make him more aware of discrimination based purely on racial factors. If so, this could lead to a rejection of the majority language and culture or dissatisfaction with the minority language and culture in the same way as if no equilibrium had been promoted by a well-designed bilingual education programme. There are, of course, no easy remedies for this situation.

Skutnabb-Kangas provides evidence of how such sentiments are perceived by a 19-year-old Turkish migrant in Sweden, clearly bringing to the fore societally determined feelings of anomie:

"It's true that in this country's terms our parents are ignorant. My mother is illiterate and though my father reads and writes Turkish fairly well, he has hardly any Swedish at all, and I don't think he even knows the name of my school. Turkish parents can't give their children any help with homework. And on the other side the school or society in general gives us no help with being Turkish. We find ourselves between two worlds, but don't really belong to either."

(Quoted in Skutnabb-Kangas, 1984: 317)

The creation of a balanced bilingual and bicultural education programme can help dispel the dangers of anomie, though it cannot eliminate them completely. It would appear that the problems of withdrawal from one of the two linguistic cultures can best be avoided if the following criteria are borne in mind:

—the rôle of parental attitudes towards bilingualism cannot be sufficiently stressed if problems of withdrawal from one of the two linguistic cultures are to be avoided. Successful results in bilingual education programmes have clearly shown a correlation between absence of anomie and positive parental support for both languages;
—bilingual education should be paired with bicultural awareness;
—monoglot linguistic and cultural reference norms should be applied with circumspection in evaluating bilingual and bicultural programmes;
—apparent linguistic retardation in one or both of the languages involved in the programme should be appraised over a sufficient period of time which takes into account the lack of opportunity to use both languages at all times and which adjusts expectancy levels accordingly;
—teachers working in bilingual programmes should be native speakers of the respective languages or bilinguals themselves and should have positive attitudes towards both of the languages and cultures in their pupils' lives, being careful not to present elements of either culture in a way that might provoke negative transfer or conflicting aspirations.

The problem of differential success in becoming bilingual is treated from a social and psychological perspective by Schumann.

Schumann (1978a, 1978b) has developed a model of second language acquisition that links up with the question of anomie, based on the social psychology of acculturation (the *acculturation model*), which draws together different strands of research and interconnects social factors, attitudinal dispositions and the outcome of bilingual achievement. This model was specifically designed to account for second language acquisition under conditions of immigration and lengthy residence in a second language environment without any language instruction, though it is likely that it could equally apply to the outcome of classroom instruction (at least in immigrant communities or stable bilingual settings).

Schumann posited the broad concepts of *social distance* and *psychological distance* as primary determinants in the relationship between acculturation and bilingual attainment. Under social distance he refers to several factors which affect the nature and amount of contact speakers of one language may have with those of another, thereby influencing the amount of input provided. The assumption is that the greater the social distance between two groups of speakers the more difficult it is for either or both of them to become bilingual. This is assessed by looking at the following:

—*social dominance patterns* where a politically, culturally, technically or economically superior group tends not to acquire the language of the inferior group, as for example when colonizing forces fail to learn the languages of the conquered territories. On the other hand the subordinate group may resist learning the language of the dominant group, e.g. certain American Indians;

—*levels of assimilation, preservation or adaptation* which determine whether speakers of language A give up their specific life style and values (assimilation), maintain these (preservation), thereby affecting the nature and quality of contacts with speakers of language B, or adaptation to the life style and values of language B group while maintaining those of language A for intragroup contact. This factor is significant in analysing intergenerational differences in bilingual proficiency in immigrant communities, whereby the first generation is the least assimilated, the second often adaptive and the third frequently assimilated and tending towards unilingualism in the majority language;

—*degree of enclosure* which refers to the sharing or separate use of such social institutions as churches, schools, recreation facilities, etc. The more these are shared the lower the degree of enclosure and the greater the possibility of cross-lingual contacts;

—*cohesiveness and size of the language group* which determine the amount of contact between speakers of different languages, the more cohesive and the larger a group is the less likely it will need to seek out opportunities to use another language;

—*congruence* or similarity of the two cultures in presence, greater

similarity making language learning potentially easier to accomplish even though it might not do so in fact;
—*attitudes* towards the other community, positive attitudes increasing the likelihood of language acquisition, negative attitude decreasing it;
—*intended length of residence* where a lengthy stay is likely to promote more contacts with the other group, and more linguistic interaction, than a short stay (Schumann, 1978a: 29–31; 1978b: 77–86).

Under psychological distance Schumann gives a series of sub-components, of which the three most important in our eyes are as follows (for others, see Schumann, 1978a: 31–34; 1978b: 86–99):

—*culture shock* relating to the ease or difficulty with which the cultural attributes borne by the second language and its speakers are assimilated. In situations where the new environment creates disorientation and stress it can lead to rejection of the new community and a minimizing of efforts to acquire its language;
—*ego-permeability* which refers to the amount of inhibition felt in using a weaker language, the more permeable one is the more likely one is to take risks in trying out the weaker language;
—*motivation*, whether this is integrative or instrumental, determining the path one takes in pursuing bilingualism.

Now it is highly likely that these sub-components of social distance and psychological distance interact in different degrees and that in applying them to specific circumstances the different elements would have to be weighted some way. However, it is also highly plausible that the sub-components represent a chain of causality whereby acculturation increases contacts with speakers of the second language leading to greater verbal interaction and enhanced potential for acquisition.

Several studies based on this model have been conducted by various scholars, revealing the significance of the different components in second language achievement (for discussion of their findings, see Schumann, forthcoming). What is interesting in this model is that it has the potential for incorporating differentiated and sometimes conflicting individual achievements into more global group patternings in a consistent, and therefore comparable, frame of reference. That is, it should be able to explain why certain individuals from a particular group apparently have problems with bilingual and bicultural proficiency whereas others from the same group do not. By the same token it should allow for comparison of group trends in widely differing circumstances, because the model is dynamic rather than static, through the weighting of each sub-component. It is interesting to speculate on its potential applicability beyond the type of population it was designed to account for.

Amongst migrant worker populations like the Turks in West Germany or Mexicans in the American Southwest the degree of social and psychological distance should highlight differentiated assimilation potential which correlates with second language proficiency or degree of bilingualism. In stable migrant enclaves, such as the Puerto Rican "barrio" in New York, it should help to account for language maintenance or language shift by highlighting intergenerational differences in such things as levels of assimilation or culture shock even though certain other features remain constant. In countries such as Wales it could be applied to the one-way bilingualism so prevalent, where Welsh-speakers learn English but few English-speakers learn Welsh and where the weighting on such features as social dominance, level of adaptation, degree of enclosure, cohesiveness and motivation is likely to be heavy, but much lighter on such features as congruence, intended length of residence, culture shock or ego-permeability; yet at the same time the model could account for individual contradictory cases (the English speaker who does learn Welsh). It could be applied to countries like Belgium where increasing mutual resistance by Walloons and Flemings to learn each other's language beyond instrumentally determined levels of proficiency is to be accounted for by maximized enclosure and cohesiveness, a denial of congruence, decreasing motivation, thereby influencing other factors in the chain to inhibit bilingualism. And although the model was not designed with classroom language learning in mind it could also be applied to success or failure of such endeavours in a variety of circumstances. For instance, by law all children in the bilingual Belgian capital receive instruction in the second national language, French or Dutch, from the age of 7 onwards, yet the majority of French speakers fail to achieve significant levels of proficiency in Dutch, whereas the majority of Dutch speakers become bilingual. This cannot be properly accounted for by simplistic attitudinal and motivational arguments, since both communities tend to share similar more or less negative or indifferent perceptions of each other, similar language loyalty and a high degree of congruence; however, they differ in terms of enclosure, level of adaptation and size, which probably affect *perceived* social distance and modify the overall patterns of social interaction.

Thus the model provides a frame of reference, based on sociological and psychological factors, which combined help to account for individual variation in analysing the background to bilingual achievement, successful or otherwise. This leads us into the next issue, which is the problem of bilingual schooling, since an awareness of the above factors to some extent explains the contradictory evidence from different types of bilingual education situations. The manifest success of the Canadian immersion programmes pioneered by Lambert & Tucker (1972) and considerably developed over the years (cf. Swain & Lapkin, 1982) is to be attributed to the care with which the different elements that influence the development of bilinguals have been reflected upon. This is not to say that no problems have been encountered, but when they have become apparent they have been squarely faced and appraised, leading to interesting implications for theory and practice. Although the children in immersion programmes are from monoglot English backgrounds, in a predominantly English environment where the second language, French, is a minority language, there is no apparent prevalence of anomie, linguistic or educational retardation arising from the bilingual context of education. It is the seriousness of the longitudinal research that has been built up over the years around the immersion programmes that is leading to the breakdown of many popularly held misconceptions about bilingualism. Although based on a different model, Dodson's work in Wales (1981) is bringing out similar conclusions.

One of the problems promoters of early bilingualism have to consider is the question of the ideal time for introducing a second language. Cases have already been quoted in preceding chapters of bilingualism beginning in the home at the onset of language learning (cf. Ronjat, Leopold, Rūķe-Draviņa), where the parents involved have carefully monitored their children's linguistic development. In these cases the home environment consisted of native-speakers from different language backgrounds who supplied the linguistic input, but a recent interesting study by Saunders (1982) relates the introduction of early bilingualism in a monoglot environment (in Australia) where neither of the parents was a native speaker of the second language. Saunders, a linguist by profession, successfully used German with his sons, even though it was not the native language of either parent, and even though the mother did not use German.

Parents and educators from non-bilingual backgrounds are sometimes worried about the conflicting evidence on the desirability of introducing a second language early in life. On the one hand there are arguments that indicate that the earlier bilingualism is introduced the more successful it will be, while others insist on the stabilization of the primary language before undertaking education in another. To test these two sides of the question Canadian experience has led to the development of different types of immersion programmes. In *early total immersion* children from monoglot English backgrounds are taught entirely in French from the very first day in school and English language instruction is introduced for approximately an hour a day from the second and third years onwards. With each successive year a larger proportion of the curriculum is taught in English until an almost equal balance is reached between the time allocated to each language. Initially the children are allowed to communicate in English with each other, though they hear nothing but French from their native-speaker bilingual teachers, while gradually they are encouraged to communicate more and more in French (Swain, 1980: 21). In *late immersion* the totality of instruction in French is postponed to about the age of 12 and is carried out for two years, followed by a period when part of the programme is continued in French, the rest in English. There are other variants of immersion education which will not be gone into here (see Swain, 1980).

The opportunity these different types of programmes have given for comparing the nature of bilingual development has led to a re-appraisal of the assumption that young children acquire a language more quickly and easily than adolescents or adults (cf. pp. 32–35). From the educative point of view, as opposed to the purely linguistic one of bilingual development discussed in Chapter 4, arguments in favour of or against instruction through the medium of a second, weaker language are still in the debating stage, depending on the type of population being provided for. Swain (1981b), in a comparison of results obtained from early and late immersion programmes, noted that the type of linguistic interaction conducted by speakers in the second language determined the rate of learning. From this investigation it appears that young children in bilingual education readily achieve basic interpersonal communicative skills (BICS) with a good accent in the second language, but that the children who started the second language later were rapidly able to achieve a comparable level of structural and lexical proficiency, thanks to their capacity to cope readily with the cognitive and academic aspects of language proficiency (CALP). Lebrun (1981) points out that the late bilingual can often perform with comparable proficiency to an early bilingual, though he adds that fatigue and stress are more likely to affect the quality of the late bilingual's production in his second language than is the case with the early bilingual.

Some arguments in favour of postponing the onset of bilingualism are based on the assumption that there is a likelihood of retardation in the primary language if schooling in a secondary language starts too early. Again this has been disproved by the early immersion programmes where careful longitudinal evaluation has shown that although there is some lag in development for a while, with time deficiencies are made good and performance in the primary language even compares favourably with that of children who have undergone monoglot education (Barik & Swain, 1975). For example, although children in early total immersion lag behind their monoglot peers in English reading skills at the end of the first year, by the end of the second year, when English has been introduced for one hour a day, they have caught up. The same children, by the end of the second year, are not comparable to peer-group monoglot French children in French but are far in advance of other English speakers who receive daily instruction in French-as-a-second-language. Thus the worries some parents express about the linguistic development of their children in the early phases of bilingualism seem to have some foundation but should also be dispelled as bilingual development proceeds. It should not be forgotten, however, that the results reported here are partly determined by the careful thought that has gone into the design of the particular bilingual education programmes and are not the consequence of chance or inadequately monitored bilingual development.

Arguments in favour of introducing early bilingualism on the assumption that the longer the exposure to two languages the better the results have also been disproved by certain of the Canadian studies. Swain (1981b) has argued that for those linguistic abilities connected with cognitive and academic linguistic proficiency (CALP) more instruction in a second language is not necessarily commensurate with higher levels of ability. In fact, it seems that the counter-intuitive opposite seems to be true, in that *less* instruction in the second language can possibly lead to *higher* levels of proficiency in those particular linguistic skills generally promoted in the school setting, such as reading comprehension and abstract reasoning. Indeed, Swain argues that in certain cases too early a shift in language usage may deny some pupils the possibility of normal cognitive and academic development and even impede the possibility of becoming bilingual.

The apparently contradictory arguments outlined above do not seem to solve the problem of deciding when the onset of bilingualism should take place and would tend to suggest that the danger of linguistic handicaps is far too evident. However, the Canadian results are not the effect of chance and do not cancel each other out. Our earlier discussion of some basic prerequisites for the avoidance of anomie point to the significance of parental support for and understanding of what is going on in the school, amongst other factors. It should be noted that the different types of Canadian immersion programmes are initiated at parental request; hence, parents favourable to the idea of early total immersion are inclined to play their necessary supportive role in this type of bilingual education, while those who are perhaps more apprehensive about the effects of a sudden home-school language switch at the age of 5 presumably select the other forms of immersion programme, early partial (i.e. where the two languages are used in equal proportions throughout elementary schooling) or late. Another point that this element of parental involvement brings with it is that there is less likelihood of cultural and linguistic clashes being exacerbated through lack of understanding. Moreover, since the teachers in these programmes are themselves bilingual and bicultural, even though they work in their dominant language, they are not likely to be the source of cross-cultural conflicts. Finally, an examination of the literature on immersion programmes (Swain, 1981b; Szamosi, Swain & Lapkin, 1979; Barik & Swain, 1978; Swain, 1976) shows to what extent the linguistic expectations are realistically adjusted to take the nature and amount of input into account, as well as the circumstances surrounding the bilingual programme, and that ability is not necessarily measured *exclusively* in terms of monoglot reference norms. For example, even though children who have undergone immersion programmes far outpace their peers from schools providing a second language in a traditional programme their knowledge of French is not nativelike. Frequent errors of gender are prevalent, periphrastic verb forms tend to replace synthetic future and past tense forms, and there are lexical gaps (Harley & Swain, 1977). On the other hand, knowledge of English matches that of monoglot peer groups after an initial lag.

One of the major problems in the evaluation of attainment in bilingual education programmes is connected with the nature of the tests and measurements used. We have often stressed the care with which monoglot reference norms should be used in talking about different aspects of bilingualism in this book. Although it is useful, even vital, to look at monoglot comparisons for evaluative purposes, two points should be borne in mind: a) the evaluative tools selected or designed should take *all* the variables into account which are likely to influence performance, and b) the results should be interpreted in the light of the specific circumstances which distinguish the groups under comparison. Although the first point is often adhered to in more recent evaluations of bilingual success, the second is still often neglected so that results are taken at face value. Shuy (1981) gives a simple illustration of this factor in a hypothetical spelling task:

> "In a right-wrong world, shades of grey are usually ignored, or worse yet, labelled as wrong. A child who spells the word *basement b-a-s-e-m-i-n-t* is a great deal closer to being right than the child who spells it *b-s-l-t-f-r-m*. His single error, in fact, may evidence the presence of a useful tool in spelling, a good ear for sound, especially since a great many Americans (mostly in the South), say the word as though it were spelled basemint."

To underline the significance of knowing how to interpret comparative scores in the measurement of developing bilinguality Shuy insists on the principles behind the idea of the sociolinguistic continuum, also referred to by Brent-Palmer (1979: 149–62) in her important critique of the role of tests in the semilingualism debate. Since most language learners are at some stage on a continuum of language acquisition, teacher expectations must be calibrated to such a continuum and not locked into an expectation of native-like perfection. Brent-Palmer (1979: 163) suggests that in assessing bilingual ability standardized tests should be viewed as a type of social activity which must be submitted to a contrastive socio/ethnolinguistic analysis for relevant interpretation. In this way one can obtain a "more-or-less" approach to bilingual ability instead of a "right or wrong" approach, which is more in line with the varying degrees of bilingual competence we have been discussing throughout this book. Schumann's (forthcoming) discussion of the type of research used to correlate with different aspects of his model of social and psychological distance underlines this point.

That unsatisfactory educational progress does arise in cases of early bilingualism with certain minority populations indicates that the Canadian model discussed earlier may not solve all bilingual education problems.

Indeed the repeated warnings provided by Skutnabb-Kangas (1984), Cummins (1981), Dolson (1985) and others (see the volume edited by Rivera, 1984, on language proficiency and academic achievement) on the inappropriateness of immersion-type education for language minority children from low-status backgrounds should not be lost sight of. The fact that many such children have been immersed in the language of the majority in the classroom has often led to subtractive bilingualism and inadequate progress in the second language for successful education.

The global environment has to be taken into account in assessing the effects of dual language education for young children, particularly the nature of pre-school parent-child interaction in the homes of minority language groups (Swain, 1981a), the social status of the recipient of the education, and the psychological variables that determine attitudes and motivation. It appears that social factors seem to be primary in determining achievement and these should be very carefully appraised before going into the purely linguistic and theoretical aspects of the question (Brent-Palmer, 1971: 141). Indeed, it appears that far too often an inadequate unravelling of the sociological from the linguistic aspects of bilingual education has led to confused and emotionally charged attacks on bilingualism in general.

It is clear that minority language groups with immigrant status and low economic well-being may well require different handling from stable, middle-class children of the type present in so many of the successfully documented bilingual schools. Brent-Palmer (1979: 141) suggests that semilingualism observed as a consequence of inadequate bilingual provision can be explained by both socio-economic status and power relationships between language groups, together with the nature of social interaction between the groups.

What the Canadian research on bilingual education has succeeded in doing is to help dispel many of the misconceptions widely held about the effects of bilingualism. McLaughlin (1978: 197-206) neatly summarizes these misconceptions and shows that there are no simple black versus white positions with reference to a number of propositions, including the following:

—The young child acquires a language more quickly and more easily than an adult because the child is biologically programmed to acquire languages, whereas the adult is not (McLaughlin, 1978: 197). Although in this book we have pointed to the apparent advantages of early versus late bilingualism, nevertheless doubts have been raised as to the explanation for any differences between the two.

Impressionistically it appears that young children learn two languages with amazing speed and efficiency, but it is difficult to prove whether this is due to cerebral plasticity or to the greater ease with which children make social contacts, leading to less inhibition, greater motivation and probably greater opportunity for use of language. It is precisely these arguments that Titone (1972: 161–65) uses in favour of promoting early bilingualism.

—The younger the child, the more he is skilled in acquiring a second language (McLaughlin, 1978: 199). Controlled experimentation has tended to prove that this is not necessarily true for all aspects of language learning. Although young children are apparently more readily able to acquire native-like phonology in two languages, on other aspects, e.g. structural complexity or lexical variety, older learners seem to progress more rapidly. This advantage to the older learner should not come as any surprise, since it fits in with what can be expected from more developed cognitive maturity. It is the often flawless accent of the young bilingual that makes so many observers neglect other aspects of his speech in a comparison with the older bilingual.

—Interference between first and second languages is an inevitable and ubiquitous part of second-language acquisition (McLaughlin, 1978: 202). Our discussion of the nature of interference in Chapter 3 has shown with what care over-hasty assumptions about this phenomenon should be made. The analysis of certain theoretical considerations in

Chapter 4 has also tried to show how what may appear to be an interference feature is not necessarily one, and may be accounted for by normal language acquisition or usage strategies.

—There is a single method of second-language instruction that is more effective with all children (McLaughlin, 1978: 203). The discussion in this chapter of different types of bilingual education programmes should clearly dispel this myth.

—The experience of early bilingualism positively (or negatively) affects the child's language development, cognitive functioning and/or intellectual development (McLaughlin, 1978: 205). On this point it is clear that the arguments can go both ways, depending on specific circumstances.

These points and others not directly related to the present discussion have been taken up again by McLaughlin in his 1984 (215–25) book on pre-school childhood second-language acquisition.

Several investigators have attempted to look very closely into what accounts for successful early bilingualism in some cases where this does not occur in others. Dodson (1981) arrives at the conclusion that the infusion of an additional language into the school at an early age has a *neutral* effect on children's development and attainment provided that a properly organized bilingual education programme is worked out and that any tests used take into account all relevant factors. His experiments with the use of Welsh and English as instructional media in Wales have been reduplicated with other languages in Japan and Sri Lanka and have confirmed his findings. To account for these successes Dodson insists on the significance of proper sequencing in the use of the two languages involved and in this differs from the type of bilingual education provided in immersion programmes where there is a fairly radical shift from home to school language. In spite of a difference in strategy, however, there seems to be a certain overlap of opinion of a theoretical nature between the thinking behind the Canadian programmes and that used in Dodson's bilingual method.

Dodson accounts for the results he achieves by making a distinction between *medium-orientated communication,* where the focus is on language, and *message-orientated communication*, where the focus is on the meaning or content of the messages, i.e. things other than language or the language-learning process. For the young speaker learning to operate in two languages the introduction of the second language may well begin with medium-orientated communication. Very quickly, however, he will find himself unable to satisfy his real needs without message-orientated communication where language has become a tool or vehicle. Dodson insists that language here is not an end in itself and that it is only in the proper phasing of these two levels for any activity that true communicative competence can flourish.

The idea that linguistic abilities acquired in one language can be put to use when a second language is introduced in schooling has been looked into by Cummins (1979), who has also tried to unravel why certain types of bilingual education for particular populations are more successful than others for different populations. Cummins (1980) was perturbed by these different findings, where home-school language switching seemed to have no detrimental effects for most middle-class children from a majority language background, whereas with many children from minority language backgrounds and less favoured socio-economic status similar circumstances often led to poor academic achievement and an inadequate command of both first and second languages. Indeed, it seems that for this latter category the home-school language switch did not represent an immersion programme but a *submersion programme* leading to subtractive bilingualism and other attendant difficulties.

Immersion programmes are suitable for a majority group wishing to become bilingual, where the mother tongue has a high status and is not threatened, where there is high motivation since the programme is optional, and where all involved in the bilingual process are striving in the same direction. On the other hand, the home-school language switch leading to a submersion programme is found when the recipients represent a linguistic minority with a low status mother-tongue, where motivation is low since there is no element of choice involved, where the second language may represent a threat to the first and where the parents, often of low socio-economic status, are not involved in their children's bilingual development (Skutnabb-Kangas, 1980). In immersion programmes the teachers are bilingual even though they use only one language, and they are positive to both cultures in the environment, while in submersion programmes the teachers are usually unilinguals and are often unwittingly hostile to the bilingual element in the child's make-up.

To account for the differentiated success patterns in both sets of circumstances Cummins examined the interaction between sociocultural, linguistic and school curriculum factors in explaining the linguistic and academic development of bilingual children. As Swain (1978a) has indicated, an important feature of the immersion programmes is that the children are consistently encouraged for their success in making progress in the second language, even when this success may be relative, whereas in submersion programmes of the type so often undergone by immigrant children they are too often made aware of their failure to match up to monoglot expectations. Another important factor is that in the successful immersion programmes all the children form a homogeneous group with regard to background and knowledge of the "new" language on entry, whereas in submersion programmes the level of attainment in the second language may vary considerably at the outset so that even within the minority group there are noticeable differences amongst the children which may affect further linguistic development.

Cummins (1979) proposed the *threshold level hypothesis* as one factor which accounts for the difference in attainment between pupils in the two sets of circumstances. This hypothesis posits that there is a minimum level of linguistic proficiency which a child must attain in order to avoid cognitive deficits. If a child has a low threshold of competence in his first language it is highly likely that a similar low level will be present in the second, thereby not allowing for the positive aspects of bilingualism to develop. Such a child, when confronted with the more academic aspects of schooling which are highly dependent on literacy skills, will very soon suffer from handicaps in attempting to assimilate the academic aspects of the curriculum. Children with a high threshold level of linguistic competence in the first language, on the other hand, are in a position to attain a sufficiently high threshold level in the second language which allows them to cope well with the more academic aspects of the curriculum and not to suffer any cognitive handicaps. Thus for minority children it would seem important to ensure that there is sufficient maintenance and support for the minority first language in order to reach the requisite level of bilingual competence to make sufficient progress in academic tasks. With majority language children entering a bilingual programme this support for the first language is likely to be automatically present, partly through the influence of the outside environment, so that a sufficiently high threshold level is more easily attained for the development of bilingual competence.

The second hypothesis put forward by Cummins (1979) is the *developmental interdependence hypothesis*, which assumes that if the outside environment provides sufficient stimulus for maintenance of the first language then intensive exposure to a second language in the school leads to rapid bilingual development with no detrimental effects on the first language. In cases where the first language is not sufficiently developed outside the school, for whatever reason, then high exposure to a second language in the school will hamper the continued development of the first language and will not necessarily help stimulate successful bilingualism. The network of European Schools designed to cater for the children of European Community civil servants from different national backgrounds has been intuitively organized to take the threshold and interdependence hypotheses into account. In these schools, subdivided into linguistic groupings, children from a wide range of socio-economic backgrounds, ranging from the offspring of porters to those of director-generals, find themselves in a country where their home language may not be spoken. All are required to become bilingual to a certain extent and receive fairly intensive instruction in a second language, sequenced according to a programme peculiar to these schools. Since the outside environment may not provide support for the primary language the majority of basic instruction in the primary school is given in this language in the appropriate linguistic group, though instruction of a second language, known as the vehicular language, is begun at the age of 7+ for roughly one hour a day (in the European School of Brussels the choice of vehicular second languages is between French, English and German). In the secondary school content matter is also taught through the medium of the vehicular language and towards the end of the programme pupils are expected to be able to take certain examinations in the vehicular language on a par with the native speakers of that language in the appropriate section of the school (Baetens Beardsmore, 1980a; 1979a). In an interesting comparison of levels of proficiency in the second language, French, between children in early total immersion in Canada and pupils from the multilingual background of a European School in Belgium highly similar results were noted, though the former had received approximately 4,500 contact hours with French whereas the latter had received approximately 1,300 contact hours (Baetens Beardsmore & Swain, 1985). These results represent a direct comparison between a majority group (English Canadians in an English out-of-school environment) receiving instruction through the medium of a second language and minority group pupils (linguistic, though not socio-economic) receiving language maintenance instruction in L1 with partial instruction through the medium of the language of the out-of-school majority. The picture that emerges from this comparison is that different strategies, determined by a variety of factors, can lead minority and majority group pupils to comparable levels of bilingual proficiency without any detriment to academic achievement, whereas in circumstances where no specific educational strategies have been developed to distinguish between majority and minority language background pupils, bilingual proficiency together with academic achievement have often failed to result.

It is interesting to note that, as with the immersion programmes in Canada, the European network of schools was built up at the specific request of parents and that the schools function with close parental involvement, two apparently significant factors not always present in less successful bilingual education. Moreover, the parents who initiated the European network of schools were particularly worried about the development of literacy skills in their children, an element underlined as significant in the developmental interdependence hypothesis.

In a further attempt to explain the rationale for different pedagogic strategies according to the majority or minority language status of children Cummins (1981) modified the BICS versus CALP argumentation into a more complex theoretical framework relating the development of proficiency in L1 to that in L2. This theory points out that the sociocultural determinants of minority language children's school failure are probably more fundamental than linguistic factors. In it Cummins distinguishes between those aspects of language proficiency involved in the development of literacy skills, which are central to scholastic progress, and other aspects of language proficiency.

After a careful appraisal of studies dealing with the schooling of immigrant children, he comes to the conclusion that those in authority often misjudge a child's proficiency in the second language by assuming that the lower threshold level, referred to earlier, indicated sufficient competence in a second language to successfully handle academic subjects. Yet Cummins noted that age-appropriate communicative skills (i.e. the lower threshold level) generally developed amongst immigrant children after two years of residence in the new linguistic environment, whereas age-appropriate academic skills in the second language (i.e. the higher threshold level) generally took between five to seven years of residence to develop. He explains this difference by looking into what constitutes language proficiency in school contexts and distinguishes, on the one hand, between "context-embedded communication" and "context-reduced communication", and on the other between "cognitively undemanding linguistic activity" and "cognitively demanding linguistic activity", to be conceptualized in the form of a quadrant as illustrated in Figure 3.

In context-embedded communication participants can negotiate meaning and rely on situational and paralinguistic cues to support interaction, while in context-reduced communication the support tends to be primarily linguistic in nature, from the text itself, with little or no non-linguistic help. Cummins suggested that learning syntax and phonology in basic human interaction is reflected in quadrant A of the model, though the greater the cognitive effort the more easily the tasks would be reflected in quadrant D as they become more cognitively demanding and rely less on contextual support from the real world, the model thereby reflecting different points along a vertical and a horizontal continuum.

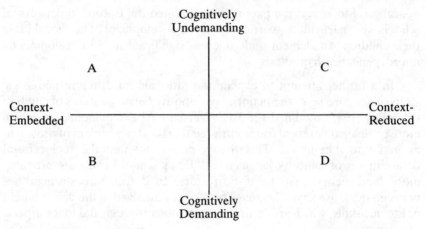

(From, Cummins, 1981: 12).

FIGURE 3 *Range of Contextual Support and Degree of Cognitive Involvement in Communicative Activities*

From the evidence of unsuccessful academic achievement in bilingual education programmes it appears that the gap between context-embedded and context-reduced communication has been underestimated in the second language, and that the latter can only be successfully built up on the former. In instruction through the medium of L1 this is a gradual and lengthy process, whereas with children receiving instruction in L2 there is often a sudden requirement to handle cognitively-demanding, context-reduced material once the lower threshold level of apparent fluency has been achieved, leading to lack of scholastic progress. Cummins believes that in order to promote academic achievement one should build up on a context-embedded language proficiency and that this will lead to a common underlying proficiency which will be interdependent across languages, thereby facilitating context-reduced activities in both L1 and L2 via transfer. This belief is based on an impressive series of studies providing evidence from results of bilingual education programmes, studies relating age on arrival and immigrant pupils' L2 acquisition, studies relating bilingual language usage in the home to academic achievement, studies on the relationship between L1 and L2 proficiency, and experimental studies on bilingual information processing.

Hence the argumentation put forward by Cummins explains the requirement for different strategies in educating majority children bilingually via classical immersion programmes or minority children via bilingual programmes that maintain the home language while gradually promoting the use of the second language over an ever-widening range of the curriculum.

To sum up the often different outcomes in bilingual education for majority and minority children Cummins (1979: 236) states:

> "In immersion programmes for majority language children the children's L1 is developed in such a way that it is unaffected by intensive exposure to L2. Consequently, as children develop high levels of L2 skills, their fluent access to two languages can give rise to enhancement of both L2 skills and other aspects of cognitive functioning.
>
> The findings in many minority language situations appear to be just the opposite... in that initial instruction in L1 has been found to lead to better results than immersion or submersion in L2. The developmental interdependence hypothesis would suggest that the relatively greater success of vernacular education in minority language situations is due, partly at least, to the fact that certain aspects of the child's linguistic knowledge may not be fully developed on entry to school."

From the arguments that have been put forward in this chapter it can be seen how a host of variables needs to be taken into account in any appraisal of the bilingual development of children. These include the type of linguistic knowledge the child brings to school, the relative status of the two languages involved, the socio-economic background of the parents, the nature of the bilingual programme being applied, the sequencing of instruction, the make-up of the group undergoing bilingual instruction and particularly its homogeneity, the expectancies and attitudes of the teachers, the extent of parental involvement and understanding of the bilingual process, the attitudes and motivations of the learners, the pressures of the outside environment in the development of anomie; this list is by no means exhaustive. It should have become apparent throughout the discussion that the problems confronting the bilingual speaker, if they arise, are primarily societally determined, but that these are not an inevitable consequence of being bilingual.

In spite of the title of this final chapter it should be clear from what has been developed that although bilinguals experience problems this does not mean to say that bilingualism itself should be automatically considered as full of problems. There is a far too prevalent tendency, particularly amongst monoglots, to consider bilingualism as a problem and unilingualism as the norm, when in fact for large portions of the world's population the opposite is probably true. Where certain difficulties have become apparent they are often due to the fact that the language element in question has made a problem case more evident. And in many situations, particularly with migrant populations, there is no choice between bilingualism and unilingualism anyway, so that it would be futile to use the fact of dual language usage as a scapegoat. It is our task to draw attention to the care with which bilingual development has to be nurtured and to point out that any pedagogic, psychological or linguistic development will be faced with risks if left to chance or well-intentioned but ill-informed improvisation. There are cases where the presence of two languages has led to unhappy consequences for the individual and there are many others where it has led to immense personal satisfaction and enrichment. The same is true for circumstances where only one language is involved. It is telling that in our interviews of 13 year-old pupils in the multilingual European School of Brussels not one would have preferred to have received education in a unilingual establishment, irrespective of the general school grades on which interviewees had been selected and reflecting a wide range of scholastic and linguistic ability. What is important for the student of bilingualism is to increase our knowledge of what is involved in being bilingual so that when problem cases arise the total picture can be seen in proper perspective.

Summary

Three major areas of discussion have been selected as clarifying questions of significance in understanding the development of bilingualism in the individual, all interconnected. The first, anomie, has shown how two sets of linguistic and cultural stimuli in the environment may cause confusion of identity and disorientation if presented as conflicting, though this confusion can be overcome. The second point, based on the acculturation model, highlights the social and psychological determinants of potential bilingual development, indicating why this is successful for some and less so for others. It specifically underlines how social circumstances link with educational strategies in the provision of adequate bilingual education. The third problem area leads on from the first two by reviewing a restricted number of bilingual educational practices which might appear contradictory if not carefully appraised. These strategies have been accounted for by the threshold level hypothesis and the developmental interdependence hypothesis as predictors of the success or failure of different bilingual education programmes. A certain number of widely held misconceptions about bilingualism have been rapidly reviewed in the light of research that still requires further development.

Bibliography

The titles preceded by an asterisk have been referred to in the text.

*ABDULLAH, P. N. A. 1979, Some Observations on Code-switching Among Malay-
–English Bilinguals, Paper presented at the Fourteenth Regional Seminar,
Seameo Regional Language Centre, Singapore, 16-21 April.

*ADLER, K. 1977, *Collective and Individual Bilingualism: A Socio-linguistic Study*.
Hamburg: Helmut Buske, Verlag.

ALATIS, J. E. (ed.) 1970, *Bilingualism and Language Contact: Anthropological,
Linguistic, Psychological and Sociological Aspects*, Washington, Monograph
Series on Languages and Linguistics, 23, Georgetown Univ. Press.

——1978, *International Dimensions of Bilingual Education*. Washington: Georgetown Univ. Press.

——(ed.) 1980, *Current Issues in Bilingual Education*. Washington: Georgetown
Univ. Press.

ALATIS, J. E. & TWADDELL, J. (eds) 1976, *English as a Second Language in
Bilingual Education*. Selected TESOL Papers, Washington, Tesol.

*ALBERT, M. L. & OBLER, L. K. 1978, *The Bilingual Brain*. New York: Academic
Press.

ALEXANDRE, P. 1971, Multilingualism. In T. A. SEBEOK (ed.), *Current Trends in
Linguistics,* vol. 7. (Linguistics in Sub-Saharan Africa). The Hague: Mouton.
654–63.

*AMMON, U. & SIMON, G. 1975, *Neue Aspekte der Sociolinguistik*. Mannheim &
Basel: Beltz Verlag.

*ANDERSEN, R. 1983, Transfer to Somewhere. In S. GASS & L. SELINKER (eds),
Language Transfer in Language Learning. Rowley: Newbury House, 177–201.

ANDERSON, N. (ed.) 1969, *Studies in Multilingualism*. Leiden: Brill.

*ANDERSSON, T. & BOYER, M. (eds) 1970, *Bilingual Schooling in the United States*.
Austin: Southwest Educational Development Lab., 2 vols.

*ANON., 1978, *Minorités linguistiques et interventions: essai de typologie/Linguistic
Minorities and Interventions: Towards a Typology*. Quebec: Les Presses de
l'Université Laval.

*ARSENIAN, S. 1937, *Bilingualism and Mental Development: A Study of the Intel-
ligence and the Social Background of Bilingual Children in New York*. New
York: Teacher's College, Columbia University.

*ASHER, J. & GARCIA, G. 1969/1982, The Optimal Age to Learn a Foreign
Language. In S. KRASHEN, R. SCARCELLA & M. LONG (eds), *Child-Adult
Differences in Second Language Acquisition*. Rowley: Newbury House, 3–12.

ATTINASI, J., PEDRAZA, P., POPLACK, S. & POUSADA, A. 1982, *Intergenerational
Perspective on Bilingualism: From Community to Classroom*. New York: Center
for Puerto Rican Studies, Hunter College, City University of New York.

*AUCAMP, A. T. 1926, *Bilingual Education and Nationalism, with Special Reference
to South Africa*. Pretoria.

BADIA-MARGARIT, A. M. 1962, Some Aspects of Bilingualism Among Cultured People in Catalonia. In LUNT (ed.), *Proceedings of the IXth International Congress of Linguists*. Cambridge, Mass. 366–77.

BAETENS BEARDSMORE, H. 1967, Quelques considérations sur le dictionnaire du dialecte bruxellois de M. Louis Quiévreux, *Reveue des Langues Vivantes*, XXXIII, 309–32.

*——1970, The Problem of Question Tags, *English Language Teaching* XXXV, 14–19.

——1971a, Aspects of Plurilingualism Amongst Lower Level Social Groups. In, L. DE COSTER *et al.*, *Aspects Sociologiques de Plurilinguisme*, Bruxelles-Paris. Aimav-Didier. 76–91.

*——1971b, The Problem of Gender in a Contact Situation, *Lingua*, 27/28, 1–21.

*——1971c, *Le français régional de Bruxelles*. Bruxelles: Presses Universitaires de Bruxelles.

*——1974a, Development of the Compound Coordinate Distinction in Bilingualism, *Lingua*, 33/2, 123–27.

——1974b, Multilingual Contacts in Brussels, *Rapport d'Activités de l'Institut de Phonétique*. Bruxelles, U.L.B., 8/1-2, 13-54.

——1977a, Anomie in Bicultural Education. In M. DE GREVE & E. ROSSEEL (eds), *Problèmes linguistiques des enfants de travailleurs migrants*. Bruxelles: Aimav-Didier. 9–23.

——1977b, An Investigation into Bilingual Education for Children from Favoured Socio-Economic Groups. In M. DE GREVE & E. ROSSEEL (eds), *Problèmes linguistiques des enfants de travailleurs migrants*. Bruxelles: Aimav-Didier. 25–45.

*——1977c, The Tolerance Level of Bilingually Marked Linguistic Cues, *Rapport d'Activités de l'Institut de Phonétique*, U.L.B. 11/12, 19–35.

*——1978a, Polyglot Literature and Linguistic Fiction, *International Journal of the Sociology of Language* 15, 91–102.

——1978b, De onbekende elementen in linguistisch onderzoek over Brussel. In E. WITTE, (ed.), *Taal en Sociale Integratie*. Brussel: Centrum Voor Interdisciplinair Onderzoek over de Brusselse Taaltoestanden. 21–31.

——1978c, L'enseignement multilingue, facteur d'harmonie psycho-sociologique, *Equivalences*, 8, 2–3, 123-31.

*——1979a, European Schools, *Mødet mellem sprogene i det dansk-tyske graensomrade*. Aabenraa: Institut for Graensregionsforskning, 38–49.

——1979b, Bilingual Education for Highly Mobile Children, *Language Planning and Language Problems*, 3,3 (9), 138–55.

*——1979c, Les contacts des langues à Bruxelles. In A. VALDMAN (ed.), *Le français*. Paris: Champion, 223—44.

*——1979d, The Recognition and Tolerance Level of Bilingual Speech, *Working Papers in Bilingualism*, 19, 115-28.

*——1980a, Bilingual Education in International Schools, European Schools and Experimental Schools: A Comparative Analysis. In LIM KIAT BOEY (ed.), *Bilingual Education*. Singapore: Singapore University Press, 3–19.

——1980b, Bilingualism in Belgium, *Journal of Multilingual & Multicultural Development*, 1, 145–54.

——1981a, De overkoepelende taalhypothese toegepast op Brussel. In E. WITTE (ed.), *Taal en Sociale Integratie*, 3. Brussel: Vrije Universiteit Brussel.

——(ed.) 1981b, *Elements of Bilingual Theory*. Brussel: Vrije Universiteit Brussel.

*——1983a, Interpreting the Scientific Literature on Bilingualism. In P. NELDE (ed.), *Mehrsprachigkeit-Multilingualism*. Bonn: Dümmler, 19–34.

*——1983b, Substratum, Adstratum and Residual Bilingualism in Brussels, *Journal of Multilingual and Multicultural Development*, 4, 1, 1–14.

BAETENS BEARDSMORE, H. & LEE, E. J. 1977, On Bilingual Competence, *Lingue e Civiltà*, 1-2, 8–10.

*BAETENS BEARDSMORE, H. & SWAIN, M. 1985, Designing Bilingual Education: Aspects of Immersion and 'European School' Models, *Journal of Multilingual and Multicultural Development* 6, 1, 1-15.

BAL, W. 1954, Francisation d'un dialecte, *Les dialectes belgo-romans*, XI, 5–19.

*BALKAN, L. 1970, *Les effets du bilinguisme franco—anglais sur les aptitudes intellectuelles*. Bruxelles: Aimav.

*BARIK, H. C. & SWAIN, M. 1975, Three—year Evaluation of a Large Scale Early Grade French Immersion Program: The Ottawa Study, *Language Learning*, 25/1, 1–30.

*——1978, Evaluation of a French Immersion Program: The Ottawa Study Through Grade Five, *Canadian Journal of Behavioural Science*, 10, 3.

BARTLY, D. E. 1971, *Soviet Approaches to Bilingual Education*. Philadelphia Centre for Curriculum Development.

*BEEBE, L. 1980, Sociolinguistic Variation and Style Shifting in Second Language Acquisition, *Language Learning*, 30, 2, 433–48.

*BENTAHILA, A. 1983. *Language Attitudes Among Arabic-French Bilinguals in Morocco*. Clevedon: Multilingual Matters.

BEN-ZEEV, S. 1977a, Mechanisms by Which Childhood Bilingualism Affects Understanding of Language and Cognitive Structures. In P. A. HORNBY (ed.), *Bilingualism: Psychological, Social and Educational Implications*. New York: Academic Press, 29–55.

——1977b, The Effect of Bilingualism in Children from Spanish-English Low Economic Neighbourhoods on Cognitive Development and Cognitive Strategy, *Working Papers in Bilingualism*, 14, 83-122.

*BERMAN, A. 1979, The Re-emergence of a Bilingual: A Case Study of a Hebrew-English Speaking Child, *Working Papers in Bilingualism*, 19, 157-79.

*BERNSTEIN, B. 1971, 1974, *Class, Codes and Control*. London: Routledge & Kegan Paul, 2 vols.

BERNY, T. & COOPER, R. 1969, Semantic Independence & Degree of Bilingualism, *The Modern Language Journal*, LIII, 182-85.

*BEZIERS, M. & VAN OVERBEKE, M. 1968, *Le Bilinguisme: essai de définition et guide bibliographique*. Louvain: Cahiers de L'Institut des Langues Vivantes.

*BICKERTON, D. 1971, Cross-level Interference: The Influence of L1 Syllable Structure on L2 Morphological Error. In J. TRIM (ed.), *Applications of Linguistics*. Cambridge: Cambridge University Press, 133–40.

BLANQUAERT, E. 1956, Taallagen en Sociale Lagen, *Tijdschrift voor Sociale Wetenschappen*, 1, 88-97.

*BLOOMFIELD, L. 1935, *Language*. London: Allen & Unwin.

BOELENS, K. 1975, *Ecoles primaires en Frise: un enseignue bilingue aux Pays-Bas*. 's Gravenhage, Ministerie van Onderwijs en Wetsnchappen.

BOILEAU, J. 1946, Le Probléme du bilingualisme et la théorie des substrats, *Revue des Langues Vivantes*, XII, 113–25, 169–93, 213–44.

*BRENT-PALMER, C. 1979, A Sociolinguistic Assessment of the Notion "Immigrant Semilingualism" From a Social Conflict Perspective, *Working Papers in Bilingualism*, 17, 135-80.

*CANALE, M. & SWAIN, M. 1980a, *Approaches to Communicative Competence.* Singapore, Seameo Regional Centre Occasional Papers, No. 14.

——1980b, Theoretical Bases of Communicative Approaches to Second Language Teaching and Testing, *Applied Linguistics*, I, I, 1–47.

*CARDINET, J. & ROUSSON, M. 1965, *Manuel de la batterie d'aptitudes scolaires collectives.* Neuchâtel: Université de Neuchâtel, Institut de Psychologie.

CARNOY, A. 1948, Le bilinguisme des noms de leiux en Belgique, *Onomastica*, 11, 3–8.

*CARROLL, B. 1980, *Testing Communicative Performance.* Oxford: Pergamon Press.

CARROW, SISTER N. A. 1957, Linguistic Functioning of Bilingual and Monolingual Children, *Journal of Speech Disorders*, 22, 371–80.

*CELCE-MURCIA, M. & HAWKINS, B. 1985, Contrastive Analysis, Error Analysis and Interlanguage Analysis. In M. CELCE-MURCIA (ed.), *Beyond Basics: Issues and Research* in TESOL. Rowley: Newbury House.

*CHILD, I. L. 1943, *Italian or American? The Second Generation in Conflict.* New Haven: Yale University Press.

*CHOMSKY, N. 1965, *Aspects of the Theory of Syntax.* Cambridge, Mass.: M.I.T. Press.

CHRISTOPHERSON, P. 1973, *Second-Language Learning.* Harmondsworth: Penguin.

*CHUMBOW, B. S. 1978, The Mother Tongue Interference Hypothesis in a Multilingual Setting. Paper presented at the Vth AILA Congress, Montreal.

*CLOSSET, F. 1963, Le problème du bilinguisme et l'enseignement des langues vivantes, *Revue des Langues Vivantes*, XXIX, 70–75.

*CLYNE, M. G. 1967, *Transference and Triggering: Observations on the Language Assimilation of Postwar German-speaking Migrants in Australia.* The Hague: Nijhoff.

*COHEN, A. D. 1975a, *A Sociolinguistic Approach to Bilingual Education: Experiments in the American Southwest.* Rowley, Mass.: Newbury House.

——1975b, Forgetting a Second Language, *Language Learning*, 25, 127–38.

——1976, The Case for Partial or Total Immersion Education. In A. SIMOES (ed.), *The Bilingual Child.* New York: Academic Press, 65–89.

COOK, V. J. 1969, The Analogy Between First and Second Language Learning, *IRAL*, 7/3, 207-16.

COOPER, R. 1969, Two Contextualised Measures of Degree of Bilingualism, *The Modern Language Review*, LIII, 172–78.

COOPER, R. & GREENFIELD, L. 1969, Language in a Bilingual Community, *The Modern Language Journal*, LIII, 166–72.

COOPER, R., FOWLES, B. & GIVNER, A. 1969, Listening Comprehension in a Bilingual Community, *The Modern Language Journal*, LIII, 235–41.

*CRYSTAL, D. 1980, *A First Dictionary of Linguistics and Phonetics.* London: Deutsch.

CUMMINS, J. 1978, Metalinguistic Development of Children in Bilingual Education Programs: Data from Irish and Canadian Ukrainian-English Programs. In M. PARADIS (ed.), *The Fourth Lacus Forum.* Columbia: Hornbeam Press, 29-40.

*——1979, Linguistic Interdependence and the Educational Development of Bilingual Children. *Review of Educational Research,* 49, 2, 221-51.

*——1980, Psychological Assessment of Immigrant Children: Logic or Intuition, *Journal of Multilingual and Multicultural Development,* 1/2, 97–111.

*——1981, The Role of Primary Language Development in Promoting Educational Success for Language Minority Students, *Schooling and Language Minority Students: A Theoretical Framework.* Los Angeles: Evaluation, Dissemination and Assessment Center, California State University.

——1984a, *Bilingualism and Special Education: Issues in Assessment and Pedagogy.* Clevedon: Multilingual Matters.

——1984b, The Minority Language Child. In S. SHAPSON & V. D'OYLEY (eds), *Bilingual and Multicultural Education: Canadian Perspectives.* Clevedon: Multilingual Matters.

——1984c, Bilingualism and Cognitive Functioning. In S. SHAPSON & V. D'OYLEY (eds), *Bilingual and Multicultural Education: Canadian Perspectives.* Clevedon: Multilingual Matters.

*CUMMINS, J. & SWAIN, M. 1983. Analysis-by-Rhetoric: Reading the Text or the Reader's Own Projections? A Reply to Edelsky *et al.,* *Applied Linguistics,* 4, 1, 23–41.

*D'ANGLEJAN, A. & TUCKER, G. 1973, Sociolinguistic Correlates of Speech Style in Quebec. In R. SHUY & R. FASOLD (eds), *Language Attitudes: Current Trends and Prospects.* Washington: Georgetown University Press. 1–27.

DARNELL, R. 1976, Language Use in Canada, Special Issue of *Papers in Linguistics,* 9/3-4.

*DAVIES, A., CRIPER, C. & HOWATT, A. 1984, *Interlanguage,* Edinburgh: Edinburgh University Press.

DAVINE, M., TUCKER, G. & LAMBERT, W. 1971, The Perception of Phoneme Sequences by Monolingual and Bilingual Schoolchildren, *Canadian Journal of Behavioural Sciences,* 3/1.

DEROY, L. 1958, *L'Emprunt linguistique.* Paris: Les Belles Lettres.

DE ZIEGLER, H. 1954, Bilingualisme et pluralisme culturel en Suisse, *Revue des Langues Vivantes,* 12–20.

*DIEBOLD, A. R. 1961, Incipient Bilingualism, *Language,* XXXVII, 97–112.

*——1962, Code-switching in Greek-English Bilingual Speech, *Monograph Series on Languages and Linguistics.* Georgetown University, 15, 53–62.

*DILLER, K. C. 1970, "Compound" and "Coordinate" Bilingualism: A Conceptual Artefact, *Word,* 26/2, 254–61.

——1972, Bilingualism and the Lexicon, *Studies for Einar Haugen.* The Hague: Mouton, 145–50.

DIMITRIJVIC, N. R. 1965, A Bilingual Child, *English Language Teaching,* XX, 23–29.

DI PIETRO, R. J. 1970, The Discovery of Universals in Multilingualism, *Georgetown University Monograph Series on Languages and Linguistics,* 13–25.

——1976, *Language Structures in Contrast.* Rowley: Newbury House.

——1977, Code-switching as a Verbal Strategy among Bilinguals. In F. R. ECKMAN (ed.), *Current Themes in Linguistics.* Washington: Hemisphere. 3–13.

*DITTMAR, N. 1976, *Sociolinguistics.* London: Edward Arnold.

DODSON, C. J. 1967, *Language Teaching and the Bilingual Method.* London: Pitman.

*——1981, A Reappraisal of Bilingual Development and Education: Some Theor-

etical and Practical Considerations. In H. BAETENS BEARDSMORE (ed.), *Elements of Bilingual Theory*. Brussel: Vrije Universiteit Brussel.

*DOLSON, D. 1985, *An Analysis of the Proposed Application of Immersion Education in the United States Context*. National Clearing House for Bilingual Education.

DOMINGUE, N. 1978, l'Usage bilingue dans le centre de Montréal. In M. PARADIS (ed.), *The Fourth Lacus Forum*. Columbia: Hornbeam Press. 278–85.

*DORIAN, N. 1982, Defining the Speech Community to include its Working Margins. In S. ROMAINE (ed.), *Sociolinguistic Variation in Speech Communities*. London: Edward Arnold, 25–33.

*DORNIC, S. 1978, The Bilingual's Performance: Language Dominance, Stress and Individual Differences. In D. GERVER & H. SINAIKO (eds), *Language Interpretation and Communication*. New York: Plenum Press.

*—— 1979, Information Processing in Bilinguals,: Some Selected Issues, *Psychological Research*, 40, 329–48.

*DOYLE, A. B., CHAMPAGNE, N. & SEGALOWITZ, N. 1977, Some Issues in the Assessment of Early Bilingualism, *Working Papers in Bilingualism*, 14, 21–30.

EDELMAN, M. 1969, The Contextualisation of Schoolchildren's Bilingualism, *The Modern Language Journal*, LIII, 179–82.

*EDELSKY, C., HUDELSON, S., FLORES, B., BARKIN, F., ALTWERGER, B. & JILBERT, K. 1983, Semilingualism and Language Deficit, *Applied Linguistics*, 4, 1, 1–22.

*EKSTRAND, L. H. 1979, *Replacing the Critical Period and Optimum Age Theories of Second Language Acquisition with a Theory of Ontogenetic Development Beyond Puberty*. Lund: Malmö School of Education, No. 69.

*—— 1983, Maintenance or Transition – or Both? A Review of Swedish Ideologies and Empirical Research. In. T. HUSEN (ed.), *Multicultural and Multilingual Education in Immigrant Countries*. Oxford: Permagon, 141–60.

ELWERT, W. T. 1959, *Das zweisprachige Individuum. Ein Selbstzeugnis*. Mainz: Akademie der Wissenschaften und der Literatur.

EMMA, D. 1968, Problèmes du plurilinguisme à l'Ecole Européenne, *Le Langage et l'Homme*.

ERIKSON, J. G. & OMARK, D. R. (eds) 1981, *Communication Assessment of the Bilingual Bicultural Child*. Baltimore: University Park Press.

*ERVIN, S. & OSGOOD, C. 1954, Second Language Learning and Bilingualism, *Journal of Abnormal and Social Psychology*, Suppl. 139–46.

*ERVIN, S. 1961a, Semantic Shift in Bilingualism, *American Journal of Psychology*, LXXIV, 233–41.

—— 1961b, Learning and Recall in Bilinguals, *American Journal of Psychology*, LXXIV, 446–51.

*ERVIN-TRIPP, S. 1964, Language and T.A.T. Content in Bilinguals, *Journal of Abnormal Social Psychology*, 68, 500–507. Reprinted in A. S. DIL (ed.), *Language Acquisition and Communicative Choice*. Stanford: California: Stanford University Press (1973).

—— 1967, An Issei Learns English, *Journal of Social Issues*, XXIII, 78–90.

*—— 1973a, Learning and Recall in Bilinguals. In S. ERVIN-TRIPP *Language Acquisition and Communicative Choice*. Stanford: Stanford University Press, 24–32.

—— 1973b, On Becoming a Bilingual. In S. ERVIN-TRIPP, *Language Acquisition and Communicative Choice*. Stanford: Stanford University Press, 78–91.

*FANTINI, A. E. 1985, *Language Acquisition of a Bilingual Child: A Sociolinguistic*

Perspective. Clevedon: Multilingual Matters.

FEITSMA, A. & VAN OVERBEKE, M. 1971, *Tweetaligheidsproblemen*. Amsterdam: Noord-Hollandsche Uitgevers Maatschappij.

*FELIX, S. 1982, *Psycholinguistische Aspekte des Zwitsprachenerwerbs*. Tübingen: Gunter Narr Verlag.

*FERGUSON, C. 1959, Diglossia, *Word*, 15, 325–40.

—— 1962, Problems of Teaching Languages with Diglossia, *Georgetown University Monograph Series on Language and Linguistics*, No. 15, Washington, 165–72.

FERNANDO, C. 1977, English and Sinhala Bilingualism in Sri Lanka, *Language in Society*, 6, 341–60.

FERTIG, S. & FISHMAN, J. A. 1969, Some Measures of the Interaction between Language Domain and Semantic Dimension in Bilinguals, *The Modern Language Journal*, LIII, 244–49.

*FISHBEIN, M. & AJZENI. 1975, *Belief, Attitude, Intention and Behaviour*. Reading, Mass.: Addison-Wesley.

FISHMAN, J. A. 1965a, Varieties of Ethnicity and Varieties of Language Consciousness, *Georgetown University Monograph Series on Language and Linguistics*, No. 18, 69–79.

*—— 1965b, Who Speaks What Language to Whom and When? The Analysis of Multilingual Settings, *La Linguistique*, 67–88.

—— 1965c, Bilingualism, Intelligence and Language Learning, *The Modern Language Journal*, 49, 227–37.

—— 1966a, *Language Loyalty in the United States*. Mouton: The Hague.

—— 1966b, The Implications of Bilingualism for Language Teaching and Language Learning. In A. VALDMAN (ed.), *Trends in Language Teaching*. New York: McGraw-Hill, 121–32.

—— 1966c, Bilingual Sequences at the Societal Level, *On Teaching English to Speakers of Other Languages*, Series II, 139–44.

*—— 1967, Bilingualism With and Without Diglossia: Diglossia With and Without Bilingualism, *Journal of Social Issues*, 2, 29–38.

*—— 1968, Sociolinguistic Perspectives in the Study of Bilingualism, *Linguistics*, XXXIX, 21–48.

—— 1969, The Measurement and Description of Widespread and Relatively Stable Bilingualism, *The Modern Language Journal*, LIII, 152–56.

—— 1970a, *Taalsociologie*. Ninove-Brussel: Steppe-Labor.

—— (ed.) 1970b, *Readings in the Sociology of Language*. The Hague: Mouton.

—— (ed.) 1971, *Advances in the Sociology of Language*. The Hague: Mouton.

*—— 1972, The Relationship Between Micro- and Macro-Sociolinguistics in the Study of Who Speaks What Language to Whom and When. In J. B. PRIDE & J. HOLMES (eds), *Sociolinguistics*. Harmondsworth, Penguin, 15–32.

*—— 1976, *Bilingual Education: An International Sociological Perspective*. Rowley: Newbury House.

—— (ed.), 1978, *Advances in the Study of Societal Multilingualism*. The Hague: Mouton.

*—— 1980, Bilingualism & Biculturism as Individual & as Societal Phenomena, *Journal of Multilingual & Multicultural Development*, 1, 1, 3–15.

FISHMAN, J. A. & CASIANO, H. 1969, Puerto Ricans in our Press, *The Modern Language Journal*, LIII, 157–62.

*FISHMAN, J. A., COOPER, R. L., MA, R., *et al.*, 1971, *Bilingualism in the Barrio*.

Bloomington, Ind.: Language Science Monographs, Indiana University.

FISHMAN, J. A. & KELLER, G. D. (eds) 1982, *Bilingual Education for Hispanic Students in the United States*. New York: Teacher's College, Columbia University.

*FITOURI, C. 1983, *Bilculturalisme, bilinguisme et éducation*. Paris: Delachaux & Niestlé.

FLINT, E. H. 1976, Language Planning in Relation to the Education of Bidialectals and Bilinguals, *Linguistic Communications: Working Papers of the Linguistic Society of Australia*, 16. Monash University, 99–114.

FLOM, G. T. 1903–1905, The Gender of the English Loan Nouns in Norse Dialects in America, *The Journal of English & Germanic Philology*, V, 1–32.

*FORSTER, J. 1970, *The Poet's Tongues, Multilingualism in Literature*. Cambridge: Cambridge University Press.

FUCHS, A. 1954, Pluralisme culturel et bilinguisme en Alsace, *Revue des langues vivantes*, 5–12.

GAARDER, A. B. 1967, Organization of the Bilingual School, *Journal of Social Issues*, XXIII, 2, 110–20.

GALINSKY, H. 1964, Stylistic Aspects of Borrowing. In H. G. LUNT (ed.), *Proceedings of the Ninth International Congress of Linguists*. The Hague: Mouton, 374–81.

GALLOWAY, L. 1977, Language Impairment and Recovery in Polyglot Alphasia – A Case Study of a Hepta-Lingual. In M. PARADIS (ed.), *The Fourth Lacus Forum*, 121–30.

*GARDNER, R. C. 1973, Attitudes and Motivation: Their Role in Second Language Acquisition. In J. OLLER, & J. RICHARDS (eds), *Focus on the Learner*. Rowley, Mass.: Newbury House. Reprinted in H. TRUEBA & C. BARNETT-MIZRAHI (eds), *Bilingual Multicultural Education and the Professional*: From Theory to Practice. Rowley, Mass.: Newbury House, 1979, 319–27.

GARDNER, R. C. & LAMBERT, W. E. 1959, Motivational Variables in Second-Language Acquisition, *Canadian Journal of Psychology*, 13, 266–72.

—— 1972, *Attitudes and Motivation in Second-Language Learning*. Rowley: Newbury House.

*GASS, S. & SELINKER, L. 1983, *Language Transfer in Language Learning*. Rowley: Newbury House.

*GEERTS, G., NOOTENS, J. & VAN DEN BROECK, J. 1978, Attitudes Towards Dialects and Standard Language in Belgium, *International Journal of the Sociology of Language*, vol. 15, "Belgium", 33–46.

GENESEE, F. 1978, Second Language Learning and Language Attitudes, *Working Papers in Bilingualism*, 16, 19–42.

*—— 1984, Historical and Theoretical Foundations of Immersion Education in *Studies on Immersion Education: A Collection for United States Educators*. Sacramento: California State Department of Education, 32–57.

*GENESEE, F., HAMERS, J., LAMBERT, W. E., MONONEN, L., SEITZ, M. & STARCK, R. 1978, Language Processing Strategies of Bilinguals: A Neurophysiological Study, *Brain & Language*, 5, 1–12.

*GHOSH, R. N. 1979, Indian Bilingualism and the Teaching of English, Paper presented at the Fourteenth Regional Seminar, Seameo Regional Language Centre, Singapore, 16–21.

GILBERT, G. G. (ed.) 1970, *Texas Studies in Bilingualism*. Berlin: de Gruyter.

*GILES, H. 1970, Evaluative Reactions to Accents, *Educational Review*, 22, 211–27.

*GLEES, P. 1961, *Experimental Neurology*. Oxford: Clarendon Press.
*GOROSCH, M. 1978, Modern Language Teaching to Adults for Professional Use. In J. RASMUSSEN (ed.), *Copenhagen School of Economics and Business Administration, Language Department*. Copenhagen, 77–122, Publication No. 4.
*GOYVAERTS, D. 1982, Over 'onduidelijke gevallen' in de taalkunde, *De Nieuwe Taalgids*, 75, 4, 348.
*GRAHAM, R. S. 1956, Widespread Bilingualism and the Creative Writer, *Word*, 12, 369–81.
GREENBERG, J., OSGOOD, C. & SAPORTA, S. 1954, Language Change, *Journal of Abnormal and Social Psychology*, Supplement 146–63.
*GROSJEAN, F. 1982, *Life with Two Languages: An Introduction to Bilingualism*. Cambridge, Mass.: Harvard University Press.
*GUBIN, E. 1978, La situation des langues à Bruxelles au XIXe siècle à lumière d'un examen critque des statistiques, *Taal en Sociale Integratie*, Vol. 1, 33–80.
GUMPERZ, J. J. 1965, Linguistic Repertoires, Grammars and Second Language Instruction, *Georgetown University Monograph Series on Languages and Linguistics*, 18, 81–90.
—— 1966, Linguistic and Social Interaction in Two communities, *American Anthropologist*, 6/2, 137–53.
*—— 1967, On the Linguistic Markers of Bilingual Communication, *Journal of Social Issues*, XXIII, 2, 48–57.
*—— 1971, *Language in Social Groups*, ed. by A. S. DIL. Stanford: Stanford University Press.
*—— 1972, On the Communicative Competence of Bilinguals: Some Hypotheses and Suggestions for Further Research, *Language and Society*, 1, 1.
*—— 1977, Sociocultural Knowledge in Conversational Inference, *Georgetown University Roundtable on Languages and Linguistics*. Washington, D.C.: Georgetown University Press, 191–211.
*—— 1982, *Discourse Strategies*. Cambridge: Cambridge University Press.
GUMPERZ, J. J. & HERNANDEZ, C. E. 1971, Cognitive Aspects of Bilingual Communication. In W. H. WHITELEY *Language Use and Social Change*. London: O.U.P. 111–25.
*GUMPERZ, J. J. & WILSON, R. 1971, Convergence and Creolization – A Case from the Indo-Aryan/Dravidian Border in India. In D. HYMES (ed.), *Pidginization and Creolization of Languages*. Cambridge: Cambridge University Press, 151–67.
GUTMANS, T. 1969, Langues et ethnies en Belgique, *La Monda Lingvo-Problemo*, 1–2, 116–19.
HADEN, E. & JOLIAT, E. 1940, Le genre grammatical des substantifs en Franco-Canadien empruntés a l'anglais, *Publications of the Modern Language Association*, 55, 839–54.
HALL, A. R. 1952, Bilingualism and Applied Linguistics, *Zeitschrift für Phonetik und allgemeine Sprachwissenschaft*, 6, 13–30.
*HALLIDAY, M. A. K., McINTOSH, A. & STREVENS, P. 1970, The Users and Uses of Language. In J. A. FISHMAN (ed.), *Readings in the Sociology of Language*. The Hague: Mouton, 139–69.
HAMERS, J. F. & BLANC, M. 1982, Towards a Social-Psychological Model of Bilingual Development, *Journal of Language and Social Psychology*, 1, 1, 29–49.
*—— 1983, *Bilingualité et bilinguisme*. Bruxelles: Mardaga.
HAMERS, J. F. & DESHAIES, D. 1978, Effets des contacts inter-groupes sur les

attitudes envers la langue seconde et les membres de ce groupe culturel chez les élèves anglophones et francophones de la province du Québec, *Ve Congrès International de Linguistique Appliquée.* Montreal, août 1978.

HAMERS, J. F. & LAMBERT, W. E. 1977, Visual Field and Cerebral Hemisphere Preferences in Bilinguals, *Language Development and Neurological Theory.* New York: Academic Press, 57–62.

HAMMARBERG. B. 1967, Interference in American English Speakers' Pronunciation of Swedish, *Studia Linguistica*, XXI, 15–36.

*HARLEY, B. & SWAIN, M. 1977, An Analysis of Verb Form and Function in the Speech of French Immersion Pupils, *Working Papers in Bilingualism*, 14, 31–46.

HASAN, R. 1974, Code, Rgister and Social Dialect. In B. BERNSTEIN *Class, Codes and Control.* London: Routledge & Kegan Paul. 253–92.

—— 1976, Socialization and Cross-cultural Education, *Linguistics*, 175, 7–25.

HASSELMO, N. 1969, How Can We Measure the Effects Which One Language May Have on the Other in the Speech of Bilinguals. In L. KELLY (ed.), *The Description and Measurement of Bilingualism.* Toronto: Univ. of Toronto Press. 122–89.

*—— 1972, Code-Switching as Ordered Selection. In E. S. FIRCHOW, K. GRIMSTAD, N. HASSELMO & W. O'NEIL (eds), *Studies for Einar Haugen.* The Hague: Mouton, 261–80.

*HATCH, E. 1976, Studies in Language Switching and Mixing. In W. C. McCORMACK & S. A. WURM (eds), *Language and Man: Anthropological Issues.* The Hague: Mouton, 201–14.

*—— 1983, *Psycholinguistics: A Second Language Perspective.* Rowley, Mass.: Newbury House.

*HAUGEN, E. 1953, *The Norwegian Language in America.* Pennsylvania: Univ. of Pennsylvania Press, 2 vols.

*—— 1954, Review of Weinreich Languages in Contact, *Language*, 30, 380–88.

*—— 1956, *Bilingualism in the Americas: A Bibliography and Research Guide.* Publications of the American Dialect Society, 26, Alabama.

—— 1958, Language Contact, *Proceedings of the VIIIth International Congress of Linguists*, 771–85, 798–810.

*—— 1962, Schizoglossia and the Linguistic Norm, *Georgetown University Monograph Series on Languages and Linguistics*, Washington, Georgetown Univ. Press, 15, 63–74.

—— 1970, Linguistics and Dialinguistics. In E. ALATIS (ed.), *Georgetown University Monograph Series on Languages and Linguistics.* 23, 1–12.

*—— 1972a, The Analysis of Linguistic Borrowings, *Language*, XXVI, 210–31.

—— 1972b, Dialect, Language, Nation. In J. PRIDE & J. HOLMES (eds), *Sociolinguistics.* Harmondsworth, Penguin. 97–111.

*—— 1972c, The Stigmata of Bilingualism. In E. HAUGEN *The Ecology of Language.* Stanford, Stanford University Press, 307–44.

—— 1972d, *The Ecology of Language.* Stanford: Stanford University Press.

*—— 1973, Bilingualism, Language Contact and Immigrant Languages in the United States: A Research Report. In T. A. SEBEOK (ed.), *Current Trends in Linguistics*, vol. 10. The Hague: Mouton.

*—— 1977, Norm and Deviation in Bilingual Communities. In P. A. HORNBY (ed.), *Bilingualism: Psychological, Social and Education Implications.* New York: Academic Press.

*HERBILLON, J. 1951, Eléments néerlandais du wallon liégeois, *Les dialectes belgo-romans*, VIII, 16–26.
*HOCKETT, C. F. 1958, *A Course in Modern Linguistics*. New York: Macmillan.
HOENIGSWALD, H. M. 1962, Bilingualism, Presumable Bilingualism, and Diachrony, *Anthropological Linguistics*, IV, 1–5.
—— 1966, A Proposal for the Study of Folk-Linguistics. In W. BRIGHT (ed.), *Sociolinguistics*. The Hague: Mouton, 16–26.
HOFFMAN, N. 1939, *The Measurement of Bilingual Background*. New York City Teachers' College, Columbia University, Contributions to Education, No. 623.
HOPE, T. E. 1962, Loan-Words as Cultural and Lexical Symbols, *Archivum Linguisticum*, 14/2, 111–21.
*HORNBY, P. A. (ed.) 1977, *Bilingualism: Psychological, Social and Educational Implications*. New York: Academic Press.
HOUSEHOLDER, F. W. 1962, Greek Diglossia, *Georgetown University Monograph Series on Languages and Linguistics*. Washington: Georgetown University Press, 15, 109–32.
*HOUSTON, S. H. 1972, Bilingualism: Naturally Acquired Bilingualism, *A Survey of Psycholinguistics*. The Hague: Mouton, 203–25.
HUERTA, A. 1977, The Acquisition of Bilingualism: A Code-Switching Approach, *Sociolinguistic Working Paper No. 39*. South-West Educational Development Laboratory, Austin, Texas.
HUGHES, E. C. 1971, The Linguistic Division of Labour in Industrial and Urban Societies. In J. A. FISHMAN (ed.), *Advances in the Sociology of Language*, vol. 2. The Hague: Mouton. 296–309.
HUGHES, J. M. 1978, Positive and Negative Tagging – Lexical Entries & Language Dominance in Bilinguals. Paper presented at the Vth AILA Congress, Montréal.
HYMAN, L. 1970, The Role of Borrowing in the Justification of Phonological Grammars, *Studies in African Linguistics*, 1/1, 1–49.
HYMES, D. 1967, Models on Interaction and Social Setting, *Journal of Social Issues*, XXIII, 2, 8–28.
—— 1971, *Pidginization and Creolization of Languages*. Cambridge: Cambridge University Press.
*—— 1972, On Communicative Competence. In J. B. PRIDE & J. HOLMES (eds), *Sociolinguistics*. Harmondsworth: Penguin. 269–93.
*—— 1974, *Foundations in Sociolinguistics: An Ethnographic Approach*. Philadelphia.
ISHWARAN, K. 1969, Multilingualism in India. In T. ANDERSON (ed.), *Studies in Multilingualism*. Leiden: Brill.
*JAKOBOVITS, L. A. 1968, Dimensionality of Compound-Coordinate Bilingualism, *Language Learning*, 3, 29–56.
*—— 1970, *Foreign Language Learning*. Rowley: Newbury House.
JONES, A. R. 1970, *Oral Facility in Bilingual and Monoglot Children*. Aberystwyth: Faculty of Education.
JONES, R. M. 1969, How and When do Persons Become Bilingual? In L. KELLY (ed.), *Description and Measurement of Bilingualism*. Toronto: University of Toronto Press. 12–77.
*KARAM, F. X. 1979, Processes of Increasing Mutual Intelligibility Between Language Varieties, *International Journal of the Sociology of Language*, 22, 115–37.

*KELLY, L. (ed.) 1969, *The Description and Measurement of Bilingualism*. Toronto: University of Toronto Press.

*KENYERES, A. & KENYERES, E. 1938, Comment une petite hongroise de sept ans apprend le français, *Archives de Psychology*, 26, 321–66.

*KESSLER, C. 1971, *The Acquisition of Syntax in Bilingual Children*. Washington: Georgetown University Press.

—— 1973, Syntactic Contrasts, in Child Bilingualism, *Language Learning*, 22, 2, 221–34.

*KJOLSETH, R. 1973, Bilingual Education Programs in the United States: For Assimilation or Pluralism? In P. R. TURNER (ed.), *Bilingualism in the South-West*. Tucson: University of Arizona Press, 3–27.

*—— 1978, The Development of the Sociology of Language and its Social Implications. In J. A. FISHMAN (ed.), *Advances in the Study of Societal Multilingualism*. The Hague: Mouton.

KLOSS, H. 1967, Bilingualism and Nationalism, *Journal of Social Issues*, XXIII, 2, 39–47.

—— 1973, *The American Bilingual Tradition in Education and Administration*. Rowley: Newbury House.

KOLERS, P. A. 1965, Bilingualism and Bicodalism, *Language and Speech*, 8, 122–26.

—— 1966, Interlingual Facilitation of Short-term Memory, *Journal of Verbal Learning and Verbal Behaviour*, 5, 314–19.

—— 1968, Bilingualism and Information Processing, *Scientific American*. March, 78–85.

*KRASHEN, S. 1973, Lateralization, Language Learning, and the Critical Period: Some New Evidence, *Language Learning*, 23, 63–73.

*—— 1975, The Development of Cerebral Dominance and Language Learning: More Evidence. In D. DATO (ed.), *Developmental Psycholinguistics: Theory and Application*. Washington: Georgetown University Press, 209–33.

*—— 1981a, *Second Language Acquisition and Second Language Learning*. Oxford: Pergamon.

*—— 1981b, Bilingual Education and Second Language Acquisition Theory, *Schooling and Language Minority Students: A Theoretical Framework*. Los Angeles: Evaluation, Dissemination and Assessment Center, California State University, 51–79.

*—— 1982, *Principles and Practice in Second Language Acquisition*. Oxford: Pergamon.

*KRASHEN, S. D., SCARCELLA, R. C. & LONG, M. H. (eds) 1982, *Child-Adult Differences in Second Language Acquisition*. Rowley, Mass.: Newbury House.

LABOV, W. 1965, On the Mechanism of Linguistic Change, *Georgetown University Monograph Series on Languages and Linguistics*. Washington: Georgetown University Press, No. 18.

*—— 1970, The Logic of Non standard English. In J. E.ALATIS (ed.), *Monograph Series on Language and Linguistics*, 22, Washington: Georgetown University Press, 1–43.

*—— 1972, *Sociolinguistic Patterns*. Philadelphia: University of Pennsylvania Press. Reprinted in 1978. Oxford: Basil Blackwell.

*LAMBERT, R. D. & FREED, B. F. (eds) 1982, *The Loss of Language Skills*. Rowley, Mass.: Newbury House.

*LAMBERT, W. E. 1955, Measurement of the Linguistic Dominance of Bilinguals, *Journal of Abnormal and Social Psychology*, 50, 197–200.

—— 1967, A Social Psychology of Bilingualism, *Journal of Social Issues*, XXIII, 2, 91–109.

*—— 1969a, Psychological Aspects of Motivation in Language Learning, *Bulletin of the Illinois Foreign Language Teachers Association*, May, 5–11.

*—— 1969b, Psychological Studies of the Interdependencies of the Bilingual's Two Languages. In J. PUHVEL (ed.), *Substance and Structure of Language*. Berkeley & Los Angeles: University of California Press, 99–126.

*—— 1972a, *Language, Psychology and Culture*, ed. by A. S. DIL. Stanford: Stanford University Press.

—— 1972b, A Social Psychology of Bilingualism. In W. E. LAMBERT (ed.), *Language, Psychology and Culture*. Stanford: Stanford University Press. 212–35.

—— 1972c, Measuring the Cognitive Consequences of Attending Elementary School in a Second Language. In W. E. LAMBERT (ed.), *Language, Psychology and Culture*. Stanford: Stanford University Press. 331–37.

—— 1972d, Developmental Aspects of Second Language Acquisition. In W. E. LAMBERT (ed.), *Language, Psychology and Culture*. Stanford: Stanford University Press. 9–31.

—— 1972e, Measurement of the Linguistic Dominance of Bilinguals. In W. E. LAMBERT (ed.), *Language, Psychology and Culture*. Stanford: Stanford University Press, 1–8.

*—— 1974, Culture and Language as Factors in Learning and Education. In F. ABOUD & R. D. MEAD (eds), *Cultural Factors in Learning*. Bellingham: Washington State College.

—— 1977, The Effects of Bilingualism on the Individual: Cognitive and Sociocultural Consequences. In P. A. HORNBY (ed.), *Bilingualism: Psychological, Social and Educational Implications*. New York: Academic Press, 15–27.

*LAMBERT, W. E. & AELLEN, C. 1972, Ethnic Identification and Personality Adjustments of Canadian Adolescents of Mixed English-French Parentage. In W. E. LAMBERT (ed.), *Language, Psychology and Culture*. Stanford: Stanford University Press. 266–89.

LAMBERT, W. E. & ANISFELD, E. 1969, A Note on the Relationship of Bilingualism and Intelligence, *Canadian Journal of Behavioural Sciences*, 1, 123–28.

LAMBERT, W. E. & FILLENBAUM, S. 1972, A Pilot Study of Aphasia Among Bilinguals. In W. E. LAMBERT (ed.), *Language, Psychology and Culture*. Stanford: Stanford University Press. 72–79.

*LAMBERT, W. E., FRANKEL, H. & TUCKER, G. R. 1966, Judging Personality Through Speech: A French-Canadian Example, *Journal of Communication*, 16, 305–21.

*LAMBERT, W. E., GILES, H. & PICARD, O. 1975, Language Attitudes in a French-American Community, *Linguistics*, 158, 127–52.

*LAMBERT, W. E., HAVELKA, J. & CROSBY, C. 1958, The Influence of Language Acquisition Contexts on Bilingualism, *Journal of Abnormal & Social Psychology*, 56, 239–44.

*LAMBERT, W. E., HAVELKA, J. & GARDNER, R. C. 1959, Linguistic Manifestations of Bilingualism, *American Journal of Psychology*, 72, 77–82.

LAMBERT W. E., HODGSON, R., GARDNER, R. C. & FILLENBAUM, S. 1972, Evaluational Reactions to Spoken Languages. In W. E. LAMBERT (ed.), *Language, Psychology and Culture*. Stanford: Stanford University Press. 80–96.

LAMBERT, W. E., IGNATOW, M. & KRAUTHAMER, M. 1972, Bilingual Organization in Free Recall. In W. E. LAMBERT (ed.), *Language, Psychology and Culture*. Stanford: Stanford University Press. 252–65.

*LAMBERT, W. E., JUST, M. & SEGALOWITZ, N. 1970, Some Cognitive Consequences of Following the Curricula of the Early School Grades in a Foreign Language. In J. E. ALATIS (ed.), *Georgetown University Monograph Series on Languages and Linguistics*, Washington University Press. 229–79.

LAMBERT, W. E. & KLINEBERG, O. 1967, *Children's Views of Foreign Peoples: A Cross-national Study*. New York: Appleton.

*LAMBERT, W. E. & MOORE, N. 1966, Word-association Responses: Comparison of American and French Monolinguals with Canadian Monolinguals and Bilinguals, *Journal of Personality and Social Psychology*, III, 3, 313–20.

LAMBERT, W. E. & PEAL, E. 1962, The Relation of Bilingualism to Intelligence, *Psychological Monographs*, 76, 27.

LAMBERT, W. E., TUCKER, G. R., PIGAULT, A. & SEGALOWITZ, N. 1972, A Psychological Investigation of French Speakers' Skill with Grammatical Gender. In W. E. LAMBERT (ed.), *Language, Psychology and Culture*. Stanford: Stanford University Press. 243–51.

*LAMBERT, W. E. & TUCKER, G. R. 1972, *The Bilingual Education of Children*. Rowley, Mass.: Newbury House.

—— 1973, The Benefits of Bilingualism, *Psychology Today*, 7, 89–94.

*LANLEY, A. 1962, *Le français d'Afrique du Nord*, Paris, P.U.F.

*LATTEY, E. 1978, Utterance Potential, Code-switching and Speech Errors. Paper presented at the Vth AILA Congress, Montreal.

*—— 1981, Individual and Social Aspects of Bilingualism. In H. BAETENS BEARDSMORE (ed.), *Elements of Bilingual Theory*. Brussel: Vrije Universiteit Brussel.

*LEBRUN, Y. & HASQUIN, J. 1971, Bilinguisme précoce et troubles du langage. In S. DE COSTER (ed.), *Aspects sociologiques du plurilinguisme*. Bruxelles-Paris: Aimav-Didier, 60–75.

*LEBRUN, Y. 1981, Bilingualism and the Brain: A Brief Appraisal of Penfield's Views. In H. BAETENS BEARDSMORE (ed.), *Elements of Bilingual Theory*. Brussel: Vrije Universiteit Brussel.

*LEE, E. 1983, Lexical Knowledge and the Use. Unpublished Doctoral Thesis, Brussel, Vrije Universiteit Brussel.

*LENNEBERG, E. H. 1967, *Biological Foundations of Language*. New York: Wiley.

*LEOPOLD, W. F. 1939–1949, *Speech Development of a Bilingual Child: A Linguist's Record*, 4 vols. Chicago: Evanston.

LEPAGE, R. B. 1968, Problems of Description in Multilingual Communities, *Transactions of the Philological Society*, 189–212.

LEVIN, S. 1978, Scholarly and Literary Bilingualism. In M. PARADIS (ed.), *The Fourth Lacus Forum*. Columbia: Hornbeam Press. 226–35.

LEWIS, G. E. 1975, Attitude to Language Among Bilingual Children and Adults in Wales, *Linguistics*, 158,103–26.

*—— 1976, Bilingualism and Bilingual Education: The Ancient World to the Renaissance. In J. A. FISHMAN (ed.), *Bilingual Education: An International Sociological Perspective*. Rowley, Mass.: Newbury House, 151–200.

—— 1977, Bilingual Education, *International Journal of the Sociology of Language*, vol. 14.

—— 1981, *Bilingualism and Bilingual Education*. Oxford: Pergamon Press.
LIEBERSON, S. 1972, Bilingualism in Montreal: A Demographic Analysis. In J. A. FISHMAN (ed.), *Advances in the Sociology of Language*. The Hague: Mouton, 231–54.
*LIKERT, R. 1932, A Technique for the Measurement of Attitudes, *Archives of Psychology*, no. 140.
*LIM KIAT BOEY (ed.) 1980, *Bilingual Education*. Singapore: Singapore University Press.
LIPSKI, J. M. 1978a, Bilingual Code-switching and Internal Competence: The Evidence from Spanish and English. Paper presented at the Vth AILA Congress, Montreal.
*—— 1978b, Code switching and the Problem of Bilingual Competence. In M. PARADIS (ed.), *Aspects of Bilingualism*. Columbia: Hornbeam Press. 250–64.
*—— 1978c, Code Switching and the Problem of Bilingual Competence. In M. PARADIS (ed.), *The Fourth Lacus Forum*. Columbia: Hornbeam Press. 263–77.
LOPEZ, M. & YOUNG, K. R. 1974, The Linguistic Interdependence of Bilinguals, *Journal of Experimental Psychology*, 102/6, 981–83.
LORWIN, V. R. 1972, Linguistic Pluralism and Political Tension in Modern Belgium. In J. A. FISHMAN (ed.), *Advances in the Sociology of Language*. The Hague: Mouton. 386–412.
MACAULEY, R. K. S. & RAMIREZ II, M. 1977, Research Priorities in Bilingual Education in the United States: Challenges for the Present and Future. In W. F. MACKEY & J. ORNSTEIN (eds), *The Bilingual Education Movement*. El Paso: Texas Western Press. 36–47.
*MACKEY, W. F. 1957, The Description of Bilingualism, *Journal of the Canadian Linguistic Association*.
—— 1967a, The Description and Measurement of Bilingualism. *The Linguistic Reporter*, 9/5, 1–3.
—— 1967b, *Bilingualism as a World Problem*. Montreal: Harvest House.
—— 1969a, Bilingual Interference: Its Analysis and Measurement, *Journal of Communication*, 15, 239–49.
—— 1969b, *Concept Categories as Measures of Culture Distance*. Quebec: CRIB, Laval.
*—— 1970a, The Description of Bilingualism. In J. A. FISHMAN (ed.), *Readings in the Sociology of Language*. The Hague: Mouton, 554–84.
—— 1970b, *Interference, Integration and the Synchronic Fallacy*. Quebec: CRIB, Laval.
—— 1971, *Literary Biculturalism and the Thought-Language-Culture Relation*. Quebec: CRIB, Laval.
*—— 1972a, *Bilingual Education in a Binational School*. Rowley, Mass.: Newbury House.
—— 1972b, *Bibliographie internationale sur le bilinguisme*. Quebec: CRIB, Laval.
*—— 1976, *Billinguisme et contact des langues*. Paris: Klincksieck.
MACKEY, W. F. & ANDERSSON, T. (eds) 1977, *Bilingualism in Early Childhood*. Rowley, Mass.: Newbury House.
MACKAY, W. F. & ORNSTEIN, J. (eds) 1977a, *The Bilingual Education Movement: Essays on its Prospects*. El Paso: Texas Western Press.
—— 1977b, Evaluating Bilingual Education Programs: Critical Variables. In W. F. MACKEY & J. ORNSTEIN (eds), *The Bilingual Education Movement*. El Paso: Texas Western Press. 48–83.
—— 1977c, Bilingual Education as an Ecology. In W. F. MACKEY & J. ORNSTEIN

(eds), *The Bilingual Education Movement*. El Paso: Texas Western Press. 96–120.

*MACNAMARA, J. 1967a, The Bilingual's Linguistic Performance: A Psychological Overview, *Journal of Social Issues*, XXIII, 2, 58–77.

—— 1967b, The Effects of Instruction in a Weaker Language, in *Journal of Social Issues*, XXIII, 2, 120–34.

*—— 1969, How Can One Measure the Extent of a Person's Bilingual Profiency. In L. G. KELLY (ed.), *Description & Measurement of Bilingualism*. 80–119.

—— 1970, Bilingualism and Thought. In J. E. ALATIS (ed.), *Monograph Series on Languages and Linguistics*, No. 23. Washington: Georgetown University Press. 25–45.

—— 1973, Attitudes and Learning a Second Language. In R. SHUY & R. FASOLD (eds), *Language Attitudes: Current Trends and Prospects*. Washington: Georgetown University Press. 36–40.

MACNAMARA, J., SVARE, J. & HORNER, S. 1976, Attending a Primary School of the Other Language in Montreal. In A. SIMOES (ed.), *The Bilingual Child*. New York: Academic Press. 113–31.

*MALHERBE, E. 1969, Comments on "How and When do Persons Become Bilingual?". In L. KELLY (ed.), *Description and Measurement of Bilingualism*. Toronto: University of Toronto Press.

*McCLOSKEY, N. & SCHAAR, J. H. 1965, Psychological Dimensions of Anomy, *American Sociological Review*, 30, 14–40.

*McCLURE, E. 1981, Formal and Functional Aspects of the Code switched Discourse of Bilingual Children. R.P. DURAN (ed.), *Latino Language and Communicative Behaviour*. Norwood: Ablex.

*McCORMACK, P. D. 1977, Bilingual Linguistic Memory: The Independence-Interdependence Issue Revisted. In P. A. HORNBY (ed.), *Bilingualism, Psychological, Social and Educational Implications*. New York: Academic Press. 57–66.

*McLAUGHLIN, B. 1978, *Second-Language Acquisition in Childhood*. Hillsdale: Erlbaum.

*—— 1984, *Second-Language Acquisition in Childhood: Volume 1. Preschool Children*. Second Edition. Hillsdale, New Jersey: Lawrence Erlbaum.

McRAE, K. 1975, The Principle of Territoriality and the Principle of Personality in Multilingual States, *Linguistics*, 158, 33–54.

MEEUS, B. 1973, Societal Bilingualism, *ITL*, 20, 1–9.

MEILLET, A. & SAUVAGEOT, A. 1934, Le bilinguisme des hommes cultivés, *Conférence de l'Institut de Linguistique de l'Université de Paris*, Vol. 2, 5–14.

MEISEL, J. M. (ed.) 1975, *Langues en contact-Pidgins-Creoles-Languages in Contact*. Tübingen: TBL Verlag Gunter Narr.

*MOSHA, M. 1971, Loanwords in Luganda: A Search for Guides in the Adaptation of African Languages to Modern Conditions. In W. H. WHITELEY (ed.), *Language Use and Social Change*. London: O.U.P. 288–308.

MOULTON, W. G. 1962, What Standard for Diglossia? The Case of German Switzerland. *Monograph Series on Languages and Linguistics*, 15. Washington: Georgetown University Press. 133–48.

*NELDE, P. H. (ed.) 1980, *Sprachkontakt und Sprachkonflikt/Languages in Contact and Conflict*. Wiesbaden: Franz Steiner Verlag.

*NICKEL, G. 1972, Papers from the International Symposium on Applied Contrastive Linguistics, Stuttgart, October 11–13, 1971, Berlin, Cornelsen-Verhagen und Klasing.

NUYTENS, E. 1962, *De Tweetalige Mens*. Assen: Van Gorcum.

OBLER, L. K. & ALBERT, M. L. 1978, A Monitor System for Bilingual Language Processing. In M. PARADIS (ed.), *The Fourth Lacus Forum, 1977*. Columbia: Hornbeam Press. 105–15.

O'HUALLACHAIN, O. F. M. 1962, Bilingualism in Education in Ireland, *Monograph series on Languages and Linguistics*, 15. Washington: Georgetown University Press. 75–84.

*OKSAAR, E. 1972a, On Code Switching. An Analysis of Bilingual Norms. In J. QVISTGAARD, H. SCHWARZ & H. SPANG-HANSSEN (eds), *Proceedings Vol. III, Association Internationale de Linguistique Appliquée Third Congress*. Copenhagen 1972. Heidelberg: Julius Groos Verlag, 491–500.

—— 1972b, Bilingualism. In R. SEBEOK (ed.), *Current Trends in Linguistics*, Vol. 9. The Hague: Mouton. 476–511.

*—— 1979, Linguistic Aspects of the Development of Bilingualism, paper presented at the Fourteenth Regional Seminar, Seameo Regional Language Centre, Singapore, 16–21 April.

*—— 1983, Multilingualism and Multiculturalism from the Linguist's Point of View. In T. HUSEN & S. OPPER (eds), *Multilingual and Multicultural Education in Immigrant Countries*. Oxford: Pergamon, 17–36.

*OLLER, J. W. 1979, *Language Tests at School*. London: Longmans.

*OLLER, J. W. & PERKINS, K. 1980, *Research in Language Testing*. Rowley, Mass.: Newbury House.

ORNSTEIN, J. 1971, Language Varieties Along the U.S.-Mexican Border. In G. PERREN & J. TRIM (eds), *Applications of Linguistics*. Cambridge: C.U.P. 1969. 349–62.

ORNSTEIN, J. & GOODMAN, P. 1974, Bilingualism Viewed in the Light of Socio-Educational Correlates. Paper presented at the 8th World Congress of Sociology. Toronto, August 18–23.

*OSGOOD, C. E. SUCI, G. J. & TANNENBAUM, P. H. 1957, *The Measurement of Meaning* Urbana: University of Illinois Press.

*OYAMA, S. A. 1976/1982, A Sensitive Period for the Acquisition of a Nonnative Phonological System. In S. KRASHEN, R. SCARCELLA & M. LONG (eds), *Child-Adult Differences in Second Language Acquisition*. Rowley: Newbury House, 1982, 20–38.

PAGE, D. 1954, Le bilinguisme au Pays de Galles, *Revue des Langues Vivantes*, 27–29.

PAINCHAUD, L. 1969, *Le bilinguisme à l'université: description du bilinguisme et du biculturalisme*. Montréal: Beauchemin.

*PARADIS, M. 1977a, Bilingualism and Aphasia. In H. A. WHITAKER & H. WHITAKER (eds), *Studies in Neurolinguistics*, Vol. 3. New York: Academic Press, 65–121.

*—— 1977b, The Stratification of Bilingualism. In R. J. DI PIETRO & E. L. BLANSITT (eds), *The Third Lacus Forum 1976*. Columbia: Hornbeam Press, 237–47.

PARADIS, M. (ed.) 1978, *Aspects of Bilingualism*. Columbia: Hornbeam Press.

PARK, R. E. 1931, *Personality and Cultural Conflict*. Publication of the American Sociological Society, 25, 95–110.

PAULSTON, C. B. 1974, *Implications of Language Learning Theory for Language Planning: Concerns in Bilingual Education*. Washington: Center for Applied Linguistics.

—— 1980, *Bilingual Education: Theories and Issues*. Rowley, Mass.: Newbury House.

*—— 1982, *Swedish Research and Debate about Bilingualism*. Skolöverstyrselsen: National Swedish Board of Education.

*PEAL, E. & LAMBERT, W. E. 1962, The Relationship of Bilingualism to Intelligence, *Psychological Monographs*, 76, (27).

*PENFIELD, W. G. & ROBERTS, L. 1959, *Speech and Brain-Mechanism*. Princeton, University Press.

PHILIPP, M. 1964, Transfert du système phonologique de Blaesheim sur une autre langue, le français. In H. LUNT (ed.), *Proceedings of the Ninth International Congress of Linguistics*. The Hague: Mouton. 392–401.

PICCHIO, C. 1954, Aspects de bilinguisme et de pluralisme culturel en Italie, *Revue des Langues Vivantes*, 1, 21–26.

PIKE, K. 1960, Toward a Theory of Change and Bilingualism. *Studies in Linguistics*, 15, 1–7.

PLATT, J. T. 1977, A Model of Polyglossia and Multilingualism (with Special Reference to Singapore and Malaysia), *Language and Society*, 6, 361–78.

*POHL, J. 1965, Bilinguismes, *Revue Roumaine de Linguistique*, 10, 343–49.

*POLLITZER, R. L. 1978, Language Development in Two Bilingual Schools: A Study in Contrastive Psycholinguistic Analysis, *IRAL*, XV1/3, 241–52.

*POPLACK, S. 1980, "Sometimes I'll start a sentence in Spanish y TERMINO EN ESPANOL: Toward a typology of code-switching, *Linguistics*, 18, 581–618.

—— 1983, Intergenerational Variation in Language Use and Structure in a Bilingual Context. In C. RIVERA (ed.), *An Ethnographic/Sociolinguistic Approach to Language Proficiency Assessment*. Clevedon: Multilingual Matters, 42–70.

PORSCHE, C. 1983, *Die Zweisprachigkeit während des primären Spracherwerbs*. Tübingen: Narr.

RADO, M. 1976, Bilingual Education in Action: The Multilingual Project, *Linguistic Communications, Working Papers of the Linguistic Society of Australia*, 16, 115–27.

RAUBICHEK, L. 1934, The Psychology of Multilingualism, *Volta Review*, 36, 17–20, 57ff.

*RAYFIELD, J. R. 1970, *The Language of a Bilingual Community*, The Hague: Mouton.

REED, C. 1942, The Gender of English Loanwords in Pennsylvania German, *American Speech*, 25–29.

REIMEN, J. R. 1965, Esquisse d'une situation plurilingue, Le Luxembourg, *La Linguistique*, 2, 89–102.

*RICHARDS, J. (ed.) 1974, *Error Analysis. Perspectives on Second Language Acquisition*. London: Longman.

*RICKFORD, J. 1986, Social Contact and Linguistic Diffusion: Hiberno English and New World Black English, *Language*, 62.

RIPOCHE, J. 1966, Résultats d'une enquête sur les réactions des élèves au plurilinguisme á l'Ecole Européene de Bruxelles, *Enfance*, No. 1, 89–98.

*RIVERA, C. (ed.) 1984, *Language Proficiency and Academic Achievement*. Clevedon: Multilingual Matters.

*RONJAT, J. 1913, *Le développement du langage observé chez un enfant bilingue*. Paris.

ROSETTI, A. 1965, Langue mixte et mélange de langues, *Linguistica*. The Hague: Mouton. 65–70.

RUDNYCKYJ, J. B. 1958, Problems in Onomastic Bilingualism in Canada and the U.S.A., *Proceedings of the VIIIth International Congress of Linguists*, Oslo.

—— 1972, Immigrant Languages, Language Contact, and Bilingualism in Canada. In T. E. SEBEOK (ed.), *Current Trends in Linguistics*, Vol. 10, 592–652.

*RUKE-DRAVINA, V. 1967, *Mehrsprachigkeit im Vorschulalter*. Travaux de l'Institut de Phonétique de Lund, Fasc. V., Lund, Gleerup.

SACHS, E. 1973, The Gender of English Loanwords in the German of Recent Immigrants, *American Speech*, 28, 256–70.

SALISBURY, R. F. 1962, Notes on Bilingualism and Linguistic Change in New Guinea, *Anthropological Linguistics*, IV/7, 1–13. Reprinted in J. B. PRIDE & J. HOLMES (eds), *Sociolinguistics*. Harmondsworth: Penguin, 1972, 52–64.

*SANCHEZ, R. 1983, *Chicano Discourse: Socio-historic Perspectives*. Rowley, Mass.: Newbury House.

SANKOFF, G. 1972, Language Use in Multilingual Societies: Some Alternative Approaches. In J. B. PRIDE & J. HOLMES (eds), *Sociolinguistics*. Harmondsworth: Penguin. 33–51.

*SAUNDERS, G. 1980, Adding a Second Native Language in the Home, *Journal of Multilingual and Multicultural Development*, 1/2, 113–24.

*—— 1982, *Bilingual Children: Guidance for the Family*. Clevedon: Multilingual Matters.

*SAVARD, J. H. & VIGNEAULT, R. (eds) 1975, *Les états multilingues: problèmes et solutions/Multilingual Political Systems: Problems and Solutions*. Québec: Les Presses de l'Université Laval.

*SAVILLE-TROIKE, M. 1973, *Bilingual Children: A Resource Document*. Bilingual Education Series, 2. Arlington: Centre for Applied Linguistics.

*—— 1982, *The Ethnography of Communication*. Oxford: Blackwell.

*SAWYER, J. 1978, Passive and Covert Bilinguals: A Hidden Asset for a Pluralistic Society. In H. KEY, G. MCCULLOUGH & J. SAWYER (eds), *The Bilingual in a Pluralistic Society*. Long Beach: California State University.

Schooling and Language Minority Students: A Theoretical Framework, 1981, Los Angeles Evaluation, Dissemination and Assessment Center, California State University.

SCHOOLS COUNCIL COMMITTEE FOR WALES, 1978, *Bilingual Education in Wales*. London: Evans-Methuen.

*SCHUMANN, J. 1978a, The Acculturation Model for Second-Language Acquisition. In R. C. GINGRAS (ed.), *Second Language Acquisition and Foreign Language Teaching*. Arlington: Center for Applied Linguistics, 27–50.

*—— 1978b, *The Pidginization Process: A Model for Second Language Acquisition*. Rowley, Mass.: Newbury House.

*—— Forthcoming, Research on the Acculturation Model for Second Language Acquisition.

*SCOTTON, C. M. & URY, W. 1977, Bilingual Strategies: The Social Function of Code-switching, *International Journal of the Sociology of Language*, 13, 5–20.

*SEGALOWITZ, N. & GATBONTON, E. 1977, Studies of the Nonfluent Bilingual. In P. A. HORNBY (ed.), *Bilingualism: Psychological, Social and Educational Implications*. New York: Academic Press, 77–89.

*SELINKER, L. 1972, Interlanguage, *IRAL*, 10/3, 219–31.

*SELINKER, L., SWAIN, M. & DUMAS, G. 1975, The Interlanguage Hypothesis Extended to Children, *Language Learning*, 25, 139–52.

*SHAFFER, D. 1976, Is Bilingualism Compound or Coordinate? *Lingua*, 40, 69–77.

*SHARP, D. 1973, *Language in Bilingual Communities*. London: Arnold.

*SHARP, D., THOMAS, B., PRICE, E., FRANCIS, G. & DAVIES, I. 1973, *Attitudes to Welsh and English in the Schools of Wales*, Schools Council Research Studies. Macmillan/University of Wales Press, 27–44, 158–69.

SHUY, R. W. & FASOLD, R. 1973, *Language Attitudes, Current Trends and Prospects*. Washington: Georgetown University Press.

*SHUY, R. W. 1981, A Sociolinguistic Perspective for Bilingualism in the Classroom. In H. BAETENS BEARDSMORE (ed.), *Elements of Bilingual Theory*. Brussel: Vrije Universiteit Brussel.

SIGUAN, M. (ed.) 1984, *Adquisicion Precoz de una Secunda Lengua*. Barcelona: Universitat de Barcelona.

SIMOES, A. (ed.) 1976, *The Bilingual Child*. New York: Academic Press.

SKUTNABB-KANGAS, T. 1975, Bilingualism, Semilingualism, and School Achievement, AILA World Congress, Abstracts.

*SKUTNABB-KANGAS, T. & TOUKOMAA, P. 1976, *Teaching Migrant Children's Mother Tongue and Learning the Language of the Host Country in the Contxt of the Socio-cultural Situation of the Migrant Family*. Tampere: University of Tampere, Dept. of Sociology & Social Psychology, Tutkimuksia Research Report 15.

*—— 1979, Semilingualism and Middle-Class Bias: A Reply to Cora Brent-Palmer, *Working Papers in Bilingualism*, 19, 181–96.

*—— 1980, Semilingualism and the Education of Migrant Children as a Means of Reproducing the Caste of Assembly-line Workers, *Tijdschrift van de Vrije Universiteit Brussel*, 21, 2, 100–36.

*—— 1984, *Bilingualism or Not: The Education of Minorities*. Clevedon: Multilingual Matters.

*SMOLICZ, J. J. 1979, *Culture and Education in a Plural Society*. Canberra: Curriculum Development Centre.

SOFFIETTI, J. 1955, Bilingualism and Biculturalism, *Journal of Educational Psychology*, 46, 222.

SOLENBERGER, R. 1962, The Social Meaning of Language Choice in the Marianas, *Anthropological Linguistics*, IV/1, 59–64.

SORENSEN, A. P. 1972, Multilingualism in the Northwest Amazon. In J. P. PRIDE & J. HOLMES (eds), *Sociolinguistics*. Harmondsworth: Penguin. 78–93.

*SPOERL, D. T. 1944, The Academic and Verbal Adjustment of College-Age Bilingual Students, *Journal of Genetic Psychology*, 64, 19–57.

SPOLSKY, B. 1972, *The Language Education of Minority Children: Selected Readings*. Rowley: Newbury House.

SPOLSKY, B., GREEN, J. B. & READ, J. 1976, A Model for the Description Analysis and Perhaps Evaluation of Bilingual Education. In A. VERDOODT, & R. KJOLSETH (eds), *Language in Sociology*. Louvain: Peeters.

*STROOP, R. 1935, Studies of Interference in Serial Verbal Reactions, *Journal of Experimental Psychology*, 18, 643–61.

*STUBBS, M. 1983, *Discourse Analysis: The Sociolinguistic Analysis of Natural Language*. Oxford: Blackwell.

Studies on Immersion Education: A Collection for United States Educators, 1984, Sacramento, California State Department of Education.

*SWADESH, M. 1941, Observations of Pattern Impact on the Phonetics of Bilinguals, *Language, Culture, and Personality*. Menasha (Wis.), 59–65.

SWAIN, M. 1968, Development of Syntactic Structures in Monolingual and Bilingual Children (A Modest Proposal), Univ. of California, Working Paper.

*—— 1972, *Bilingualism as a First Language*. Unpublished doctoral thesis, Univ. of California at Irvine.

*—— 1976a, Bibliography: Research on Immersion Education for the Majority Child, *Canadian Modern Language Review*, 32, 5, 592–96.

*—— 1976b, English-Speaking Child + Early French Immersion = Bilingual Child? *The Canadian Modern Language Review*, 33, 2, 180–92.

—— 1977, Bilingualism, Monolingualism and Code Acquisition. In W. F. MACKEY & T. ANDERSSON (eds), *Bilingualism in Early Childhood*. Rowley, Mass.: Newbury House. 28–35.

*—— 1978a, Home-School Language Switching. In J. C. RICHARDS (ed.), *Understanding Second Language Learning: Issues and Approaches*. Rowley, Mass.: Newbury House. 238–51.

*—— 1978b, School Reform through Bilingual Education: Problems and Solutions in Evaluating Programs, *Comparative Education Review*, 22, 3, 420–33.

*—— 1978c, French Immersion: Early, Late, or Partial? *Canadian Modern Language Review*, 34, 3, 577–88.

*—— 1980, Bilingual Education for the English-Canadian: Three Models of "Immersion". In LIM KIAT BOEY (ed.), *Bilingual Education*. Singapore: University Press, Singapore, 19–35.

*—— 1981a, Linguistic Expectations: Core, Extended and Immersion, *Festschrift for H. H. STERN, Canadian Modern Language Review*, March.

*—— 1981b, Time and Timing in Bilingual Education, *Language Learning*, 31.

*SWAIN, M. & BARIK, H. C. 1978, Bilingual Education in Canada: French & English. In B. SPOLSKY & R. L. COOPER (eds), *Case Studies in Bilingual Education*. Rowley, Mass.: Newbury House, 22–71.

*SWAIN, M. & LAPKIN, S. 1982, *Evaluating Bilingual Education: A Canadian Case Study*. Clevedon: Multilingual Matters.

*SZAMOSI, M., SWAIN M. & LAPKIN, S. 1979, Do Early Immersion Pupils "Know" French? *Orbit*, October, 49.

TABOURET-KELLER, A. 1962a, Incidences psychologiques du bilinguisme, Journée d'Etudes, No. 24, Ministere de l'Education Nationale et de la Culture, Bruxelles-Mons, 95–109.

—— 1962b, Contribution à l'étude sociologique des bilinguismes, *Proceedings of the IXth International Congress on Linguistics*, 612–21.

—— 1963, L'acquisition du langage parlé chez un petit enfant en milieu bilingue, *Symposium de l'Association de Psychologie Scientifique de Langue Française, Neuchâtel, 1962*. Paris: P.U.F. 205–19.

—— 1969, La motivation des emprunts, *La Linguistique*, 1, 25–60.

TANNER, N. 1972, Speech and Society Among the Indonesian Elite: A Case Study of a Multilingual Community. In J. B. PRIDE & J. HOLMES (eds), *Sociolinguistics*. Harmondsworth: Penguin. 125–41.

TAYLOR, D. 1956, Language Contacts in the West Indies, *Word*, 12, 399–414.

—— 1977, Bilingualism and Intergroup Relations. In P. A. HORNBY (ed.), *Bilingualism: Psychological, Social and Educational Implications*. New York: Academic Press. 67–75.

THE SECOND FOUNDATION, 1977, Relational Network Approaches to Code-switching. In M. PARADIS (ed.), *The Fourth Lacus Forum*. Columbia: Hornbeam Press. 250–62.

*THIERY, C. 1976, Le bilinguisme vrai, *Etudes de linguistique appliquée*, 24, 52–63.

*THURSTONE, L. L. 1931, The Measurement of Attitudes, *Journal of Abnormal and Social Psychology*, 26, 249–69.

*TIMM, L. A. 1978, Code-switching in *War and Peace*. In M. PARADIS (ed.), *The Fourth Lacus Forum*. Columbia: Hornbeam Press.

*TITONE, R. 1972, *Le bilinguisme précoce*, Bruxelles: Dessart.

—— 1973, *Bilingui a tre anni*. Roma: Armando.

—— 1977, *Teaching a Second Language in Multilingual/Multicultural Contexts*. Paris: UNESCO.

*TITS, D. 1948, *Le mécanisme de l'acquisition d'une langue se substituant à la langue maternelle chez une enfant espagnole agée de six ans*. Bruxelles: Veldeman.

*TOURET, B. 1973, *L'aménagement constitutionnel des Etats de peuplement composite*, Québec, CRIM, Laval.

TOUSSAINT, J. 1935, *Bilinguisme et éducation*. Bruxelles.

*T'SOU, B. K. 1981a, Triglossie et réalignement sociolinguistique, *La linguistique*.

*—— 1981b, The Language of Swonals (Speakers Without a Native Language): A Study on Semilingualism and Accelerated Creolization. In H. BAETENS BEARDSMORE (ed.), *Elements of Theory*. Brussels: Vrije Universiteit Brussel, 125–65.

TUCKER, G. R. 1977, Some Observations Concerning Bilingualism and Second-Language Teaching in Developing Countries and in North America. In P. A. HORNBY (ed.), *Bilingualism: Psychological, Social and Educational Implications*. New York: Academic Press. 141–46.

TUCKER, G. R. & D'ANGLEJAN, A. 1971, *An Approach to Bilingual Schooling: The St. Lambert Experiment*. Montreal: McGill Univ.

TUCKER, G. R. & GEDALOF, H. 1970, Bilinguals as Linguistic Mediators, *Psychological Sciences*, 20, 6, 369–70.

*TUCKER, G. R. & LAMBERT, W. E. 1969, White and Negro Listeners' Reactions to Various American English Dialects, *Social Forces*, 47/4, 463–68.

UNIVERSITY COLLEGE OF WALES, 1953, *A Review of Problems for Research into Bilingualism and Allied Topics*, Pamphlet No. 1 Aberystwyth, Faculty of Education.

—— 1971, *Bilingualism: A Bibliography of 1000 References with Special Reference to Wales*. Cardiff: University of Wales Press.

*URE, J. 1974, Code-switching and Mixed Speech in the Register Systems of Developing Languages. In A. VERDOODT (ed.), *Proceedings of the 3rd AILA Congress*. Copenhagen, Heidelberg: Groos, 222–39.

*VALKHOFF, M. 1931, *Les mots français d'origine néerlandaise*. Amersfort: Valkhoff & Cie.

VAN HAMME, M. 1939, La question des langues dans l'éducation en Belgique, *Revue des Sciences Pédagogiques*, VI, 25, 24–32.

VAN LOEY, A. 1951, Over tweetaligheid, *Handelingen van het XIXe Vlaamse Filologencongres*, 21–32.

*—— 1958, Les problèmes du bilinguisme en Belgique, *Etudes Germaniques*, XXIII, 289–302.

VAN OVERBEKE, M. 1968, La description phonétique et phonologique d'une situation bilingue, *La Linguistique*, 93–109.

—— 1969, A propos d'une interférence due au bilinguisme, *Revue de Phonétique appliquée*, 10, 65–78.

—— 1970a, *Modèles de l'interférence linguistique*. Unpublished doctoral thesis, Université Catholique de Louvain.

—— 1970b, *Inleiding tot het tweetaligheidsprobleem*. Ninove-Brussel: Steppe-Labor.

*—— 1976, *Mécanismes de l'interférence linguistique*. Madrid: Frangua.

VERDOODT, A. 1968, *Zweisprachige Nachbarn*. Wien-Stuttgart: Braumüller.

—— 1972, *Etude sur les problèmes linguistiques des travailleurs migrants adultes et les problèmes sociolinguistiques des enfants de travailleurs migrants scolarisés dans le pays d'accueil*. C.E.E. Contrat No. 17/72.

—— 1973, *Les problèmes des groupes linguistiques en Belgique*. Louvain: Centre de Recherches Sociologiques, Université Catholique de Louvain.

—— 1976, *Les problèmes communautaires belges à la lumière des études d'opinion*. CRISP, Courrier Hebdomadaire, 742.

—— 1977a, *Linguistic Tensions in Canadian and Belgian Labor Unions*. Quebec: CIRB.

—— 1977b, *Education in a Multilingual and Multicultural Context*. Paris: UNES-CO.

—— 1978, *International Journal of the Sociology of Language: Belgium*.

VERDOODT, A. & KJOLSETH, R. 1976, *Language in Sociology*. Louvain: Peeters.

VIDOS, B. 1960, Le bilinguisme et le mécanisme de l'emprunt, *Revue de linguistique romane*, XXIV, 93–94.

VILDOMEC, V. 1963, *Multilingualism*. Leyden: Sythoff.

—— 1971, Multilingualism. In A. BAR-ADON & W. F. LEOPOLD (eds), *Child Language, A Book of Readings*. New Jersey: Prentice-Hall. 300–1.

*VOGT, H. 1954, Language Contacts, *Word*, 10, 2–3, 365-74.

WALD, B. 1974, Bilingualism. In B. J. SIEGEL, A. R. BEALS & S. A. TYLER (eds), *Annual Review of Anthropology*, 3, 301–21.

WARLAND, J. 1940, *Glossar und Grammatik der germanischen Lehnwörter in der wallonischen Mundart Malmedys*. Liège: Faculté de Philosophie et Lettres.

*WARNANT, L. 1973, Les parlers région aux, *Langue Française*, 18, 100–25.

WEIJNEN, A. 1943, *Tweetaligheid*. Tilburg: Opvoedkundige Brochurenreeks.

*WEINREICH, U. 1953, *Languages in Contact*. The Hague: Mouton.

—— 1957, Research Frontiers in Bilingual Studies, *Reports of the Eighth International Congress of Linguists*. Oslo, Vol. 1.

—— 1962, Multilingual Dialectology and the New Yiddish Atlas, *Anthropological Linguistics*. IV, 6–20

—— 1963, Four Riddles in Bilingual Dialectology, *American Contributions to the 5th International Congress of Slavists*. The Hague: Mouton, 335–58.

WEST, M. 1958, Bilingualism, *English Language Teaching*, XII, 94–97.

*WHITTAKER, H. A. 1978, Bilingualism: A Neurolinguistic Perspective. In W. C. RITCHIE (ed.), *Second Language Acquisition Research*. New York: Academic Press. 21–32.

WHITELEY, W. H. 1971, *Language Use and Social Change*. London: Oxford University Press.

WILLARD VON MALTITZ, F. 1975, *Living and Learning in Two Languages: Bilingual-Bicultural Education in the United States*. New York: McGraw-Hill.

WILLEMYNS, R. 1984, Bilingualism, Diglossia and Language Planning: Three Major Topics of Sociolinguistic Concern in Belgium, *Handelingen der Koninklijke Zuidnederlandse Maatschappij voor Taal – en Letterkund en Geschiedenis*, XXXVIII, 253–72.

WOOLFORD, E. 1983, Bilingual Code-Switching and Syntactic Theory, *Linguistic Inquiry*, 14, 3, 520–36.

Working Papers in Bilingualism/Travaux de Recherches sur le Bilinguisme. Ontario: Ontario Institute for Studies in Education.

YAP, A. (ed.) 1978, *Language Education in Multilingual Societies*. Singapore: Singapore University Press.

YOUNG, R. W. 1977, Semantic Categories of Bilingual Children. In W. F. MACKEY & T. ANDERSSON (eds), *Bilingualism in Early Childhood*. Rowley: Newbury House, 174–84.

ZIERER, E. 1977, *Second-Language Teaching in a Plurilingual Context*. Paris: UNESCO. Ref. ED–77/CONF. 613/5.

Index